William Shakespeare: Comedies, Histories, and Tragedies

Peter Saccio, Ph.D.

THE
GREAT
COURSES®

PUBLISHED BY:

THE GREAT COURSES
Corporate Headquarters
4840 Westfields Boulevard, Suite 500
Chantilly, Virginia 20151-2299
Phone: 1-800-832-2412
Fax: 703-378-3819
www.thegreatcourses.com

Copyright © The Teaching Company, 1999

Peter Saccio, Ph.D.
Leon D. Black Professor
of Shakespearean Studies
Dartmouth College

Peter Saccio has taught at Dartmouth College since 1966. He chaired the English department from 1984 to 1988; in addition, he has won Dartmouth's J. Kenneth Huntington Memorial Award for Outstanding Teaching. He has served as visiting professor at Wesleyan University and at University College in London.

He received a B.A. from Yale University and a Ph.D. from Princeton. He is the author of *The Court Comedies of John Lyly* (1969) and *Shakespeare's English Kings* (1977), the latter a classic in its field. He edited Middleton's comedy *A Mad World, My Masters* for the Oxford *Complete Works of Thomas Middleton* (1996). He has published or delivered at conferences more than twenty papers on Shakespeare and other dramatists.

Professor Saccio has directed productions of *Twelfth Night*, *Macbeth*, and *Cymbeline*. He has devised and directed several programs of scenes from Shakespeare and from modern British drama, and he served as dramaturg for the productions of his Dartmouth colleagues. He has acted the Shakespearean roles of Casca, Angelo, Bassanio, and Henry IV as well as various parts in the ancient plays of Plautus and the modern plays of Harold Pinter, Tom Stoppard, and Peter Shaffer. ■

Table of Contents

INTRODUCTION

Professor Biography i
Course Scope 1

LECTURE GUIDES

LECTURE 1
Shakespeare Then and Now 3

LECTURE 2
The Nature of Shakespeare's Plays 16

LECTURE 3
Twelfth Night—Shakespearean Comedy 28

LECTURE 4
Twelfth Night—Malvolio in Love 41

LECTURE 5
The Taming of the Shrew—Getting Married in the 1590s 54

LECTURE 6
The Taming of the Shrew—Farce and Romance 66

LECTURE 7
The Merchant of Venice—Courting the Heiress 79

LECTURE 8
The Merchant of Venice—Shylock 92

LECTURE 9
Measure for Measure—Sex in Society 104

LECTURE 10
Measure for Measure—Justice and Comedy 116

Table of Contents

LECTURE 11
Richard III—Shakespearean History 127

LECTURE 12
Richard III—The Villain's Career 139

LECTURE 13
Richard II—The Theory of Kingship 151

LECTURE 14
Richard II—The Fall of the King 163

LECTURE 15
Henry IV—All the King's Men 175

LECTURE 16
Henry IV—The Life of Falstaff 187

LECTURE 17
Henry V—The Death of Falstaff 199

LECTURE 18
Henry V—The King Victorious..224

SUPPLEMENTAL MATERIAL

Chart of Shakespeare's Plays 237
Timeline 239
Glossary 248
Biography of William Shakespeare..253
Bibliography...255

William Shakespeare:
Comedies, Histories, and Tragedies

Scope:

In thirty-six half-hour lectures, *William Shakespeare: Comedies, Histories, Tragedies* introduces the plays of Shakespeare and delineates the achievement that makes Shakespeare the leading playwright in Western civilization. The key to that achievement is his "abundance," not only the number of plays he wrote and the length of each one, but also the variety of human experiences they depict, the multitude of actions and characters they contain, the combination of public and private life they deal with, the richness of feelings they express and can provoke in an audience and in readers, and the fullness of language and suggestion.

The first two lectures are introductory. They consider how Shakespeare's plays have been found valuable by four centuries of readers, and how they have been interpreted and reinterpreted by the generations who have read and seen them. The lectures consider the kind of theater for which he wrote, the characteristic structures of his plays, and the way the plays easily mingle events from different realms: different social levels, different levels of realism, different metaphysical contexts.

The course then proceeds to consider the plays in terms of genre. Lectures 3 through 10 discuss four comedies. *Twelfth Night* offers an example of basic Shakespearean comic structure and subject matter: courtship by several young couples. Renaissance courtship practices are discussed, together with their implications about the place of romantic love in human life as a whole. Shakespeare also includes in his survey of lovers Malvolio the ambitious steward, for whom courtship is a means of social advancement. *The Taming of the Shrew* provides a more realistic look at bourgeois marriage customs and the place of a strong woman in a patriarchal society. It shows as well Shakespeare experimenting with an unusually sharp collision of romance and farce. *The Merchant of Venice* entails a particularly lofty form of romantic idealism in the courtship plot, but it confronts that idealism with the problematic, possibly tragic, character of Shylock, who has forced generations of actors into reinterpretation of Shakespeare. *Measure for Measure* shows Shakespeare on the verge of breaking out of comic conventions altogether. The characters marry at the end, as is customary, but the route to their unions is a gritty path entailing near-rape and near-execution via the courtrooms and the sexual underground of a corrupt modern society.

Lectures 11 through 18 deal with five plays drawn from English history. The nature of the history play is explained. Richard III is followed through the arc of his villainous and entertaining career. *Richard II* raises constitutional problems that vex us still: what can be done with a ruler who is undoubtedly entitled to rule and is also damaging the realm? The two plays named after Henry IV show Shakespeare's widest scope in depicting the realm of England from throne room to tavern to countryside, and they introduce Shakespeare's most remarkable comic creation, Falstaff. In *Henry V*, Shakespeare kills Falstaff in a scene of extraordinary artistic skill and emotional effect, and then takes the king to a military victory that still arouses all our conflicted convictions about the morality of warfare.

Lectures 19 through 36 deal with Shakespeare's tragedies. They show him taking Romeo and Juliet, who should be the leading pair of lovers in a comedy, and plunging their private bliss in the public violence of a city torn by feud. Why ancient Rome was important to Shakespeare (and to the Renaissance as a whole) is explored in two lectures on *Julius Caesar*. Two lectures on *Troilus and Cressida* show Shakespeare re-writing Homer into a bitter satire on vainglorious men and unfaithful women. Finally, three lectures apiece are devoted to each of the four greatest tragedies, *Hamlet*, *Othello*, *King Lear*, and *Macbeth*, so that the richness and variety of each can be explored. Emphasis falls on the scope of the tragic effect: Shakespeare's acute development of the inner consciousness in his tragic soliloquies, placed within the far-ranging philosophical and theological implications of tragic events for the whole of human life.

As with his students at Dartmouth, Professor Saccio expects his listeners and viewers to have some familiarity with the plays (he does not waste time on basic plot summary), but otherwise he provides the critical tools necessary for the appreciation of Shakespeare's world, his artistry, his significance, and his emotional power. ■

Shakespeare Then and Now

Lecture 1

This is a course in the plays of William Shakespeare. It will explore some of the most powerful works of art available to us in the Western tradition. They first filled theaters in London 400 years ago, and they continue to please, to move, and to enlighten many people today.

Shakespeare was an extremely prolific playwright, composing 38 surviving plays as well as 154 sonnets and several other poems. In about the year 1601, the scholar Gabriel Harvey said *Hamlet* pleased "the wiser sort." Several years earlier, the hack writer Thomas Nashe had described Shakespeare's effect on his audiences. Puritans said plays were pretense and provided bad examples of immoral behavior. Nashe countered that the plays honored history and provided good examples of valor and heroism.

English actor Edmund Kean in *Richard III.*

Shakespeare's plays have enriched many generations of readers and listeners. They have encouraged patriotism. They have provided a livelihood for actors; e.g., following the Puritans' closure of England's theaters between 1642 and 1660. They have become important in school and university curricula. They have assumed centrality in the culture of the English-speaking world—indeed, in all European-based cultures. John Dryden and Samuel Johnson found Shakespeare to be the greatest modern writer. Matthew Arnold and Ralph Waldo Emerson found him to be semi-divine.

Different generations have interpreted him according to their own interests. The most influential scholarship of the 1940s and 1950s saw Shakespeare as a conservative figure who upheld the "Elizabethan World Picture." More recent critics interpret Shakespeare as an advocate of liberal or even radical positions in favor of underprivileged classes and feminism. Shakespeare is a "culture hero": a mythical figure, a founder of the society, a lawgiver, a prophet. Each age must reinterpret such a figure according to its own needs.

The most extreme reinterpretation is anti-Stratfordianism, which argues that someone other than Shakespeare wrote the plays attributed to him.

The most extreme reinterpretation is anti-Stratfordianism, which argues that someone other than Shakespeare wrote the plays attributed to him. There is no factual basis for such arguments. Anti-Stratfordianism stems from false expectations. People expect great playwrights to be celebrities whose lives are recorded in detail. People expect plays about aristocrats to be written by an aristocrat. People expect plays with learned allusions to have been written by a university graduate.

Anti-Stratfordianism is an extreme version of a natural response to Shakespeare's abundance: the desire to reconceptualize him to meet the expectations, interests, or fancies of the present. ■

Essential Reading

Schoenbaum, *William Shakespeare: A Compact Documentary Life.* If a briefer account is preferable, most one-volume complete Shakespeares include the basic facts in the introduction.

Supplementary Reading

Schoenbaum, *Shakespeare's Lives*, Part 6: "Deviations."

Taylor, *Reinventing Shakespeare.*

1. Discuss the sorts of things that readers and audiences nowadays expect of a person who is labeled a "great writer."

2. Do stage performances run the risk of immorality? Explore the issues involved.

Shakespeare Then and Now

Lecture 1—Transcript

Hello. My name is Peter Saccio. I teach Shakespeare at Dartmouth, where I have been for more years than I care to count, and this is a course in the plays of William Shakespeare. It will explore some of the most powerful works of art available to us in the Western tradition. They first filled theaters in London 400 years ago, and they continue to please, to move, and to enlighten many people today. Just how they please, move, and enlighten us is our business in this course.

Thirty-eight plays of Shakespeare survive. They are not all that Shakespeare wrote; there's a sequence of 154 sonnets, some half dozen other poems, long and short. We know he had a hand in several other plays whose texts survive, and others whose texts are lost, apparently forever. Since he was the house playwright for a busy theatrical company, I'm sure that he also did lots of other writing, of which we have no record now, doctoring other playwrights' plays, putting in a scene here, a speech there. "Hey Will, we're doing this terrible old thing for kids next week. Could you put in some stuff to juice up the betrayal scene?"—That kind of stuff. That's what a house playwright does.

All this work was done in the space of about a quarter of a century, from about 1589, when Shakespeare was in his mid-twenties, to about 1612, as he approached the age of 50. If you have trouble remembering dates, perhaps an easy way to remember is this; this is four centuries ago. Take the year 1600 as the midpoint; it is the midpoint of Shakespeare's career. It's the date of *Hamlet*; he was working 12 years before that and about 12 years after that. *Hamlet* is the great crossing place.

He was a productive man, and was appreciated in his own time. About the year 1601, a Cambridge scholar named Gabriel Harvey scribbled some notes evaluating current English writing. Among his comments was the following, on a certain poet and playwright who had been gaining attention: "The younger sort takes much delight in Shakespeare's *Venus and Adonis*, but his *Lucrece* and his *Hamlet, Prince of Denmark* have it in them to please the wiser sort." Now, Gabriel Harvey was a vain and waspish man, the sort of nasty, argumentative shrew that gives academics a bad name. In fact, he was so quarrelsome, that he couldn't get promotion even in his own university, let alone a decent job outside when he tried to do that. And you can see his condescension toward "the younger sort," who like love poems, amorous poetry like *Venus and Adonis*. But his remark is also reassuring, the remark about *Hamlet*. A play that we find great now was appreciated in its own time by a demanding critic. In fact, the remark flatters us; "Hamlet pleases the wiser sort." Well, I like *Hamlet*; I must be one of the wiser sort.

Shakespeare, in his time, pleased tastes less demanding than that of Gabriel Harvey. Some 10 years before Harvey jotted down his notes, a much more genial man, a hack writer called Thomas Nashe, wrote the earliest surviving description of an audience at a Shakespeare play. Nashe describes a direct, open-hearted response the audience gave to plays dramatizing English history. He's speaking in particular about the death of Lord Talbot, one of the generals of the Hundred Years War against France and the hero of Shakespeare's play *Henry VI, Part I*. This is what Nashe writes:

> What if I prove plays to be no extreme vice, but a rare exercise of virtue? First, for the subject of them, it is, for the most part, borrowed out of our English chronicles, wherein our forefathers' valiant acts that have lain long buried in rusty brass and worm-eaten books, are revived, and they themselves, raised from the grave of oblivion and brought to plead their ancient honors in open presence, than which what could be a sharper reproof to these degenerate, effeminate days of ours? How it would have joyed brave Talbot, the terror of the French, to think that after he had lain two hundred years in his tomb, he should triumph again on the stage, and have his bones new embalmed with the tears of ten thousand spectators at least, who in the tragedian that represents his person imagine they behold him fresh bleeding.

Now, as the first sentence indicates, Nashe has his own axe to grind. He wants to prove that stage plays are a virtue, not a vice. He is an occasional playwright himself, and he's defending the stage against Puritan attack. The extract I have quoted is part of a debate over the morality of the stage that extends from the 1560s, when Shakespeare was a toddler, to 30 years after his death, when, in 1642, the Puritans gained a majority in Parliament and passed an act forbidding all theatrical performance in England.

The Puritans are the radical Protestants. They're the left wing of the political religious spectrum. They want to carry the Reformation further, to turn England into the new Jerusalem, to make it as much like a primitive church as possible, and they held that the stage was immoral. The stage was immoral in itself because acting is pretense, passing yourself off as something other than what God made you to be. It is also immoral in its effect, since the plots of practically every play involve some sinful behavior, and the audience might be tempted to go home and imitate those sinful acts. Nashe is trying to answer both points. He argues that the pretense, in fact, honors the subject, that Talbot would be delighted to know that his heroic deeds of a century and a half earlier are being reenacted on the stage. Moreover, the effect of this impersonation is highly moral, not immoral at all; the audience is inspired by the heroic example and reproved for its modern degeneracy.

But at the heart of this polemic, Nashe records a fact, and it's that fact that I'm chiefly interested in at the moment. At several performances, large audiences were deeply moved by the valor and heroism of Talbot. They were so drawn in to the theatrical illusion that they momentarily believed that they were witnessing the real thing, that they behold—"in the tragedian that represents his person, they behold him fresh bleeding." They see the death of Talbot himself, and it's an interesting linguistic fact that I just discovered this past fall, that in English the word "personate," meaning "take on the identity of another individual," comes into common use in this decade of the 1590s, when Nashe is writing about Shakespeare's early performances.

By starting with two contemporary quotations in praise of Shakespeare, I do not mean to suggest that while he was still alive, he was held in the extraordinary esteem that he is now. Now, he is a cultural icon, the biggest name there is in Western literature. But I do want to establish that his plays were successful, that they earned him both profit and credit in his own time. He was not a closet genius unknown to his contemporaries. And some of the ways in which the Elizabethan audience appreciated him continue now. The association of his work with English patriotism, which Nashe makes clear in talking about Talbot, has continued to this day. The best known twentieth-century use of Shakespeare for the building of patriotic morale has been the film of *Henry V*, made by Laurence Olivier in 1944, to which the British government contributed some funding, and which Olivier dedicated to the British troops. It was a project in which Winston Churchill himself was deeply interested. He was aware of the value of cinema for public morale. I know a woman—in fact, I've been directed in the theater by her—who is now in her late eighties. At the end of the war in 1945, when that film opened in London, she was a very young mother living in London, and she told me she went back to see that film every two weeks. It gave her the necessary boost to carry on in London when Hitler's V-2 bombs were still falling on the city.

But Shakespeare had been many other things to his own time and to later generations, many other things than a patriot. He has been the source of livelihood to actors. The theatrical company of which he was part for most of his years in the theater became the most successful of his time. They were called the Lord Chamberlain's Men. When they were founded in the year 1594, their official patron was the Lord Chamberlain of the court of Queen Elizabeth I. When Elizabeth died nine years later and was succeeded by her cousin, King James I, there was a reshuffling of all the patronage at court, and a new patron of Shakespeare's company was the new King James himself. So they were called the King's Men, and under that name they lasted for another 39 years, until the Puritans closed the theaters in 1642.

When the theaters opened 28 years after that, in 1660, after the Puritan interregnum, the old companies had, of course, long since fallen apart. But there were actors here and there who wanted to get back on the stage as soon as they could. Of course, nobody had been writing new plays; nobody writes plays if there's no chance of getting them produced. So for a while, the actors had to resort to the old repertoire, which meant Ben Jonson, Beaumont and Fletcher, and Shakespeare. This carries on into the eighteenth century, the next century, when Ben Jonson and Beaumont and Fletcher begin to be less interesting to current audiences, but Shakespeare goes on being revived again and again. Indeed, by the eighteenth century, English actors have come to be evaluated chiefly on their ability to perform Shakespeare's leading characters. Their portraits come down to us painted in the costumes and the scenes of his plays. We see Garrick as Richard III; we see Mrs. Siddons as Lady Macbeth. And it is still the case; English actors do many things besides Shakespeare, of course, but Shakespeare is where you achieve real distinction and fame. I cut out a clipping of this morning's paper, which quotes Dame Judi Dench, one of the really distinguished senior Shakespearean actresses currently at work. She says, "Shakespeare is known in our house as the gentleman who pays the rent." Now, Shakespeare is a source of livelihood to more than Dame Judi. He is a source of livelihood to Britain as a whole. Much of the Royal Shakespeare Company's audience at Stratford-on-Avon consists, of course, of overseas tourists: Europeans, Japanese, North Americans. The plays are a magnet that brings money, not only to the theaters, but to the restaurants, the hotel keepers, the airlines, the souvenir shops.

He has also become an educational staple. This began to happen in the nineteenth century, as the British, step by step, extended the franchise, the ability to vote, to more and more classes of people. As they did that, the British government realized they also had to expand the schools; these new voters from the lower middle classes and the working classes had to be educated. What should they learn? Well, working-class people cannot really be expected to learn Latin or Greek, like their upper-class betters, so English literature begins to replace the classics in the curriculum. If they can't read Julius Caesar in his original writing, they can at least read about Julius Caesar in Shakespeare's play.

By the end of the century, English had become an acceptable subject of study in the universities as well as the schools, and that meant that research on Shakespeare—editing his plays, commenting on them (an activity which had formerly been in the province of private scholars and societies)—moved into the hands of academics. Shakespeare is the gentleman who pays my rent, too. Players, shopkeepers, schoolmasters, college professors—we all have a heavy vested interest in Shakespeare. But beyond the economic argument, Shakespeare has assumed a massive centrality to English-speaking cultures, indeed to all the European-based cultures. There are, after all, Italian operas and Russian novels that make heavy use of Shakespeare, West Indian poets who rewrite *The Tempest*. Shakespeare gets quoted the way the Bible is quoted, to settle some important issue in human affairs. That means, of course, he gets quoted by crackpots as well as by the wiser sort, but I'll mostly ignore the crackpots.

This begins late in the seventeenth century, when Shakespeare is not yet 100 years dead. The poet John Dryden wrote that Shakespeare was "the man who of all modern, and perhaps ancient poets, had the largest and most comprehensive soul." Of all modern and perhaps ancient poets; that slight hiccup "perhaps" comes in because Dryden doesn't quite dare say that Shakespeare is greater than Homer. That's a real step for a seventeenth-century man to take. In the eighteenth century, Dr. Samuel Johnson echoes that: "Shakespeare is, above all writers ..., the poet of nature, the poet that holds up to his readers a faithful mirror of manners and of life." And that phrase, "of manners and of life," indicates that what he means by nature is not rocks and trees and everything outside; he means human nature, the way people behave.

Now, so far, Shakespeare's superlative talents have been said to lie in observation and feeling: "a comprehensive soul," "a faithful mirror of life." He is the most widely observant and expressive of writers. A jump happens in the nineteenth century when, in England, Matthew Arnold in a famous sonnet compares Shakespeare to a "lofty hill," whose top is perceivable only to the stars; it is hid from mortals by clouds. A few years later in America, Ralph Waldo Emerson, in supposedly silver prose, declares that Shakespeare is "inconceivably wise." This, I find, rather dangerous. The nineteenth-century Shakespeare, the Shakespeare of Arnold and Emerson, is no longer human, a mortal playwright working with theaters and actors; he has become a god beyond our kin. The attitude that they are expressing is called Bardolatry.

Now, just what Shakespeare is wise about depends on the reader. In matters of philosophy, he has been enlisted on behalf of idealism; he has also been enlisted on behalf of nihilism. In matters of religion, he has been found in favor of Roman Catholicism; he has been found to favor Protestantism; he has been found to favor agnosticism and skepticism. In our own century, readers have found him particularly suggestive in political matters. The most influential scholarship of the mid-century, the 1940s and -50s, argues that Shakespeare reflected what was called the "Elizabethan world picture." This is a strongly conservative view of the world; God created all things in a vast vertical order, the great chain of being; angels in their ranks at the top, then human beings, then animals, then plants, and then stones, and then down to the smallest mote of dust. Maintaining that order is essential to virtue—all sin can be defined as trying to get out of your place in that order. Shakespeare's plays, particularly the history plays and the tragedies, show conflict to be the result of individuals breaking out of their places, and resolution to be possible only when they return to the proper order. So argued scholars like E.M.W. Tillyard, in the middle of the century, who had an enormous influence on subsequent scholarship.

On the other hand, some of the most energetic criticism of the past 15 years is liberal and indeed radical in its direction, greatly concerned with the injustices perpetrated upon people through distinctions of race, gender, class. Readers influenced by ideas of Marxism and cultural materialism point to passages that appear to sympathize with unprivileged classes rather than with kings and lords. Readers influenced by feminism stress the strength of some of his female characters, or stress the ways in which most women are marginalized or even silenced by a social system that gives power to husbands and fathers. I'm trying to wrap up, in a few sentences, the painstaking work of scores of scholars, and therefore doing them an injustice; this course is accompanied by a bibliography that can guide you into the libraries of Shakespearean scholarship.

My point is a simple but big one. For many generations, Western culture, particularly English-speaking culture, has found Shakespeare important, found it necessary to relate to Shakespeare on those issues that seem to us to matter most: what we believe, what we find good or evil, how we should organize our relations with each other. Shakespeare is what the anthropologists call a culture-hero, a mythical figure who may or may not be based on a real person, a founder of the society, a lawgiver, a prophet. Such a figure each age must reinterpret according to its own needs. This applies not only to what is written by scholars, to be read in libraries, and what is said by teachers in classrooms, but also to productions of the plays in theaters and in films. When patriotism is needed in World War II, Laurence Olivier films a highly patriotic *Henry V*. When warfare becomes deeply suspect because of Vietnam and the Falklands, Kenneth Branagh films a skeptical and gritty *Henry V*.

The most extreme form of reinterpreting Shakespeare is to say that he was someone else, to deny that he wrote the plays at all. This is a famous topic; people who know nothing else about Shakespeare know there's been a dispute over this. If I fall into conversation with a stranger at a cocktail party, and let it be known that I teach Shakespeare for a living, I'm almost certain to be asked, "Tell me, did he really write those plays?" I shouldn't complain; people with any kind of job have to get used to some idiot question or other, and it's better to be a Shakespearean than a proctologist.

No one doubts that there was a William Shakespeare who was born in Stratford-on-Avon, went on to act in the London theaters, and eventually died back in Stratford. What is contested is whether that man wrote the plays that have come down under his name, and the people who contest it propose various different alternatives: Francis Bacon, the earl of Oxford, Christopher Marlowe, there's a long list. So instead of calling them Baconians or Oxfordians et al, I refer to them under the blanket title of anti-Stratfordians. The one thing they agree on is it wasn't the guy from Stratford. Anti-Stratfordianism is fascinating because it tells us a great deal about what people look for in a superlative writer. They see a wonderful poet, or a remarkable psychologist, or a great philosopher, or a man capable of expressing the views of an aristocratic class, or a man deeply concerned about the status of women and the oppressed, or any number of things, for which there is some basis in the text of Shakespeare's plays. Then they note that the image they've constructed of the writer doesn't seem to cohere with a guy who was born the son of a country glover. The glover himself was probably illiterate, and the son never got beyond grammar school in Stratford, so it must have been somebody else.

I must, therefore, assert at the start of a course of lectures on Shakespeare that there is no mystery here. There is no subject for debate. The facts of Shakespeare's life are as well recorded as anyone could expect—of his domestic life in Stratford, of his professional life in London. We'd like to know more, of course, but we don't know a great deal about the life of any person in his time, except for a few great figures of state and church, like the Queen and the archbishops and the lords and generals, whose activities were naturally given a great deal of attention. We know as much about Shakespeare's life as we know about any other commoner of the time. The Elizabethans did not live filling out the records, keeping the forms the way we do. We do have documents that say, or that make sense only if you assume, that the actor from Stratford and the playwright in London were the same man. If they were not—if those documents are forgeries or lies—then quite a number of people would have to have been engaged in a great conspiracy, for which there is no positive evidence and no attested reason.

Anti-Stratfordianism is, in fact, just crazy if you know anything about how the theater works as a profession at all. Theater is a collaborative art, and people in the theater always know what other people in the theater are doing. Even now, in the much larger world of the New York theater, everybody in it knows everybody else. Everybody knows if someone is ghostwriting someone else, everybody knows if a new director has been brought in to fix a play, everybody knows who's understudying such and such a play. Everybody knows who are sleeping together. In the much smaller world of Shakespeare's theater—in London of 1600, when probably no more than 200 people were trying to get a living out of putting on plays at any given time—it is unimaginable that three dozen successful plays could be written by someone other than the man to whom they were publicly attributed, without someone leaving some statement about the hoax.

Anti-Stratfordianism (it's a horrible word) stems from false expectations. People expect that a great playwright would attract curiosity, that we would inherit diaries and personal reminiscences and the like, which we don't have for Shakespeare. But we expect that because successful playwrights today are celebrities. They are interviewed; they are invited to speak on college campuses. Elizabethan playwrights did not attract that kind of attention; they merely provided stage entertainment. If they were very good, they might have aroused the interest of what Gabriel Harvey calls "the wiser sort," or one's scribbled note in his study, but it would be the plays that would provoke interest, not the personality.

We expect, or at least some people expect, plays to reflect the personal experience of the writer. Specifically, it is assumed that plays about kings and queens and lords must have been written by an aristocrat. How else would he know how they behaved at court? Hence the suggestion that it was really Bacon, who grew up at court and became Chancellor of the Realm, or Oxford, an aristocrat whose lineage goes back to the Norman conquest. But that is to mistake the nature of Shakespeare's art, which does not pretend to represent a realistic transcription of behavior in high places. No real king or duke ever spoke in spontaneous blank verse. And to suppose that a middle-class boy could not grow up to write tragedies about princes is sheer social snobbery. Most Elizabethan plays are about princes, yet none of the anti-Stratfordians ever suggested that the plays of Shakespeare's contemporaries—the plays of Webster or Kyd or Beaumont and Fletcher—were really written by lords.

We expect, or at least some of us do, that plays rich in literary allusions and classical references and historical knowledge, must have been written by a man with a university education. After all, we need a college education to understand them, or parts of them. Shakespeare did not attend a university; Christopher Marlowe did, so he must have written the plays. But education was different then. Grammar school provided a rich literary training: grammar, composition, rhetoric, poetry, figurative language, the classics. The universities, then, were like graduate schools; they were meant for specialized training in theology or medicine or law. From a good grammar school education, and the Stratford grammar school was good, a smart boy could have developed his verbal skills and also learned how to look things up, how to acquire specialized knowledge that he might want to use. Marlowe went to university, true; so did other playwrights like Robert Greene. Ben Jonson did not; he taught himself, and he was the most learned playwright of the time. Thomas Kyd did not go to university, and Thomas Middleton went to Oxford, but dropped out.

Anti-Stratfordianism is the extreme case of reconceptualizing Shakespeare to meet the interests or needs or expectations or fancies of the present. And some of it is really crazy in its methods. But however mad it may be, its fundamental impulse is one common to all readers of Shakespeare; confronted with enormously stimulating artistic achievement, achievement that encompasses a wide variety of human experience, those of us who are stimulated are bound to find something that speaks to our needs, our preoccupations. Those who fear a breakdown of social order find in his works a celebration of hierarchy and harmony as it supposedly existed at some time in the past, because his kings do desire peace. Those who desire to shake up the current establishment enlist him as a social critic on behalf of marginalized people. He writes with equal eloquence for the rulers and the oppressed, for women and men, for young and old. He can speak for each character with such authenticity that when it strikes a particular chord in us, we think we hear Shakespeare himself speaking.

Of course, it is all Shakespeare, and we all find in his riches something we need to stay in contact with him.

The Nature of Shakespeare's Plays
Lecture 2

Aristotle observed that it was a principle of Greek drama to have a single unified action, but Shakespeare regularly has multiple plots; three or four couples court one another in a comedy. ... Three or four parties are scheming against each other in a history or a tragedy. And the number of dead bodies at the end of a tragedy is ultimately controlled only by the absence of a front curtain; you have to have enough living people standing up to carry off the corpses.

Shakespeare was a professional man of the theater. His dramatic genius could flourish because he lived at a time when theater itself flourished. He was by no means a solitary genius. Shakespeare's plays are abundant in their contents. They have five acts and many scenes, lines, characters, and plots. The plots are derived from diverse sources. Originality lay less in one's invention of stories than in his treatment and development of existing stories. *Measure for Measure*, for instance, was based on a basic plot that had been often retold. Shakespeare gave the familiar story a new twist, and therein lay his genius.

The size of the stage in Shakespeare's time invited both epic and intimate effects. The stage features known as the heavens and the hell provided a potential supernatural context. The size of the stage invites setting personal lives in a wide social context. For instance, the large stages of Shakespeare's time allowed the depiction of eavesdropping. There is a case of double eavesdropping in *Troilus and Cressida*, in which a single event means five different things to three different sets of characters.

Shakespeare found brilliant ways to make the complex inner self speak.

Shakespeare keeps both the private and the public in interplay. He presents the title character of *Richard II* in both his private and public roles. Shakespeare found brilliant ways to make the complex inner self speak. For instance, he invented the modern soliloquy. *Romeo and Juliet* offers another example of this dichotomy between public and private identities. Romeo's desire to be altogether private in his love for Juliet is thwarted by his public identity as a Capulet. Despite the centrality of the feelings, motivations, and desires of Shakespeare's characters, we are continually aware that their lives are intertwined with the condition of the societies in which they live.

Shakespeare keeps the down-to-earth and the imaginative in interplay. In *Much Ado About Nothing*, Beatrice refers at once to the pain her mother suffered in giving birth to her and to the fantastic vision of a star dancing over the scene of her birth. Cleopatra's dream of Antony romanticizes her dead lover but also refers to qualities that Antony genuinely had.

Hemmings and Condell first collected Shakespeare's plays under the title *Mr. William Shakespeare's Comedies, Histories and Tragedies*. Nevertheless, Shakespeare strains at the boundaries of generic definition. Shakespeare's tragedies and comedies are quite different from those of ancient Greece. There is no ancient Greek analogue to Shakespeare's history plays. ■

Essential Reading

Shakespeare, *Antony and Cleopatra*, Act 5, scene 2.

———, *Richard II*, Act 3, scene 2.

———, *Romeo and Juliet*, Act 3, scene 1.

———, *Troilus and Cressida*, Act 5, scene 2.

Supplementary Reading

Beckerman, *Shakespeare at the Globe*.

Questions to Consider

1. Compare the characteristic form and structure of a Shakespeare play with a play of another period, ancient or modern. What is gained or lost by the "abundance" of the former as opposed to the more disciplined focus of the latter?

2. Do the multifarious contents of a Shakespearean play make it unreasonably difficult to grasp?

The Nature of Shakespeare's Plays
Lecture 2—Transcript

I ended the last lecture by stressing Shakespeare's extraordinary eloquence in speaking for all sorts and conditions of people. That, indeed, is the theme that will link all these lectures together—the variety and richness of his work, and the variety and richness of the ways in which it affects us.

Each play is abundant in its contents. There are five acts; usually there are somewhere between 15 and 25 individual scenes, although *Antony and Cleopatra* has over 40. The total length of the play is always more than 2,000 lines, and with *Hamlet* gets close to 4,000. The total length is, indeed, more than our modern customs of theatergoing normally tolerate, which is why, in modern productions, the texts are almost always cut. The cast list is long. Greek tragedy permits only three speaking actors onstage at any given time, plus, of course, the chorus. Many modern plays are similarly small in focus, for example, the family dramas of Ibsen, of O'Neill; the isolated figures in Beckett. But Shakespeare has never less than 15 characters, and sometimes nearly 50.

There's a lot happening in the plot. Aristotle observed that it was a principle of Greek drama to have a single unified action, but Shakespeare regularly has multiple plots; three or four couples court one another in a comedy. Their paths sometimes cross, but also sometimes diverge. Three or four parties are scheming against each other in a history or a tragedy. And the number of dead bodies at the end of a tragedy is ultimately controlled only by the absence of a front curtain; you have to have enough living people standing up to carry off the corpses.

A similar multiplicity appears in the storylines themselves, the kinds of stories that get told. Greek tragedy stuck almost exclusively to Greek mythology. Medieval drama stuck to Biblical stories, to saints' lives, and to moral struggles in allegorical form. The Elizabethans, however, Shakespeare among them, pillaged any narrative source they could find: classical stories; medieval collections like Chaucer; Italian Renaissance stories like those of Boccaccio; history, whether it be English or European or classical; romances; folktales. You name it, they lifted it.

Shakespeare did not invent his stories. That sort of originality was not especially valued in his time; what mattered was the originality in handling the stories, in restructuring them, in finding new significances in them, in combining stories from different sources, developing new characters and incidents. That is why it can be useful to the serious student of Shakespeare to read Shakespeare's sources, all of which have been collected in a magnificent set of eight volumes by a British scholar named Geoffrey Bullock under the title of *The Narrative and Dramatic Sources of Shakespeare.* By learning the sources, you can make good guesses, you can even deduce what was important to Shakespeare about those stories by looking at what he stresses, keeps, omits, where he brings in something else.

For example, the main plot of *Measure for Measure* is a story that had been many times retold before Shakespeare got a hold of it. A man is condemned to death; a woman who is devoted to him—his wife, his daughter, his sister, what have you—goes to the judge and begs for a pardon. The judge looks at her and says to himself, "I want that woman," and makes a bargain with her: "If you sleep with me, I'll issue the pardon." The woman agrees to the bargain, but after the judge has had his pleasure, he double-crosses her and executes the convict anyway. The interest of the story lies in what the woman does next. Now, when the story reached Shakespeare, he made a drastic change. His is the first version of the story in which the woman rejects the bargain, refuses to sleep with the judge, and her convict brother, who values his sister's honor, at first applauds her decision, and then, in terror of death, begs her to change her mind. "Please, sister, let me live." But the woman is a young nun, a novice in a nunnery, and her chastity is of great significance to her, so the whole focus of the story has been changed so that the struggle between two rival values is pursued. Which is more important, chastity or charity?

Also contributing to the abundance of Shakespeare is the theater itself. The typical Elizabethan theater was an amphitheater, a polygonal building with 16 or 20 sides, designed rather like a tall donut. The stage projected from the inner wall of one side out into the central space; the cheapest audience accommodation was to stand around that space around the stage. If you could afford more, then you sat in one of the galleries that went up along the sides. The stage was both wide and deep, with two doors in the rear for entrances, and between the doors a booth or discovery space that could be used for special effects. This large stage, about 40 feet wide, could accommodate many actors. You can do crowd scenes, court scenes, battle scenes, fencing displays; the duel at the end of *Hamlet* is a real duel between people who know how to use those weapons. That is, the stage could be epic in its scale. Yet because the audience stood or sat about three-quarters of the way around, and because those galleries go straight up instead of being recessed, like in a modern Broadway theater, all the audience is really quite close to the stage. Nobody is more than 40 feet away from an actor standing downstage center. Therefore, it is possible to do very intimate scenes, to have scenes between two people, or to have a quiet soliloquy, one character like Hamlet meditating on the meaning of his experience. You get quite closely inside his mind. This is an extraordinarily flexible stage; nothing more flexible in entertainment was invented in the West, at least until the movies came along. The movies, of course, can give us the epic scale and the intimacy, even better than the stage, but they do so at the price of putting it all on film; the action and the actors are no longer live.

The stage also had trap doors; characters could descend beneath the stage floor into what was called the hell. It was also partly roofed over, the front part of the roof being supported by columns or pillars. And those pillars go all the way to the top level, so that most of the audience standing in the pit or seated in the galleries can see the underside of that canopy roof, and that was painted with stars and constellations and was sometimes called the heavens. (They have built a couple of years ago, in London, a full-size replica of Shakespeare's Globe. It is called Shakespeare's Globe, and they are putting on a full summer season of plays there now. I strongly recommend that you go there if you can.) Those two terms, the ""heaven above and the "hell" below the stage, remind us of the Christian heritage of this Elizabethan theater. Men and women work out their destiny on earth between the alternatives of heaven and hell.

The world of the Elizabethan stage was not only vertical; it was also horizontal. Let me go back for a moment to the size of the stage, to those crowd and court and battle scenes. This is a stage big enough to accommodate what Rosalind, in *As You Like It*, calls "the full stream of the world," what Macduff calls "pleasures in a spacious plenty." Unlike Greek plays, unlike most modern drama, where one family may stand for society only by metaphor, this stage really can present a large population. The big stage goes along with the multiple plots of the play; people dwell in a broad society, different kinds, different social levels of men and women. We focus not just on their personal lives; we are also made to focus on them in a large social context. And the big stage goes along with kinds of scenes that Shakespeare writes—the thronerooms and battlefields that I mentioned, but also, to take an odd example, eavesdropping scenes. Eavesdropping is frequent in Shakespeare; it's hard to stage when Shakespeare's put on television, because the television screen is small, but on the Elizabethan stage, eavesdropping is a natural activity. You can have one pair of characters doing something stage left, and other characters watching them, a sufficient distance apart for it to be credible, but both groups are within our view so that we have the event and the commentary simultaneously.

There's even a case in *Troilus and Cressida* of multiple eavesdropping. In the Greek camp, Cressida is reluctantly yielding to the seduction of Diomedes. Watching them is Cressida's lover, Troilus, to whom she has sworn fidelity, who is horror-struck by this event and thinks the whole world is falling to pieces because his girl is unfaithful. He is accompanied by an older, wiser, worldly Greek Ulysses, who keeps telling Troilus, "Don't make so much fuss about it. This is the sort of thing that happens. It's the way of the world." And there's a fifth character watching also, Thersites, the complete cynic, who tells us in the audience, "This just proves what I always said; all people are whores and knaves." In other words, we have an event that means five different things simultaneously. To Cressida, who is being seduced, she is alone and scared, and needs male protection, and is finally reluctantly willing to pay a price for it. Diomedes just wants the girl for the night. And it means three different things to each of the three male observers. The event no sooner happens but it's got five interpretations. That's an example of the abundance of Shakespeare.

Let me expand on this; a Shakespearean play gives us a sense of panorama, a view of life in breadth and in depth. We are concerned with the private lives of people, their inner natures; there's the depth. We are also concerned with the worlds, the nature and fate of the societies in which they live. At the end of the most famous speech Shakespeare gives to King Richard II, Richard insists that he is not a king at all; he is a man as other men are, a man quite like those he is talking to: "I live with bread like you, feel want, / Taste grief, need friends: subjected thus, / How can you say to me, I am a king?" It is a characteristic Shakespearean moment when we look through the king to see the Richard, look through the political position and see the human being who occupies that position and, in this case, does not fit it very well.

Shakespeare's plays provide us with some of the most intense personal experience available in drama or in any other form of literature: the anguished soliloquies of Macbeth; the angry confrontation of Hamlet with his mother; the balcony scene between Romeo and Juliet; or the teasing affection between the pairs of lovers in the comedies. These scenes make us acquainted with characters of remarkable fullness, with emotions of power and subtlety and depth. Playgoers and readers find him intimately acquainted with the human condition, with the human heart.

Indeed, it has been said by several modern critics, of whom Harold Bloom is the best known, that Shakespeare invented that thing that we call the self, the complex psyche, the private identity, that is partly, but not wholly, self-aware, tremulous and changing. I'm going to shy away from a bold statement like that, that Shakespeare invented the self. There are other writers before Shakespeare who had some awareness of the self and its instabilities. But Shakespeare certainly found brilliant ways of making that self speak. He gave artistic form to the notion that people are complex selves, that they have private lives that stand in opposition to their public appearance and to the social circumstances and forces that surround them. He found means in dialogue, monologue and subtext for the complications of private life to be revealed.

Later in this course, when we get to *Macbeth*, I will try to demonstrate that he invented the modern soliloquy, a form of speech in which the complexities of the self are revealed to an eavesdropping audience, even more fully than the speaker himself realizes. And because Shakespeare has become a kind of culture- hero, because he is one of the founders of modern Western culture, and his plays have remained central to our artistic and educational practices, we derive from him important notions about our private selves.

Opposed to Richard II, moving from divine right king to privately suffering man, let me pose Romeo. Early in the third act, Romeo would like to be altogether private, to deal with the world solely on the basis of his love for Juliet. Romeo and Juliet have declared their love for each other, have been secretly married, and are only waiting for nighttime fully to consummate their union. In the hot midday sun, Romeo encounters Tybalt, and wants to treat him with the love that he feels for the whole world in his happy, newly-married state. But Tybalt is a Capulet and sees Romeo not as a loving man, but simply as a Montague, a member of the rival family, an opponent in the feud that divides Verona. And Tybalt's antagonism leads quickly to the death of Mercutio and of Tybalt himself, and Romeo's own banishment from Verona. The personal feelings of the hero of the play are erased; what happens to him thereafter is determined by his public position as the son of one of the two feuding families who dominate the city. The personal feelings of one man cannot deflect a city full of social history. Young lovers are part of a multigenerational social order.

Likewise Hamlet, the most famous soliloquizer in Shakespeare, whom we usually think of as standing alone, or talking to the skull of Yorick, also has a position as crown prince, a mother, a stepfather, and a dead father who, from the grave, imposes upon him the duty of purging the rottenness of Denmark. And Macbeth himself is the rottenness that infects all Scotland. We are fascinated by the feelings and motives and decisions, the psychology of Shakespeare's characters, but we are also made aware that their lives are interlocked with the health or ill health of the societies in which they live. The characters of Shakespeare live out their private lives in public places, and their lives are dramatized in such a way that it is hard to say whether the private concerns or the public ones are the more important.

Shakespeare deals not only with the private and the public, but also with the imaginative. Indeed, his ability to combine ordinary, earthbound fact with imaginative vision is another of his characteristic talents. Let me give you two examples. In *Much Ado About Nothing*, the witty heroine, Beatrice, is happily jesting away when it occurs to her that she may be giving offense by speaking so frivolously in the presence of the prince, Don Pedro. So she says to him, "I beseech your grace, pardon me. I was born to speak all mirth and no matter." And Don Pedro replies, "To be merry best becomes you, for out of question, you were born in a merry hour." And she replies, "No, sure my lord, my mother cried. But there was a star danced, and under that was I born."

When Shakespeare mentions childbirth, he always refers to the groans of the mother in labor; he never forgets the pain of delivery, which was unrelieved by anesthetics at that time. But it was equally characteristic of him that he should leap from the pain of the mother, to the fantasy of a star dancing over his witty heroine's birth. He adapts the current belief in astrology, in which I doubt he put any serious stock, to make a charming and appropriate account of Beatrice's first moment on earth.

Let me take a more sustained and serious example. This is Cleopatra in the last act of her play, mourning her dead lover Antony and preparing to face her conqueror, Octavius Caesar. She is speaking to one of Caesar's captains, Dolabella:

> *Cleopatra*: I dream'd there was an Emperor Antony
> O, such another sleep, that I might see
> But such another man!
> *Dolabella*: If it might please you.
> *Cleopatra*: His face was as the heavens; and therein stuck
> A sun and moon, which kept their course, and lighted
> The little O, the earth.
> *Dolabella*: Most sovereign creature—
> *Cleopatra*: His legs bestrid the ocean; his rear'd arm
> Crested the world: his voice was propertied
> As all the tuned spheres, and that to friends;
> But when he meant to quail and shake the orb,
> He was as rattling thunder. For his bounty,
> There was no winter in't; an autumn 'twas
> That grew the more by reaping: his delights
> Were dolphin-like; they show'd his back above
> The element they liv'd in: in his livery
> Walk'd crowns and crownets; realms and islands were
> As plates dropp'd from his pocket.
> *Dolabella*: Cleopatra—

> *Cleopatra:* Think you there was or might be such a man
> As this I dream'd of?
> *Dolabella:* Gentle madam, no.
> *Cleopatra:* You lie, up to the hearing of the gods.

Now, it is understandable that a bereaved woman should romanticize her dead lover in this way, and natural that the worldly Roman soldier would keep hold of reality. But Cleopatra's dream is based on qualities Antony genuinely had. He was a great general, and he was generous to his friends. He ruled half the known world, and although he was given to sensual pleasures, one never forgot his greatness; even when he wallowed in pleasure, his back showed above them like a "leap-feeding" dolphin.

And the grandeur of Cleopatra is manifest in her ability to hold on to that vision of Antony, even in defeat. And if Dolabella is kindly in his soft denial of the dream, like a man speaking to a deluded person—"Gentle madam, no"—Cleopatra is majestic in her rejection of his denial; "You lie, up to the hearing of the gods." This is not a petty matter; it is not a fib or white lie. Antony's reputation is of universal import. This woman, who at times has been down-to-earth, flirting, scheming, deceiving, squabbling, brawling, is now preparing to meet death as a great queen. The romance here is as real as the ordinary daily facts.

Finally, let me speak of the genre of these plays. Seven years after Shakespeare's death, two of his theatrical colleagues, actors named Hemmings and Condell, gathered 36 of his plays together—only 36, they didn't quite get them all—and published them, collected in one large volume, a volume that scholars now refer to as the First Folio. They tried to organize the profusion of these plays by arranging them in three categories: comedy, history and tragedy. The organization was reflected in the title they gave the book, *Master William Shakespeare's Comedies, Histories and Tragedies.*

Now, many modern "complete Shakespeares" follow this same arrangement, and I will follow it also in these lectures. I follow it because it is useful and suggestive, but it is not definitive. Shakespeare keeps straining at the bounds of these genres. The mixed nature of Shakespeare's plays leaps into prominence if we compare them with ancient Greek plays. Greek plays fly like arrows to their targets in under 1500 lines each. A Greek tragedy; things start bad, get worse, reach bottom, and the chorus winds up by telling you the best thing that can happen to a man is never to have been born. Shakespearean tragedy' a great many people die, too, but they do all sorts of other things. They triumph, they clown, they crack jokes. Hamlet is one of the wittiest characters in Shakespeare.

In comedy, the Greeks cracked jokes, they told dirty stories, and they ended with a revel of food and wine and sex, and Shakespeare has those things in his comedies. But he also has serious things. Many people find Shylock a tragic character, even though he appears in a comedy, and *Measure for Measure* certainly deals with serious issues in a gritty world.

As for the third genre, history, the Greeks didn't write plays of this mixed nature at all. It's difficult to say what constitutes a Shakespearean history play. Some history plays end happily for the leading characters, like *Henry V*; others end with defeat and death, like *Richard II*. My point here is that the abundance of Shakespeare overflows the traditional generic boundaries. He is restless; he is experimental in the sorts of plays he writes. Life doesn't come packaged as comedy or tragedy, so Shakespeare strains at the boundaries of the traditional forms to get in as much as he can.

No artist can reflect all of life. Art, after all, involves some selection from life, a selection manifesting a form, a form either imposed by the artist or believed by the artist to be inherent in the material. But of all the artists I know, Shakespeare manages to get the most in, and still be coherent. His prodigality, his abundance, gives us pleasures and griefs in a spacious plenty.

Twelfth Night—Shakespearean Comedy
Lecture 3

Comedy is concerned with desire and fulfillment. People are in a state of yearning, which of course entails a state of frustration, and eventually, they arrive at a condition of satisfaction.

Shakespearean comedy centers on the human desire for romantic love, which moves through courtship to marriage. This comedic pattern is as basic as the tragic pattern of decline and fall. Shakespeare has helped to establish modern Western ideas about courtship and marriage. The plots of comedies concern overcoming the barriers to the fulfillment of desire. In *A Midsummer Night's Dream, As You Like It,* and *The Merchant of Venice,* these obstacles to desire-fulfillment are external to the characters; in *Much Ado About Nothing* and *The Taming of the Shrew,* they are internal to the characters. These obstacles generate the major plot patterns of the plays. The external barriers lead to an action of escape from the place where the barriers rule; internal barriers lead to an action of invasion into the deadlocked situation.

Foolish behavior arises particularly because societies invent highly artificial codes of conduct and speech for lovers.

Shakespeare especially perceives that love is both foolish, prompting us into behavior that looks silly to the rest of the world, and wonderful, a profound and character-changing experience. Romantic comedies are thus both funny and moving. Foolish behavior arises particularly because societies invent highly artificial codes of conduct and speech for lovers. Courtship involves a highly stylized and ritualized set of behaviors. Early twentieth-century Americans courted with restraint, formal visits, and chaperones. Late twentieth-century American lovers converse in psychobabble. Late sixteenth-century English lovers courted in ballads, formal speeches of praise drawing classical mythology from Ovid, and sonnets drawing stylized descriptions from Petrarch.

The main plot of *Twelfth Night* illustrates and contests these sixteenth-century conventions. Orsino in 1.1 praises Olivia and compares himself to the hunter Actaeon, the main character in a story from Ovid's Greek mythology. Orsino describes himself as a stag pursued by hounds representing his unsatisfied desires. Acting at Orsino's behest, Cesario (Viola in male disguise) approaches Olivia with a formal speech of praise, but Olivia rejects the praise and mocks the method. Speaking more directly, Cesario addresses Olivia with masculine appreciation *and* feminine insight.

Cesario rebukes Olivia for cloistering herself from human relationships. According to the parable of the talents in the Gospel of Matthew, we do not own our possessions, merits, virtues, and other natural gifts and abilities. Instead, we hold them in trust from God and must put them to work in the world. The movement from self-absorption to generosity and reciprocal interaction with others is a basic measure of character in Shakespeare, especially for lovers. ■

Essential Reading

Shakespeare, *Twelfth Night*.

Supplementary Reading

See the film of *Twelfth Night*, directed by Trevor Nunn, or the BBC-TV videotape.

Hawkins, "The Two Worlds of Shakespearean Comedy."

Warren and Wells, Introduction to *Twelfth Night* (Oxford edition).

Questions to Consider

1. During the play, we see Orsino, Cesario, and Malvolio court Olivia, and Olivia court Cesario and Sebastian. Compare and contrast modes of courtship within the play.

2. What varying tones do you find in the play? Is it purely comic? Are there moments of melancholy, anger, and other feelings that qualify the comedy? How does this affect our experience as we read or see the play?

Twelfth Night—Shakespearean Comedy
Lecture 3—Transcript

When I was a graduate student and a young professor, I learned an enormous amount about Shakespearean comedy from the essays of the Canadian scholar Northrop Frye, and I still am deeply indebted to him. What follows, follows from Frye's theories.

Comedy is concerned with desire and fulfillment. People are in a state of yearning, which of course entails a state of frustration, and eventually, they arrive at a condition of satisfaction. Now, we desire many things: food, money, freedom, pleasure, what you will. Shakespearean comedy concentrates on love, the desire for another person, which meets fulfillment in both spiritual and physical union. Shakespeare is the great playwright of romantic love, one of the great exponents of the idea or myth that for every young man out there, there is a young woman; and they will meet, and they will court, and perhaps get through some difficulties, but they will marry; and they will produce young of their own, who will meet, and court, and marry, and produce young of their own. The notion that romantic love is the normal prelude to marriage gains tremendous strength in the sixteenth century, and of course has dominated the Western imagination ever since.

Comedy, then, has a basic pattern that is related to the rhythm of the human race. The aesthetic philosopher Suzanne Langer pointed this out many years ago; the human race as a whole reproduces generation by generation, it works in the rhythm of renewal. This is as opposed to the rhythm of tragedy, where each of us individually rises to some peak or platform, and then descends to death. I would add, at this point, that many people think, generally people who have not thought about the matter very much, that somehow, inherently, tragedy is more profound than comedy. I disagree with that. What is profound is an individual play. There are great and profound tragedies; there are also cheap and superficial tragedies. I have read some of them. There are, likewise, great and profound comedies; *Twelfth Night* and *The Tempest* have lasted for centuries by now. There are also cheap and superficial comedies; a movie you saw last week at the multiplex and won't remember more than another day or two. It isn't the form that is profound; both forms are related to basic things in life—desire and fulfillment for comedy, decline and death for tragedy. It's the individual plays that can be achievements.

The plots of Shakespearean comedy concern the obstacles to fulfillment, the barriers that stand in the way. Usually the characters fall in love very quickly in Act I; they are united in Act V, so they spend the time of the play trying to get over, around, and through the various obstacles. In some cases, those obstacles are external. There is a domineering father, who says to his daughter, "You may not marry the guy you want; I pick out for you this other guy." Or there is a law that stands, somehow, between the lovers. Or there is a rival lover, usually someone less attractive but more powerful within the society, who wants the desired object. This is the case in *A Midsummer Night's Dream* and *As You Like It* and *The Merchant of Venice*. In fact, *A Midsummer Night's Dream* is a very good example, where all three occur. Hermia wants to marry Lysander, but her father says, "No; you must marry Demetrius." Her father is backed up by a law in the ancient Athens, in which *A Midsummer Night's Dream* is set, a law that says you must marry the man your father picks out for you, or you will die the death, or go into a convent. Pretty extreme law. And there is the rival, because Demetrius, the man her father has picked out, does want to marry her, so she has all three of those things to struggle with.

In other comedies, the barrier is internal. In *Much Ado about Nothing*, the sexual antagonism between Benedick and Beatrice is as great as the sexual attraction. And in *The Taming of the Shrew*, Kate is a raging termagant who is hostile to all the men she has met so far. Sometimes, there is a failure in love, and when this is the case, it is nearly always the man who is at fault. Most of Shakespeare's women are pretty steadfast in love, and wise about love. Some of the men, however—Proteus in *Two Gentlemen of Verona*, Claudio in *Much Ado About Nothing*, Posthumus in *Cymbeline*, Leontes in *The Winter's Tale*—are fickle or skittish or easily deluded into thinking that the woman they love has been unfaithful, when she hasn't.

Now, from these possible obstacles come the major patterns of the plots of Shakespearean comedies. When the barrier is external, the characters usually cope with it by escaping the jurisdiction in which the barrier prevails. We begin in a city or a court, the characters run away. In *A Midsummer Night's*

Dream, they leave Athens and go outside into the wood outside Athens. In *As You Like It*, the characters leave for the forest of Arden. In a place closer to nature, they may work out their relationships undeterred by the power of the father or the law.

When the barriers are internal, the pattern is not escape, but invasion. The home city is caught in a state of deadlock; what it needs is fresh people to come in from outside, fresh characters to upset the deadlock. In *The Taming of the Shrew*, Padua is caught in a state of deadlock. Everybody wants to marry Bianca, but her father has said her older sister, Kate, must marry first. Nobody wants to marry Kate, so everybody is unhappy. We need someone to come in and woo Kate. This is also the case in *Twelfth Night*. Duke Orsino loves the countess Olivia, but she has vowed to honor her dead brother by seven years of ritual mourning, which leaves the Duke mooning around in hopeless melancholy with no one to address his passion to. Illyria, where they live, is locked in entropy; what it needs is outside people to come in and establish new relationships. Those outside people turn up as the shipwrecked twins, Viola and Sebastian.

One other generalization I must get into, before I discuss *Twelfth Night* in detail—Shakespeare's special insight into love. For him, pretty regularly in the comedies, love has this unique and paradoxical quality. It is both foolish and wonderful. We behave foolishly when we're in love; we sigh, we pine, life is not worth living unless we're with the beloved, or thinking about the beloved, or trying to get to the beloved. And other people laugh at us. At the same time, love is wonderful. It is the most profound experience a young person can undergo, short of being mixed up in some catastrophe, some war, or the early death of one's parents, or something truly dreadful. Love is the most moving, the most changing, experience a person in the late teens or the twenties can undergo, the discovery that there is another soul out there that fits our soul, another we admire that admires us; a profound and personality-altering and life-altering experience for most of us. And this combination of folly and wonder means that a comedy about romantic love can be both funny and deeply moving.

Once of the reasons why love looks foolish is that it produces highly artificial behavior in lovers. Courtship is an extremely stylized set of actions. This is another great paradox of love. To the lover, love feels natural; what could be more natural than the response of desire to a desirable person? Desire is an instinctive response; the biologists would say it is a hormonal response. The pheromones start vibrating in the air between two people. That's why Shakespeare can so often use the plot of love at first sight. But however spontaneous and genuine the emotion feels, the expression of it is very sharply codified. Love needs a language, a set of behaviors. The first product of love is artifice. Every society I know of has invented a standard code of speech and action, conventions that are thought appropriate for young lovers. After all, in decent society, you can't just jump on the person you want. You have to approach and speak and behave in a particular way.

For example, early in the twentieth century in America, a young, well-brought-up, middle-class American man would court a young woman by formally calling on her at her house. He might sit on the front porch with her; he might bring to her some small gift of flowers, a slim volume of poetry, something small. You don't want to suggest you're going to buy the girl or something like that, just an expression of your feeling. And the conversation would be discretely chaperoned by her mother or her aunt—not sitting on the porch with them, that's a little gross. Perhaps sitting on the front room, not even seeing them, but hearing occasionally the conversation through an open window to make sure the proprieties were being observed.

Now, we don't do that any more. It seems silly to us. We don't have chaperones; we probably don't have front porches. And young people courting now think that they behave far more freely than their grandparents or great-grandparents did. And in some ways, they do. But, in fact, we have a different set of conventions that are equally rigid. I look at my students at college courting. What do they do? They go to the campus café or to some eatery downtown, and they order tacos and diet Coke, and they sit at the table gazing into each other's eyes, and they proceed to analyze the psychological ramifications of what they call "our relationship." They talk about their needs and their anxieties and their inhibitions and how their parents brought them up and the struggles they are going through. The Coke and the tacos aren't obligatory; beer and pizza would do as well, but the psychobabble is obligatory. It's the language we have for love these days.

If you were a young Englishman at the end of the sixteenth century, trying to express your spontaneous and overflowing passion for a young Englishwoman you've met, you would take your language and your conventions not from diluted Freud, but from art, especially from literature. In *As You Like It*, in the "Seven Ages of Man" speech, Jaques describes the characteristic behavior of the lover as "sighing like a furnace and making a ballad to his mistress' eyebrow" A ballad, a song in praise of some feature of his mistress' beauty. Or, if you can't sing well, a speech, either to be written out in an elegant hand and delivered by a messenger, or to be recited orally when you see the lady. And these compositions are written in elaborately rhetorical prose, really fine compositions, and they invariably draw on classical mythology, the love affairs written up by the Greek and Roman poets, particularly one Roman poet, Ovid, whose collection, *The Metamorphoses*, was a convenient anthology of all the famous classical stories. Lucentio in *The Taming of the Shrew*, Benedick in *Much Ado About Nothing*, Orsino in *Twelfth Night*, Orlando in *As You Like It*, they all refer to one myth or other—Leander being drowned as he swam across the Hellaspont on his way to see his beloved Hero; or Dido pining for Aeneas as he sailed away to found Rome; or Troilus and Cressida pining for each other, separated by the armies of Troy.

And if speeches and song are not enough, and you have real literary talent, you write sonnets. And sonnets have a very standard form, not only the 14 lines and particular rhyme scheme; they have a very standard language. The sonnet is almost always uttered by the man, and he speaks of himself as burning and freezing alternately, in hope and in despair, swearing he'll die if his mistress doesn't grant him mercy. And he describes the lady in an elaborate language of praise, which is very set, very formal. The lady always has a white hand, whiter than snow. Her hair is like fine-spun gold. Here eyes shine like the stars or the sun. Lilies and roses war in her cheek, her lips are like coral, her teeth are like pearls, her breasts are like globes. Spontaneous feeling, upheaving within the lover, produces very scripted roleplaying of one kind or another.

Now, that is how Orsino is behaving in the first scene of *Twelfth Night*. Act I, Scene I, Orsino has sent yet another messenger to Olivia, and Olivia rejects the messenger at the gate, will not even listen to the message. She is going to go on mourning her dead brother, and Orsino is melancholy and simply meditates upon his feelings: "O, when mine eyes did see Olivia first, / Methought she purged the air of pestilence! / That instant was I turn'd into a hart;"—that is, a stag—"And my desires, like fell and cruel hounds, / E'er since pursue me."

Olivia is so beautiful, she is so radiant, that she purges the air of all pestilence, all the plague germs around. She clarifies the atmosphere. And then the business of "When I saw her I was turned into a stag, and my desires pursued me like hounds," is a deliberate allusion to a very famous Greek myth out of Ovid—the myth of Actaeon. Actaeon was a hunter who, while out on the chase, accidentally stumbled across the goddess Diana, who was bathing in a pool. Now, Diana is a virgin goddess. She has nothing to do with men, and she was outraged that this male mortal should see her naked. Therefore, she transformed Actaeon into a deer, and he was run down and killed by his own hunting hounds. And that story is moralized throughout the Middle Ages and into the Renaissance, as a story about how desire unsatisfied will devour the desirer. If our desires do not reach fulfillment, we are torn to pieces.

Orsino's suit has been rejected by the countess Olivia. He tries one more time; the shipwrecked Viola turns up in his court in male disguise, dressed as a pageboy, calling herself Cesario. This Cesario is employed by Orsino, once more, on embassy to Olivia; he sends Cesario, thinking that the freshness and youth of the pageboy may cause the countess to have a change of heart. And it does—it causes the countess to fall madly in love with the pageboy. And the scene in which they first meet is one of the best demonstrations of characteristic action in love in *Twelfth Night*, and I will spend the rest of this lecture on it.

Essentially, Cesario does three things. He comes with a prepared text, the kind of speech of praise I've been saying is characteristic of sixteenth-century lovers. I'm going to call Cesario "he" because he's supposed to be a man, but it's very confusing; you don't know whether to say "he" or "she". The androgynous appeal of this person works, in fact, for both Olivia and Orsino; it's one of the rather magical things in the play. Cesario begins, "Most radiant, exquisite and unmatchable beauty," but then he interrupts himself. Olivia has several ladies-in-waiting around, and is wearing a veil. He doesn't know which one Olivia is, so he undercuts the formal convention himself of making the speech of love, and says, "I pray you, tell me if this be the lady of the house, for I never saw her: I would be loathe to cast away my speech, for besides that it is excellently well penned, I have taken great pains to learn it."

You see what's going on; there is the formal behavior of love here, but the messenger himself is making fun of it, and saying he's not going to waste his efforts on it. He's not behaving like the standard lover, and that rather interests Olivia. Instead of getting just another suit from Orsino, just another fancy piece of verse or prose, we've got someone with some personality. As the conversation goes on, Cesario tries once more to deliver this speech of praise. By this time, they've gotten rid of the ladies in waiting, and Olivia says, "Now sir, what is your text?"

> *Cesario (Viola)*: Most sweet lady—
> *Olivia*: Oh, an excellent text, and much may be said of it. Where lies your text?
> *Cesario*: In Orsino's bosom.
> *Olivia*: In his bosom! In what chapter of his bosom?
> *Cesario*: To answer by the method, in the first of his heart.
> *Olivia*: O, I have read it: it is heresy."

Now, Olivia is mocking the convention of delivering a formal speech; she's treating it as if it were a sermon. "You've got a text? OK, what's the chapter, what's the verse? Oh no, you can't build a sermon on that chapter and verse; it would be heretical." Both of them are mocking the method. Something is beginning to happen between these two people. That's the first stage, to set up the formal convention and start to undercut it.

The second thing that Cesario does is to talk in two different voices, and this is why I mentioned the androgyny in particular, because one voice is that of a man, and the other is that of the woman whom Cesario really is, Viola. When Cesario asks for Olivia to take off that veil—"Good madam, let me see your face."—Olivia hesitates and then finally does take it off. "Look you, sir, such a one was I this present: is it not well done?"

And Cesario replies, "Excellently done, if God did all." I think that's a wonderful line; the "excellently done" is the voice of a man, who genuinely admires this womanly beauty. The "if God did all" is a woman's voice saying, "My dear, is that all you? How much of it is cosmetics? Let me look a little closer." And that double voice thing happens a little bit later in the scene, when Cesario gets rather exasperated with Olivia: "I see you what you are, you are too proud; / But, if you were the devil, you are fair." The first line, "I see you what you are, you are too proud," is a woman's insight into another woman's vanity. After all, Viola knows she's already falling in love with Orsino herself, and she's sizing up the competition. The next line, "But, if you were the devil, you are fair," is a very masculine kind of line, a guy saying, "By gum, she's pretty." Both voices are going there, so the scene becomes quite electrical in its sexual relationship.

The third, and most important, thing that Cesario does in this courtship scene is to rebuke Olivia, to rebuke her quite stiffly, for secluding herself from human relationships. And in that rebuke, she advances a theory that lies at the heart of all Shakespeare's ideas about love. Cesario tells Olivia, "What is yours to bestow is not yours to reserve." And in a later speech, " Lady, you are the cruelest she alive / If you will lead these graces to the grave / And leave the world no copy." That is, you are a very cruel woman if you will die a virgin, not having had a child who will carry on your beauty to another generation.

Now, these rather odd compliments—"You are beautiful, therefore, you should reproduce;" "What is your to give, to bestow, is not your to reserve, to hold back"—are based ultimately on a fundamental text in Western civilization. They're based on the parable of the talents in the Gospel according to Matthew. As the story is told in Matthew, a rich man went off on a long journey, leaving three of his servants with sums of money, 10 talents for one, five for another, one for the third. And the 10-talent servant went out and invested his money, and when the lord returned, was able to give him back 20. Likewise, the 5-talent man doubled his. But the 1-talent man buried his in the ground and returned only the single talent. The first two servants were praised. "Well done, thou good and faithful servant." The third servant was rebuked. "Thou wicked and slothful servant. You will be cast into outer darkness."

Now, the point of this parable, as it is understood in Shakespeare's time at any rate, is this; that we do not own our possessions, our merits, our virtues, our graces, the things we are given by birth, anything that can be called a "talent." This, by the way, is where the word "talent" in modern usage comes from, in all the original Western European languages. In the original Greek of the Gospel, it's simply "a sum of money," and because of this parable, it has come to mean any gift, any ability that we are born with, whether it be beauty, or an artistic skill, or a business skill, or whatever. We do not own these things; they were given to us by God. We are only stewards of them; we hold them in trust. It is our job to put them to use in the world. A virtue, a grace, a skill, an ability does not fully exist unless it is put into action. It merely withers away.

Now this is a general Christian idea. It is still in practice. In an Episcopal church, when the collection is taken up, the congregation recites together, "All things come of Thee, O Lord, and of Thine own have we given Thee." Of Thine own have we given Thee; that's our job, to give God's gifts back to Him, to make God's gifts work in the world on His mission. And it was a doctrine particularly important in the sixteenth century in England. In the English Renaissance, there was a general turn against the enclosed monastic way of life. Henry VIII abolished the monasteries, and he did it, of course, for personal gain and for political reasons. But he was able to do it, the population went along with it, because there was a general sense that the monastic, or conventional, way of life, the enclosed cloistered way of life, was not the highest way for people to use their abilities. They should go out and work in the world; young, humanistically educated, able people should be active in the world. A life of prayer and contemplation is okay if you're old; this is what you do toward the end of your life. But young people ought to be active.

Now, by translating this idea of stewardship into the highest realms of religious thought—I may be overplaying my hand, or it may sound that way to you; after all, Viola is only talking about Olivia's physical beauty, not her moral virtues—but the idea is pervasive in Shakespeare, not a message that he wants to preach, just part of his basic mental equipment. Excellence of any kind must be given generously to the world, shared with the world, or it loses its value as an excellence, and that includes beauty. It is selfish merely to sit and look in a mirror, or to enclose yourself in a self-made cloister, as Olivia is doing. Our talents are the gifts of God and nature, and we must render an accounting for our use of them.

Olivia should not be living a barren life, and in fact, the effect of this scene is to persuade Olivia of this truth. Within the next 60 lines, she falls head over heels in love with Cesario, agrees that "ourselves we do not own"—I am not my own to seclude—and starts giving him gifts. All the real lovers in this play act with extraordinary generosity. The effect of Viola, this androgynous, charming creature, is to cause Olivia and, in a later scene, Orsino, to undertake a journey from self-absorption to generosity, from self-absorption to a reciprocal love with other persons.

Twelfth Night—Malvolio in Love
Lecture 4

Shakespeare is a comprehensive writer. Comprehensiveness is one of his great virtues. He closes this comedy with predominant happiness, but reminds us that there are always some people who decline to join the supposedly universal celebrations of common humanity.

In this discussion of *Twelfth Night*, we take a closer look at the characters of the play. This enables us to contrast the young lovers with the one character who is clearly outside their circle, yet would like to be in it. That character is Malvolio (whose very name gives us a hint of his true nature). Malvolio is also placed in contrast with a group of lesser characters who plot—and achieve—revenge as he plots for the hand of Olivia. We will see that this is a comedy with a bite, which does not necessarily resolve itself into the characteristic "happy" ending of Shakespearean romantic comedy in general.

In his soliloquy in Act 4 Scene 3, Sebastian acknowledges the bizarre quality of events in Illyria, and he argues for Olivia's sanity nonetheless. The real point of the speech lies, however, in his eager embrace of the good things of the world: the sun, the air, the Countess. This is a vital part of the view of life in Shakespearean comedy. The scene of Sebastian in the sun contrasts directly with that of Malvolio confined to the darkhouse, which represents his inability and unwillingness to see beyond himself.

In a great Elizabethan country house, the upper servants were significant

Malvolio in the dark (Act 4, Scene 2).

people, perhaps members of the lesser gentry themselves. Malvolio is a person of consequence, conscientious in his job as estate manager. His concern for the estate contrasts with Sir Toby's merry-making. This is one of the instances, recurring in Shakespeare, of opposition between festival and duty, Carnival and Lent, merry-making and Puritanism. Twelfth Night, or Epiphany (January 6), is the festive occasion that follows the solemnity of Christmas. Malvolio has the Puritan desire for power and the Puritan repressiveness but not the Puritan religious zeal or devotion. He is negatively virtuous; he wants to do away with all festivity.

Malvolio's concern with decorum and order is especially repressive because it coexists with the indecorum in his soul, his wish to rise above his place by marrying Olivia. Shakespeare does not consider it wrong to desire a desirable woman, but Malvolio wants her not for herself but for the worldly position he would achieve through her. Worldly position is not wrong either, except that Malvolio wants it only to exert trivial power over others. His fantasy of the marriage to Olivia in 2.5 consists entirely of tinpot tyranny.

The darkhouse is a symbol of Malvolio's self-ignorance and egomania.

The plot of Toby, Maria, Andrew, Feste, and Fabian to punish Malvolio for his repressiveness and threats is a precisely measured piece of comic revenge. Their revenge is exact and just. They tyrannize over him and make him appear to be mad. The darkhouse is a symbol of Malvolio's self-ignorance and egomania. At some point, however, we begin to feel sorry for Malvolio. The comic revenge turns slightly sour as we perceive his genuine suffering. His fate is exact and just, but few if any of us can endure such strict justice. At the end, Malvolio achieves some dignity in his blank-verse appeal to Olivia for some explanation of why he has been abused.

Malvolio refuses to acknowledge his faults, and he rejects Fabian's peace-making overtures. Shakespeare's inclusion of one unreconciled person who still wants revenge in the otherwise happy and harmonious ending is a characteristic mark of his comprehensiveness. Malvolio's refusal to be reconciled dilutes our pleasure slightly at the end of the play. Shakespeare thereby anchors the play in real life. ■

Shakespeare, *Twelfth Night*.

Barber, *Shakespeare's Festive Comedy*, chapter 10.

Leggatt, *Shakespeare's Comedy of Love*, chapter 9.

1. Malvolio is a somewhat problematic character for a Shakespeare comedy. Is his punishment, stimulated by revenge, condign? Why do you think Shakespeare fails to redeem him at the end of the play?

2. After listening to the lectures on *The Merchant of Venice* (Lectures 7 and 8), compare and contrast Malvolio and Shylock in terms of their character, actions, and downfall. Is one more sympathetic than the other? More realistic? More justified in his actions?

Twelfth Night—Malvolio in Love
Lecture 4—Transcript

Several years back, a film version of *Twelfth Night* came out, directed by Trevor Nunn, with Imogen Stubbs as Viola and Nigel Hawthorne as Malvolio. It's a very good movie; I do recommend it. *The New York Times*, reviewing it, had to struggle a bit with the plot of *Twelfth Night*; in fact, the reviewer referred to the plot as being "a Renaissance ramshackle plot." Apparently, it was a bit too much for *The New York Times* that there are identical twins, and a sex disguise that is successful, and switching about of lovers, and so forth.

I will talk about realism and fairy-tale qualities in Shakespearean plots in another lecture in this course, but I want you to know, at this moment, that Shakespeare is perfectly well aware of the improbabilities in this story. In fact, he writes for Sebastian, Viola's twin brother, a soliloquy that acknowledges the unlikelihood of what is going on. Sebastian has turned up late in the play, just in time to take over the man's role in Cesario's love affair with Olivia. Olivia, to him a totally strange, but beautiful, rich and desirable woman, has swept down on him in the street and said, "At last, I have found you. Come and marry me," and Sebastian is responding to this extraordinary development.

> This is the air; that is the glorious sun;
> This pearl she gave me, I do feel't and see't;
> And though 'tis wonder that enwraps me thus,
> Yet 'tis not madness. Where is Antonio, then?
> I could not find him at the Elephant:
> Yet there he was; and there I found this message,
> That he did range the town to seek me out.
> His counsel now might do me golden service;
> For though my soul disputes well with my sense,
> That this may be some error, but no madness,
> Yet doth this accident and flood of fortune
> So far exceed all instance, all discourse,
> That I am ready to distrust mine eyes
> And wrangle with my reason that persuades me

To any other trust but that I am mad
Or else the lady's mad; yet, if 'twere so,
She could not sway her house, command her followers,
Take and give back affairs and their dispatch
With such a smooth, discreet and stable bearing
As I perceive she does.

Shakespeare has Sebastian acknowledge the bizarre quality of events, the unprecedented accident and flood of fortune, and has him work out an argument for Olivia's sanity. She rules her house well; she takes and gives back affairs with a smooth, discreet and stable bearing. She must be sane. That's his concession to realism here.

But the point of the soliloquy is really Sebastian's openness to experience, his readiness to embrace new developments. He is eager; he welcomes the good things of life. It is not just the sun up there, it is the glorious sun, and the sun *is* glorious, unless we are so jaded or so self-absorbed that we've forgotten about it, that we take it for granted. He describes himself as enwrapped with wonder, and he is, that such a thing as the sun should exist, that the air should exist, that pearls exist, that a beautiful woman like Olivia exists. This is a vital part of the view of life in Shakespearean comedy, that life is wonderful, and to be embraced.

And Sebastian's soliloquy is all the more impressive because of where it comes in the play: the middle of Act IV, directly following the scene in which Malvolio has been confined to the dark. Malvolio is thought to be mad and put in a dark-house, which was the customary medical treatment for madmen in Shakespeare's time. Sebastian is in the sun; Malvolio is in the dark. Now, Malvolio really can see nothing beyond himself; he cannot see or appreciate other things. His only interest in the sun is that it enables him to see his own shadow. Maria, Olivia's lady-in-waiting, has a line about him doing that: "He hath been yonder in the sun practising behavior to his own shadow this half hour." "Behavior" means courtly gestures, bowing, and gestures with the arms, flinging the cloak around.

Malvolio is the center of the second plot of *Twelfth Night*. He is the steward of Countess Olivia, and he is tricked into believing that the Countess is in love with him, and will marry him and this make him Count Malvolio—if he courts her in yellow stockings and crossed garters. Before I talk about him personally, let me talk about servants here in general. Because we live in an age and culture that largely does without servants, we are apt to misconstrue their position and think that all servants in the sixteenth century are menials who scrub pots. No. The Elizabethan country house is a very large establishment. It would be an estate of thousands of acres, with farms and tenant farmers and all sorts of people dependent on it in various ways. An Elizabethan manor house was the center of the social, legal, and agricultural organization for the whole district, probably for the whole county. That's where the title of Count and Countess come from.

The upper servants in such an organization were vital and responsible people. They would not be peasants; they certainly wouldn't scrub pots. They might come from the ranks of the lesser gentry themselves, and the gentry are the top five percent of the population in Shakespeare's time. Probably that is the case with Maria and with Malvolio. Malvolio is called a gentleman, and Maria is referred to, or addressed by Malvolio, as "Mistress Mary." They might be, say, the younger son of a gentleman, the one who didn't get the inheritance of course, and the younger daughter or the one who didn't have enough dowry to attract a husband or something like that. The younger offspring of gentry, of good family but no particular fortune, who would make a career in service to the really great lords.

Malvolio is the steward; he runs the whole estate. He has charge over everything, keeps the books. If this were the twentieth century, we would call him an estate manager, and he would probably have a degree in business or law. That's the kind of rank we're thinking about here. Olivia has great respect for him. When told that Malvolio has gone mad, she is very disturbed. "I would not have him miscarry for half my dowry." And since her dowry is her whole estate—she is the only heiress—that's a considerable amount. He's a figure of visible important onstage; he would have a steward's staff on hand and a chain around his neck, a chain of office. He's very good at his job, devoted to the Countess, carrying out the business of the household very carefully, and a great household needs such a steward.

Sir Toby, the wastrel cousin who just gets drunk every night, says in his first scene, "Care is an enemy to life," and that is very true. Being burdened with cares means you don't enjoy yourself. But so also, one might say, carelessness is an enemy to life. Both views can be taken. If you do not take care of an inheritance, you will end up like Sir Andrew, who has a small inheritance, but is going through it very rapidly. Maria describes him as "a very fool and a prodigal." Here is one of the great oppositions that occurs in a number of Shakespearean plays; I'll come back to it when we get to Falstaff, the opposition between merrymaking and devotion to duty. In this case, in *Twelfth Night*, the opposition gets into the title of the play itself. Twelfth Night is one of the great festivals of the Elizabethan year. It is the Feast of the Epiphany, January 6, the Twelfth Night of Christmas and as the Elizabethans did these things, Christmas was kept as a religious occasion; the big parties and the gift giving happened on New Year's and Twelfth Night.

Twelfth Night, in particular, was an occasion for games, and putting on plays, and other entertainments, and the merrymaking and festivals that are associated with Twelfth Night as an occasion in the Elizabethan year are embodied by Sir Toby and Sir Andrew and Maria and Fabian and the clown, the jester, whose very name recalls the idea of festival. His name is Feste. And when they have that impromptu party in the second act, the party that Malvolio tries to close down, saying it's too loud, it's too late, you're all behaving in an unbecoming way, then we have the full opposition between the spirit of festival and the spirit of repression, Carnival versus Lent. Malvolio is a Puritan.

Now this is a very interesting point about Malvolio. Maria, in fact, does, at one point, call him a kind of a Puritan. Then, five lines later, she says he is not a Puritan at all, but merely a time-pleaser, and an affected ass. He is, and is not, a Puritan. Shakespeare is being very careful with a volatile contemporary subject. The Puritans, whom I've already mentioned in an earlier lecture, were the left wing of the political and religious spectrum, and they were a powerful group, both in the city of London and at court. They desired to carry the Reformation further, to purify the church, to do away with some of the remaining elements of Roman Catholicism that still existed in the Church of England, like bishops and elaborate ceremonies.

They desired to create a wholly virtuous commonwealth, to build the new Jerusalem.

Now Malvolio is not a Puritan, because he has none of that true Puritan zeal, religious devotion. He is a Puritan in the sense of being repressive. He has all that hatred of holiday and reveling. He is virtuous—negatively virtuous—and so desires to set the standard of virtue for other people. Toby asks him the crucial question, "Dost thou think, because thou art virtuous, there shall be no more cakes and ale?" Because you are virtuous, shall we do away with all the things that are fun, all the rest of us? Cakes and ale are central to all festivals. Indeed, Malvolio's concern with order, with decorum, with not getting drunk and staying up too late at night, with virtue, is particularly repressive because it coexists with a monstrous indecorum in his own soul. He desires the Countess. Now that's not bad in itself; there's nothing wrong with that, the Countess is a desirable woman. It's quite natural to desire her. But he doesn't desire her for herself; he never speaks of her beauty, or her virtue, or her graces. Like many repressive people, he is himself repressed. When he has a fantasy of being married to Olivia, she plays actually very little role in the arrangement. He desires not love, but a vertiginous rise in social position. He wants to be Count Malvolio.

Now there's nothing wrong with that either, I think, or certainly Shakespeare didn't think so. He himself rose socially. He managed to get a coat of arms for the Shakespeare family, to have them declared gentry. That was a rise from the origins of his parents, and he had the money to do it; he earned the money in his work in the theater in London. But Malvolio desires worldly position, not because it makes possible comfort and grace and benevolence to others; he desires worldly position because it would give him power over other people, the power to rebuke and expel Toby and Andrew and Feste and Maria. He's a tinpot tyrant.

When he is deluded into believing that Olivia is in love with him, he expresses a feeling that none of the other lovers in this play ever express—a smug satisfaction in finding himself the object of love. All the other lovers give when they fall in love; he only takes. The best way to demonstrate this is to look at his fantasy. This is Malvolio daydreaming, unaware that he is overheard by the other characters, and I'll leave out their lines and just do this as a soliloquy in Act II, Scene V:

> To be Count Malvolio! Having been three months married to her, sitting in my state, —

Now, a state is a raised chair with a canopy over it; he's going to look like a king when he's a count.

> Calling my officers about me, in my branched velvet gown; having come from a day-bed, where I have left Olivia sleeping,—

That's very interesting. He's got a fantasy about marriage to her, but first he thinks of the chair, and then he thinks of the officer who he'll summon, then he thinks of his own clothes, and only then does Olivia come into the relationship. And she's lying on a day-bed, apparently sexually exhausted by his exertions and demands of her.

> And then to have the humour of state; and after a demure travel of regard, telling them I know my place as I would they should do theirs—

That's just outrageous. You're having an enormous fantasy about getting out of your place, and in this fantasy, you say "I know my place" and squash the officers.

> To ask for my kinsman Toby,—

Oh, this is going to be the great delight of being a count; you don't have to call cousin Toby Sir Toby anymore. You just call him "my kinsman Toby."

> Seven of my people, with an obedient start, make out for him—

Seven? He needs seven people to go get one drunken old sot?

> I frown the while; and perchance wind up my watch, or play with— some rich jewel.

I assume he's playing with his steward's chain, and then he remembers, he wouldn't be wearing his steward's chain anymore. He would be having something grander ornamenting his doublet.

> Toby approaches; courtesies there to me,—I extend my hand to him thus, quenching my familiar smile with an austere regard of control,—

My goodness, when have we ever seen Malvolio smile, let alone quench it with an austere regard of control? He's got an austere regard of control all the time. One of the funny things about the delusions is that they make him smile all the time; the forged letter tells him to do so. That is the way he behaves.

This is the thematic opposition. The theatrical result of this thematic opposition between the Puritan repressed daydreamer on the one hand, and the festival drinkers on the other, the theatrical results are two of the funniest scenes in Western comedy; the scene when Malvolio actually picks up that letter and swallows its absurd command whole, and begins to delight that Olivia loves him; and the later scene when he follows out the commands of the letter to appear in yellow stockings and cross-gartered and be impudent to everybody in the household except Olivia. In these scenes, Sir Toby and Sir Andrew and Fabian and Feste and Maria are all getting revenge for particular threats and disservices that Malvolio has done them. We are told why each one has a motive to exact some kind of comic revenge upon him, and the result is a piece of precisely measured comic revenge.

He had been dreaming of greatness, to be Count Malvolio. He had imagined Toby curtsying to him. Well, at the end of the play, his bitter complaint to the Countess is that Toby has been given rule over him when he was thought to be mad. He asked the revelers in the midnight party scene, "My masters, are you mad?" Are you out of your minds to be drinking and making noise at this late hour? The revelers make him appear to be mad and put him in the dark-house. He had spurned and criticized the fool, Feste, going so far as to suggest to Olivia that she get rid of him. "I don't see why my lady should be troubled with so barren a fool as this; he's not even funny." The fool spurns him in the dark-house.

The whole revenge is exact and just, and the locking up of Malvolio alone in the dark-house is a stage picture, a precise emblem of Malvolio's spiritual condition. He is locked in his own dark, isolated ego, and the fool tells him truly, "I say there is no darkness but ignorance; in which thou art more puzzled than the Egyptians in their fog." The ignorance of knowing no one but yourself, of not going forth of yourself—the contrast to the generosity of all the other lovers in the play.

Having said that, I must pull back just a little; I've got to add an "except." Except, somewhere along this process, the comic revenge, funny as it is, begins to turn slightly sour. Not wholly sour, but Toby himself begins to worry if *he* will get in trouble with his cousin, the Countess, for bedeviling her steward in this way, and he's living off Olivia. He's got to be careful about that. And somewhere along the process—I don't know at what point, it may be a different point for every one of us—but somewhere along the process of what Malvolio goes through, we in the audience may be struck by the fact that Malvolio is genuinely suffering. For a sane man, and of course, Malvolio really is sane, to be locked up in the loony bin, and to have his pleas for help derided, is of course a nightmare. The revenge upon Malvolio I described a moment ago as being exact and just. But exact justice may be something that none of us can endure. As Portia says in *The Merchant of Venice*, "In the course of justice none of us should see salvation."

The pathos of Malvolio's position late in the play has earned attention in productions of the late nineteenth and the twentieth centuries. The dark-house scene has lent itself to anguished playing. The most famous modern version, perhaps, has been with the actor Michael Hordern, and in the production in which he played Malvolio, there was no structure on the stage to represent the darkhouse. We didn't, in fact, see Hordern himself; the dark-house was a trap door in the stage floor. He was down under the stage floor, so that all the audience saw was his anguished hands as he reached up, begging the fool for help. "Please, get me pen, ink and paper, that I may write the Countess and get myself out of here. Don't mock me." And that we didn't see him, but just saw the gesture calling for help, was indeed moving.

In the final scene, when Malvolio has been released and comes before all the other characters, who have sorted out their various love problems and gotten properly matched up with each other, when he comes forth to make his complaint about how he has been abused, he does so with a kind of dignity. He still thinks that it is Olivia who is responsible for that letter that misled him so much. And he speaks to her:

> Tell me, in the modesty of honour,
> Why you have given me such clear lights of favour,
> Bade me come smiling and cross-garter'd to you,
> To put on yellow stockings and to frown
> Upon Sir Toby and the lighter people;
> And, acting this in an obedient hope,
> Why have you suffer'd me to be imprison'd,
> Kept in a dark house, visited by the priest,
> And made the most notorious geck and gull
> That e'er invention play'd on? tell me why.

There is a dignity in that speech, and a pathos, and an emotional impression that is partly created by the way it is written; this is the only time that Malvolio speaks in blank verse. Everything else of his is written in ordinary prose. But he rises to the level of blank verse as he demands to know why he's been so notoriously abused. Then it is all explained, and Fabian, in particular, explains how they made fun of him, and they didn't mean any harm, and it would be a nice thing if we could all laugh about it and forget. You hurt us, we hurt you. Quits are even; let us laugh about it instead of being angry about it.

But Malvolio will not give up; he will not be reconciled. He refuses to recognize his own faults, he refuses to admit his deeds brought these revenges on. He refuses the peacemaking efforts of Fabian. And that leaves us with some bit of dissatisfaction. He exits from the final scene, instead of joining the happiness there. He exits with a terrible line, "I'll be revenged on the whole pack of you," a line not only refusing reconciliation, but indicting people who haven't even had anything to do with this, because onstage at that time are, as well as the people who have put him in the dark-house, Sebastian and Viola and the Duke, who have nothing to do with it. We want this man to relax, to try for a more satisfactory connection with people. Why does he give himself over to such wholesale resentment?

It would really be very comforting to forget all about Malvolio, to conclude merely that he deserves what he gets, which is fundamentally what I've been saying in this lecture, and then to dismiss him from further consideration so that we can thoroughly enjoy the end of the play. But we can't. The suffering, the isolation of his ego are there, even if it is his own choice to isolate himself. That is the real vexation about Malvolio's stubbornness at the end, is that he wounds our pleasure.

This is a comedy; it ends in happiness, in the still silent wonder of the marvelous recognition scene, when Sebastian and Viola finally see each other, and each knows that the twins are both alive; in the still silent wonder of the recognition that fortune is benevolent, the salt waves have been fresh in love, that there is no quarrel to taint the condition of the present tide, that each has found a spouse, and all are happy. Malvolio injures our pleasure slightly. Not as much as Shylock does at the end of *The Merchant of Venice*—I'll come to that in a later lecture—but slightly. And by doing so, he anchors the play in real life.

If the play were just lovers and benevolent fortune, it would be too sweet, a cotton-candy confection. I don't mean to knock the love plot; I said it's improbable, but I think that it contains truth, that the things it deals with are part of life: love and generosity. But, of course, they're not all of life, and Shakespeare is a comprehensive writer. Comprehensiveness is one of his great virtues. He closes this comedy with predominant happiness, but reminds us that there are always some people who decline to join the supposedly universal celebrations of common humanity. Some Scrooges don't join the party at the end of the book.

Malvolio is wrong, by the values of the play, which are the values of love, warmth, forgiveness and generosity. But he's true to himself, and his enclosed egoism is a part of life, also.

The Taming of the Shrew—Getting Married in the 1590s
Lecture 5

Lots of people have disliked [*The Taming of the Shrew*], and the play has caused considerable amount of argument and hard scholarly research from feminist scholars in the last 25 years.

*T*he Taming of the Shrew presents problems about both doctrine and action. The play is realistic in its survey of courtship practices of the 1590, though many of these practices appear odd or even offensive to the modern reader. Propertied parents often arranged marriages for their children. Dowries and dowers were expected as we now expect college degrees, for economic security. The source of wealth for young people of the upper classes lay in the family, not in working at a career. In individual cases, arranged marriages might succeed or fail.

Some preachers and moralists in late sixteenth-century England discouraged arranged marriage and argued for more consideration of personal affection. Romancers and poets could elevate personal affection among young couples to an absolute. In *Shrew*, the arranged marriage of Baptista's daughter Kate with Petruchio works better than the romantic one of his other daughter Bianca with Lucentio.

Some preachers and moralists in late sixteenth-century England discouraged arranged marriage and argued for more consideration of personal affection.

Kate closes the play with a 44-line speech in which she emphatically agrees with the doctrine of male supremacy in marriage. Actresses have played the speech for irony. This can be done either crudely or elegantly. Actresses can contradict the speech with gestures. Difficulties arise when the literal meaning of the speech is undercut or ignored. The doctrine of male supremacy requires careful statement. *Shrew* exemplifies the usefulness of old plays in reminding us that people have not always behaved or thought as we do today.

Kate's speech may be done sincerely but framed to acknowledge a variety of views. In Andrei Serban's production of *Shrew*, Kate recites the speech slowly and uncertainly, as if discovering something new. In the epilogue of the Serban production, the actors appear in their ordinary clothes and embrace each other in ways that suggest a multiplicity of relationships among them. Thus Serban supplements Shakespeare's portrayal of the "full stream of the world" by suggesting that heterosexual union with female submission, as depicted in the play, is not the only relationship possible. ∎

Essential Reading

Shakespeare, *The Taming of the Shrew*.

Supplementary Reading

See Zeffirelli film with Burton-Taylor or ACT video directed by Ball.

Cook, *Making a Match: Courtship in Shakespeare and His Society*.

Kahn, "*The Taming of the Shrew*: Shakespeare's Mirror of Marriage."

Saccio, "Shrewd and Kindly Farce."

Questions to Consider

1. How does Bianca either reflect or contrast with Kate?

2. Is Kate straightforward or ironic in her long final speech?

The Taming of the Shrew—Getting Married in the 1590s
Lecture 5—Transcript

Some 15 years back, the distinguished British actor Sir Anthony Quayle visited a Shakespeare class I was teaching at Dartmouth. Since he has acted a great deal of Shakespeare and, for most of the 50s, was the artistic director of the Shakespeare Festival at Stratford-on-Avon, he was able to share very generously with my students all sorts of stories about Shakespeare interpretations of particular scenes, parts he had played, work that he had done with fellow actors on Shakespeare. He was really extremely kind and gave us many perceptive comments and a wonderful stream of theatrical anecdotes. This went on for over half an hour, until a student of mine brought up *The Taming of the Shrew*, which we had read several weeks earlier. At that point, this genial fountain shut up. Quayle declared *The Shrew* to be a hateful play and said, "Ask me about something else," and we had to clear our throats and collect ourselves and think quickly of another topic.

Now, in fact, *The Shrew* has nearly always been a popular play, both in Shakespeare's texts and in any number of adaptations. There is, for example, another Elizabethan play called *The Taming of a Shrew*, that is so close to Shakespeare's in date, that we don't know which is first, whether Shakespeare was ripping that one off, or the anonymous author of *A Shrew* was ripping Shakespeare off. In that one, Kate has two younger sisters, so there are more suitors and the plot differs a bit, but there are many parallel scenes. In the eighteenth century, David Garrick wrote a short version of it called *Katherine and Petruchio*. In the twentieth century, Cole Porter wrote a musical version of it called *Kiss Me Kate*.

But Anthony Quayle has hardly been alone in his dissent from the play. Lots of people have disliked it, and the play has caused considerable amount of argument and hard scholarly research from feminist scholars in the last 25 years. Feminist scholarship has mattered a lot in recent Shakespearean work, and they have worked a lot on this play. Now, at the end of the twentieth century, it poses still two large problems: a problem of doctrine, and a problem of action. The problem of doctrine is that it appears to preach male supremacy in marriage. The problem of action is that it appears to humiliate its spirited heroine by making her the victim of farce. In this lecture, I'll talk about the marriage. In the next one, I'll take up farce.

As in other Shakespearean comedies, the action focuses on bringing together several couples: Kate and Petruchio; her sister Bianca and Lucentio; and, in a small variation introduced very near the end, Hortensio marries a widow. But the way in which the story is handled is rather more realistic than is usually the case in Shakespearean comedy. Here, there are no shipwrecks on remote shores, no identical twins, no heroine wearing a male disguise, as in *Twelfth Night*. There is no rushing off to dwell in a pastoral forest, as in *As You Like It*; no mysterious lottery by which the heroine will find the right husband, as in *The Merchant of Venice*. Instead, we are in a familiar, bourgeois, commercial society. In this case, it is the Italian city of Padua, and there is a wealthy gentleman, Baptista Minola, who has a problem that would be completely recognizable to the Elizabethan audience for whom Shakespeare was writing in the 1590s. He's trying to find suitable husbands for his two daughters; that's his job as a responsible father.

In the propertied classes—that is, amongst the nobility, the gentry, the bourgeois of the towns and cities—marriage in the 1590s was very often a matter of arrangement, the parents arranging suitable matches for their children, an arrangement in which property, inheritance, family, a title if there was one, were important constituents. Fathers were expected to provide a dowry for their daughters, a sum of money, specified in the marriage contract, which would go to the husband and make the daughter a more desirable match. The prospective husband, or his father, in turn would also provide a sum of money. This sum was called the dower, or jointure, and it was meant to be set aside for taking care of the wife if the husband died first. It's widow money.

Now, this kind of arrangement—drawing up marriage contracts on the basis of sums of money provided by their fathers—may seem strange and even offensive to our modern assumptions about marriage. Since Shakespeare's time, we've been through dozens of nineteenth-century novels and seen dozens of twentieth-century plays and movies, in which people who marry for rank or money are bound to be miserable. And fathers who force their children into matches that they don't like are cruel, heartless people. But arranged marriage could be regarded as quite a reasonable social practice. This is the way in which an adequate income was provided for a young couple. Young members of the propertied classes were not expected to go forth and earn salaries, as we expect our children to do now. Wealth lay chiefly in land; if wealth was earned by large-scale trade, the merchants tried to convert it to land or other property as soon as possible, and property passed by inheritance. Therefore, the source of wealth for most young persons lay in their family, not in taking up a career.

Parents who failed to provide for their children, who left a daughter unbestowed or a son unendowed, would be criticized for parental neglect by the other relatives, by the neighbors, by the children themselves. These parents had not provided adequately for the economic future of their children. It would be exactly the same kind of criticism that we would give to a middle-class pair of parents now, if they failed to provide a college education for their children, since nowadays, a college degree is what you need in order to have economic comfort.

Now any social practice can be well- or ill-carried out by particular people. Individual sixteenth-century fathers may have acted tyrannically in matching their offspring, just as nowadays, particular offspring may choose badly in selecting their spouses. Generally, it was thought decent of the father to consult the wishes of the children, to give a daughter at least the right of refusal to a suitor she found repulsive. But since women were, by and large, expected to marry, it would take a strong-minded young woman to go on refusing possibility after possibility. She might get scared that she would never have a husband, and then what would become of her?

Some parents seem to have favored older spouses for their daughters. This would have the advantage that the man in the match would have gone past his wild, young years of adulthood. Indeed, his father might have died, and he would have come into the inheritance, and therefore he would be a stable and prosperous citizen. So it was possible for a young woman in her 20s, and that was the usual age of marriage—mid-20s—to marry a man of 35 or 40. Sometimes it happened that way just for biological reasons. Infant mortality was high. Women died in childbirth frequently, so that a man might be several times widowed before he got a wife who, in fact, gave him children and survived, before he established a family.

Now, in the 1590s, in Shakespeare's England, arranged marriage was not the only courtship practice for the propertied families. Some preachers and moralists discouraged arranged marriage, considering it largely to be a manifestation of parental greed, likely to create unsuitable unions, incompatible marriages. And incompatible marriages would lead to jealousy and infidelity, and they automatically assumed that infidelity would lead to murder. Such moralists advised a greater attention to the preferences of the young people. Poets and other tellers of romantic tales elevated the personal affections of the young people to an absolute: the course of true love might not run smooth, but it should run. It should triumph, eventually.

So, there were a number of social models available to a playwright in Shakespeare's time. The situation was a rich one for the playwright to exploit. You can get an interesting plot if the choices of the parents conflict with those of the children. Modern social historians have disputed what percentage of marriages in the 1590s were governed by personal affection, what percentage by family considerations. But fortunately for us, we don't need to know what percentage it actually was; all we need to know is that both arrangements were possible, so you could get an interesting family, like that of the Minolas.

Baptista's problem lies in the unpopularity if his elder daughter. With the younger, Bianca, there's no trouble; she's attractive, apparently very meek, men flock around her. The elder, Kate, is also attractive, but she's an ill-tempered shrew and nobody wants to court her. Under these circumstances, Baptista does a fair to middling job. He tries to even the odds between the two daughters by specifying that the elder must marry first, thereby creating pressure on those who want Bianca to find a husband, or to help him find a husband, for Kate. He also provides money for the dowries of the daughters and educates them to make them more attractive. Of course, he doesn't really understand them, and he favors one of them unfairly, and his early insistence that the daughters really love the men that they marry, that everything depends on winning their love, just evaporates wordlessly when moneyed men actually turn up to court them. So, I suppose in a world where arranged marriages could happen, were common, Baptista earns the grade of B, perhaps, maybe B-.

The interesting complications occur with the younger generation. At the start, Petruchio, coming to Padua, clearly has in mind a marriage of the old, arranged kind. "I come to wive it wealthily in Padua," he says, a line that Cole Porter stole bodily from him and made the lead line of a song. He tries to seal the match with Kate's father, even before he's met Kate. At the wedding in Act III, when he's behaving with deliberate outrageousness, he announces a doctrine of male supremacy in marriage so extreme that it amounts to outright ownership: "She is my goods, my chattel, / My horse, my ox, my ass, my anything." And oddly enough, Kate eventually falls in with this; although she is rebellious for most of the play, at the very end, she articulates at length the correspondent principle of female obedience to the husband: "Wives are bound to serve, love and obey."

In the other plot, however, Bianca and Lucentio, they behave with romantic independence. Bianca makes her own choice of mate, disregarding entirely her father's auction of her to the highest bidder. She marries in secret, and not until the knot is securely tied do the young lovers try to get the approval of their fathers. Now, although in later romantic comedies Shakespeare favors romantic young lovers over the authority of the family, here the marriage of Kate and Petruchio, although arranged in the first instance for property reasons and with parental authority, turns out to be the happier one. And, in fact, Kate and Petruchio are the more interesting people, much more interesting than Bianca and Lucentio.

So the situation seems a little paradoxical, and it's difficult to say that Shakespeare is making any judgment about whether romantic union or arranged matches are preferable. Once the marriages have been contracted, however, the play does seem to take a stand. At least it ends with that long speech of Kate's in which a wife declares obedience to her husband. And it is a long speech, 44 lines. A wife should serve, love, and obey; a wife owes duty to her husband as a husband owes duty to a prince, and this duty is properly symbolized by the wife placing her hand beneath her husband's foot, a gesture that must occur onstage in that final scene. That is pretty uncompromising doctrine. And to many people in the late twentieth century, it is quite unattractive doctrine. Many men are embarrassed to sit there and hear these words; many women are angered by them.

Now, it is the practice of literary critics and theatrical artists, when they confront something they dislike, to reinterpret it. For the past 50 years or more, critics and directors have regularly attempted to revise the plain doctrine of Kate's final speech under the all-saving name of irony, claiming that Kate doesn't mean what she says. There are various ways to do this. Kate may do it crudely, simply by winking at the audience somewhere during the speech, or she can do it elegantly. There was a famous production in England with the great actress Edith Evans, who played Kate as if Kate were the heroine of a high comedy, something by Congreve or Oscar Wilde, very artificial and elegant. And by the extreme stylization with which she delivered the speech, made it clear, "This is just a social ritual that I am going through. I have to satisfy the men by saying these silly things. I don't mean a word of it." Lately, I've seen a new addition to this repertoire of ways of evading the final speech, a postmodern way of doing it. It was a *Shrew* set in the American Wild West, and Kate delivered the final speech while holding the entire wedding party at gunpoint. That's what postmodern is, the total cognitive dissonance between words about obedience and those six-shooters.

This can be done, as I've said; you can ironize it. I don't think it works very well. With the winking or any other form of deceit, it seems to me to turn Kate into a sly sort of person, and what we had liked about Kate was her openness, as opposed to her sister's slyness. More largely, I think these methods are simply cheating. You can subvert any passage in Shakespeare by reading against the lines, or contradicting it with a gesture. It's a familiar form of theatrical humor; it's great fun if you do it at a cast party. But when you're actually doing a production, and you want to suppose that someone is lying or deceiving someone else, you've got to find some basis in the text for that supposition. Shakespeare's liars and deceivers regularly alert the audience to their little plots. And if you look in the text for such basis, I don't think you'll find it. In the final speech, you will find a few lines, individual lines, that look ironical. For example, that business about Kate saying that a husband "commits his body by painful labor" at sea and land to the care of the wife. Well, the Petruchios I've seen all have looked slightly startled at the phrase "painful labor," and rightly so. Petruchio's a country gentleman. He doesn't dig the ditches; he may manage the estate, but he doesn't dig the ditches. There may be local ironies like that. But a 44-line irony? That seems to me a bit much.

In any case, verbal irony is far less important in drama than irony of event. When Shakespeare wants to set up a long, doctrinal speech, that will somehow be examined, ironized, contradicted, or at least qualified, he puts it early in the play. That's the case with the divine rights speeches in *Richard II*, and with Ulysses' speech on degree in *Troilus and Cressida*, both of which I'll talk about later in this course. But Kate's speech comes at the very end of the play, when nothing else can contradict it. The play ends with Kate asserting her belief that she should obey.

Now, Shakespeare is not as anti-feminist as he could be. The sources are much more violent in the way that Kate herself is treated, and Kate's profession of obedience could be stronger than the way Shakespeare wrote it. That anonymous *Taming of a Shrew* that I mentioned earlier has Kate swear obedience because Eve betrayed Adam in the Garden of Eden; she's the crooked rib, she's the source of evil, she should be ruled by her husband. Shakespeare doesn't have that theological justification for obedience of wives. Instead, his Kate talks about a political arrangement; husband and wife have distinctive roles in a cooperative and companionate union. But, however much we go into this, and we have gone into it—Shakespearean scholarship has gone into it a lot in the last quarter century—I think it's impossible to turn Shakespeare into a modern feminist. The assumptions of his time were not egalitarian, they were hierarchic. St. Paul explicitly endorsed the authority of husbands, and it would have been hard for people who believed in the literal inspiration of the Bible to directly fly against that. How the authority should be exerted is another question, but that the authority should be there is the assertion with which Kate closes the play.

And is the case, generally, when such matters are handled in our older literature. There's a great marriage debate in Chaucer's *Canterbury Tales*. Who should have the mastery in marriage? The wife of Bath has it over five husbands. Patient Grizelda yields it, even though her husband treats her in what seems to us a horrible fashion. But no one ever suggests abolishing the mastery, saying that the matter should be equal. Someone's got to be in charge. One can accept this, rewrite the play, or leave it on the shelf.

The Taming of the Shrew thus furnishes a good example of the ways in which old plays can be instructive to us. If you don't try to rewrite it, if you accept it as it is, you'll find out a lot about the past. You think beyond the assumptions that you take for granted in the present. People did not always act as we would like them to do now. Why should they? We don't act the way they would like us to have done when they were thinking several centuries ago. Why should the living tyrannize over the dead any more than we want the dead to tyrannize over the living? The past is, in fact, a great reservoir for us all. It is useful to know that lives were organized in different ways, that we need not be trapped in the customs that happened to prevail at any given time. If we know that, we may be encouraged to forge new ways of coping with problems that seem to recur, by combining elements of the present with elements of the past, with innovation.

There is more to be said about how Shakespeare handles Petruchio's taming of Kate, and in particular, how Kate can believably arrive at the final speech. I must postpone talking about that until the second lecture because I have to develop another line of approach first. But in what remains to me of this lecture, I want to tell you about one production in which Kate said the final speech, meaning it totally, accepting the doctrine that it preaches. And it worked unexpectedly well. I was really surprised; I didn't know this was going to happen. I had heard nothing about the details of the production before I went to the theater. This happened at the American Repertory Theater in Cambridge last winter, January of '98, and the director was a distinguished director named Andrei Serban.

Kate's manner in delivering the final speech was quite different from the way that she had played earlier scenes. Hitherto, she had been quick, loud, assertive, spontaneous. In this case, she spoke slowly. She spoke uncertainly. She was thinking out what she was saying, discovering it for the first time.

> Thy husband is thy lord, thy life, thy keeper,
> Thy head, thy sovereign; one that cares for thee,
> And for thy maintenance commits his body

To painful labour both by sea and land, …
Whilst thou liest warm at home, secure and safe;
And craves no other tribute at thy hands
But love, fair looks, and true obedience…
I am asham'd that women are so simple
To offer war where they should kneel for peace;
Or seek for rule, supremacy, and sway,
When they are bound to serve, love, and obey.

This slow, thoughtful delivery meant that she was really thinking out the words, and the pause after "serve, love and obey", one heard, or could hear, if you know the source, the echo. The source is the marriage rite in the Book of Common Prayer, where you swear to serve, love and obey. It was extraordinarily moving to watch a person arrive at this new set of convictions, something that was unexpectedly true for her. Whether or not I personally agreed with it, I was watching someone's mind change and find a secure resting place in a doctrine that made sense to her.

Then something else happened. This discovery of hers was placed in a frame. *The Taming of the Shrew* is, as a matter of fact, a framed play. It opens with a couple of scenes concerning a drunken tinker called Christopher Sly, who's accosted by an anonymous lord, who picks him up (he's been thrown out of a tavern) and takes him home and decides to have a practical joke. This drunken beggar/tinker will wake up from his drunken stupor and discover that he's really a lord himself, that he's been out if his mind for some years, and doctors are taking care of him, and he's going to be restored to health and wealth and wisdom. And part of the health treatment is that he be shown a merry play, because comedy is health-giving. And the play, put on by the lord's own company of players, is *The Taming of the Shrew*.

Now, as a matter of fact, we never get the end of this frame. In Shakespeare's *The Taming of the Shrew*, it just doesn't appear in the folio text at the end; we never go back to the tinker and the lord. But Andrei Serban, in this production I'm talking about, invented an extended wordless action to replace the loss. The actors came forth in their ordinary clothes, full of good cheer and warmth toward each other, the kind of enthusiasm that actors always have when they've given a performance that has been well-received, when they feel satisfied with their work. And in the hugging, something odd about the pairing was very noticeable, that Kate was hugging the actor playing Lucentio, and Bianca was hugging the actor playing Petruchio. The casting apparently had switched the real-life relationships that were going on offstage. And they certainly did hug, embrace, kiss, fondle in a very thorough way. Then, they switched, Kate embraced Petruchio, Bianca embraced Lucentio, and you thought, "The casting is in accord with the offstage relationships that are happening." Then they switched once more, and it was the two guys who went hand in hand off one way, and the two women who went off, arms around each other, in the other direction. It was, in fact, a gay male couple and a lesbian couple.

It was perfectly charming. The play preaches a heterosexual union with female submission, and it did so quite sincerely and movingly. Then this wordless epilogue added, quite simply, that's not the only kind of relationship there is. Other kinds of relationship seem to work too. Serban had added, in other words, to Shakespeare. This is an early Shakespeare play, Shakespeare is not full of quite as much abundance yet as he later will have; Serban is adding to that abundance now.

The Taming of the Shrew—Farce and Romance
Lecture 6

The verbal wit of the play is often farcical. Compared to the lyrical strain of speeches in later Shakespearean comedies like *Twelfth Night* or *As You Like It*, the wit of *The Taming of the Shrew* comes near wisecracking.

In *The Taming of the Shrew*, an early comedy, Shakespeare adventurously combines farce with romance. The romantic thread lies in Kate's discovery of herself and of love for her husband. The bulk of the action, though, is farce. The play has many farcical elements and characters. Tranio displays the trickery and disguising inherited from ancient Roman farce. Grumio is a pantaloon out of the Italian Commedia dell'Arte. Petruchio and his servants engage in slapstick. The verbal wit consists of wisecracks and grotesque catalogues. The script invites farcical invention from directors and actors.

Farce has a poor reputation with critics, and it is often described negatively. Robert Heilman has averred that farces typically depict limited personalities that operate in mechanical fashion. Those having this sort of personality cannot feel or think deeply, and they are not moved by scruple. According to Heilman, farce represents a selective anesthetizing of the person. Such a mode of critical description could be applied to tragedy or any other genre with equally devastating effect. Characters in many of Shakespeare's tragedies show personality traits that Heilman attributes to characters in comedic farces: they rush to extremes, they fail to pause or reflect on their actions (or do so faultily), they lack a sense of humor about their problems.

In *The Shrew*, farce celebrates the virtues of energy, ingenuity, and resilience.

Farce deserves a positive description. In *The Shrew*, farce celebrates the virtues of energy, ingenuity, and resilience. These virtues are especially demonstrated by the male characters arriving in Padua: Petruchio, Lucentio, and Tranio. Petrochio's speeches exemplify energy. Ingenuity is exemplified by the suitors' use of unconventional means to attain their ends. Both Petruchio and Tranio illustrate resilience in their stubbornness and adaptability, and in their ability to endure repeated setbacks. Kate also has verbal and physical energy and determination, but at the start she suffers from compulsiveness and destructiveness. Over time she grows in farcical range. Petruchio teaches her to play, thus releasing her energies more fully.

Play—game or pastime—is the dominating activity and metaphor of *The Shrew*. At first Kate's understandable anger prevented her from playing games, and she has not met any men worth her respect. She is "curst," and thus she cannot play and is not fully human. There are faint suggestions in the second and third acts of her interest in Petruchio.

The development of her mind is more carefully traced in the fourth and fifth acts. She becomes sympathetic with the victims of Petruchio's temper-tantrums, such as Grumio and the other servants. She is perplexed by Petruchio's claim that he acts out of love. She resorts to anger and insists on obvious facts. In 4.5, the scene of the sun and the moon, she realizes that Petruchio is playing games. She starts playing with him, and she quickly learns to keep up with his rule-changing, to exaggerate, and to mock. Games have a cathartic effect. They release Kate from her compulsiveness and her insistence on literal fact.

Since the story of the shrew is a play enacted by the anonymous lord's players for the tinker Christopher Sly, it is all a game. Theater is Shakespeare's great game, in which he persuades audiences that the sun is the moon and that a thirteen-year-old boy is a nubile virgin named Kate or Bianca. Such games may be therapeutic. Once Kate loses her anger, she becomes a very effective *farceuse*. ■

Essential Reading

Shakespeare, *The Taming of the Shrew.*

1. In view of the (often) negative view of farce expressed by critics, how can we explain its enduring appeal across time, language and even culture?

2. The basic premise of this play has been adapted, with greater or lesser effect, into Broadway musicals (*Kiss Me Kate*), westerns, television sit-coms and even updated versions of the Bard's play set in contemporary times. You are a producer/director for a new movie version. Which contemporary actress-comedienne would cast for Kate? How would you direct her to bring out the farcical elements discussed in this lecture?

The Taming of the Shrew—Farce and Romance
Lecture 6—Transcript

The Taming of the Shrew is an early comedy of Shakespeare's, probably the second or the third. I put *Twelfth Night* before it in this course only for pedagogical reasons, because *Twelfth Night* so clearly demonstrates Shakespeare's characteristic comic structure, the way he developed his leading comic theme of romantic love. But *The Shrew* comes eight, possibly even 10, years before *Twelfth Night*, and as I've suggested in the last lecture, *The Shrew* does not have all the variety that Shakespeare later developed. But *The Shrew* does display an adventurous young Shakespeare, trying out new things that other people hadn't tried.

The play is fundamentally a farce, but it combines farce with a strain of romance in a way worth exploring if we wish to understand the richness of the young Shakespeare's talent. In the romantic thread of the play, Kate discovers her inward self, and comes into a loving relationship with her husband. This can be quite moving on the stage, but the bulk of the action is certainly farcical.

Tranio, a servant of Lucentio, who as a matter of fact, is the second largest part of the play, Tranio exemplifies the trickery and disguise that Renaissance farce inherited from ancient Roman comedy. Gremio, the elderly suitor to Bianca, is the stock old man, the pantaloon, out of the Italian *commedia dell'arte*. Petruchio and his servants display the physical knockabout, the slapstick, that occurs in farce of all ages. He is introduced beating his servant Grumio, he carries Kate bodily off out of her own wedding reception, food and water are tossed around at Petruchio's country house, the clothes that are made for Kate are abused, the tailor himself is abused.

The verbal wit of the play is often farcical. Compared to the lyrical strain of speeches in later Shakespearean comedies like *Twelfth Night* or *As You Like It*, the wit of *The Taming of the Shrew* comes near wisecracking. Even the names are jokes; although I only realized it recently, Grumio isn't an Italian name at all. It's simply the English "groom"—he's Petruchio's servant—with an Italian ending tacked on to it. The funny speeches in this play are one-liner exchanges, as in the courtship scene between Kate and

Petruchio, or grotesque catalogs, such as Biondello's list of the diseases from which Petruchio's horse suffers, or accounts of physical roughhouse, such as Grumio's story of the horse that fell on him in the mud. Actors and directors, of course, add to the farcical element. There are not many stage directions in this play; there are not many stage directions in all of Shakespeare. But actors and directors respond to the obvious competitiveness within the script by inventing farcical routines that go with that script.

Now, all this farce has distressed some thoughtful people. I've been collecting descriptions of farce for a number of years, mostly in connection with this particular play, but also from other places. I've written an article on this particular play; that's how this started. I was looking around for people to define or at least describe farce. And I found farce described as "unnatural," "rigid," "depersonalizing," "mechanical," "inhuman." This is in work from scholars of repute. Farce may be amusing for a careless evening in the theater, but it isn't real; we don't take it seriously. That's the keynote of the descriptions I have accumulated, the use of the negative terms— "unnatural," "depersonalizing." Farce is described in terms of what it isn't, or it's diminished. It's called something small. We say the thing is "just a farce," as if it were easy to write a good farce.

Perhaps I can sum this up best if I quote from an article by a scholar I very much respect. Robert B. Heilman wrote an essay on *The Shrew* that moved me into response. According to Heilman, farce deals with "limited personality that acts and responds in a mechanical way and hence moves toward a given end with a perfection not likely if all the elements of human nature were really at work." Or another quote: "Those who have this personality are not really hurt, do not think much, and are not much troubled by scruples. They lack, largely or totally, the physical, emotional, intellectual and moral sensitivity that we think of as normal. Farce simplifies life by a selective anesthetizing of the whole person."

Now, each of these sentences is couched in negatives, or privitives: "limit," "without," "not," "lack," "simplify," "anesthetize," and it seems to me very strange. No work of art can contain all the possibilities of life; all works of art have to simplify to some extent, by selection and emphasis. One could describe any genre this way and thus make it sound unattractive to those of us who are interested in doing serious justice to the possibilities of human character. What would happen if tragedy were described in this fashion? Tragedy concerns persons unnaturally ready to rush to extremes. They do not pause to reflect; see King Lear. Reflecting, they do so faultily; see Othello. By a selective anesthetizing of the whole person, they lack a sense of humor or balance; Macbeth could certainly do with a sense of humor about his problems. They will not sit down with a sympathetic friend or a good therapist, or at least a Valium, to get to the root of the matter, but instead dash around with drawn swords. In short, a collection of paranoid hysterics who refuse to live like sensible adults. And as for moving toward a given end with a perfection foreign to human nature, what real royal court has, short of armed revolution or war, suffered the simultaneous and total extermination that happens in Elsinore at the end of *Hamlet*?

The farce that is presented in Petruchio's wooing of Kate, and in the efforts of Tranio and Biondello to win Bianca from the master Lucentio, deserves a positive description. That farce arises, as I said in the previous lecture, from a relatively realistic situation. Bianca's popularity, and Baptista's preference for her, credibly motivates Kate's shrewish behavior. Baptista's behavior within the realistic circumstances of the upper middle class in Elizabethan times, to even the odds between his popular daughter and the unwanted elder sister, by vowing that Bianca shall not marry before Kate does, only creates a frustrating stalemate for everybody concerned: for himself, for his daughters, and for Bianca's suitors.

Within this situation, farce does something positive. It celebrates three virtues: energy, ingenuity and resilience—virtues that disrupt the static dilemma in Padua and work to resolve it. The energy is obvious in the eagerness in the male characters who arrive in Padua—Petruchio, Tranio, Lucentio—and the way they take on a set of problems regarded by the Paduans as hopeless, and the demands they confidently make upon themselves in solving those problems. The energy is verbally elaborated in Petruchio's speeches. He boasts of his career amid roaring lions and clanging trumpets.

Ingenuity, that is, mental independence and resourcefulness, lies in the suitors' adoption of unconventional means to gain their ends, notably in Petruchio's behavior at the wedding and, above all, his great pretense of being a worse shrew than Kate, but also in the fertile inventiveness of Lucentio and his servants in the Bianca plot.

And the third quality, resilience, by that I mean a special combination of stubbornness and adaptability. This is a virtue that often occurs in farcical characters, but most people don't recognize it as a virtue. We're too ready to describe farce as mechanical or rigid. The ability to endure or initiate repeated confrontations, pratfalls, beatings, can be testimony to the determination of the characters to get what they're after. And the determination loses any mechanical quality it might have, when it is combined with the cleverness, the ready resourcefulness, displayed by Petruchio in the taming, and the numerous schemes that Tranio comes up with. In civilized life, of course, adults avoid the shouting and the knockabout that is characteristic of farce. We don't go in for that sort of physical activity. But the energy, the ingenuity, the resilience, these three virtues, embodied in such activities are valuable qualities. We do not honor lassitude, mental barrenness, or defeatism.

Now, so far, I have attributed these farcical virtues only to male characters. That, indeed, is one of the complaints that feminist critics have made about this play. A distinguished Shakespearean at Brown University, my friend Coppélia Khan, has weighed in particularly strongly and has written in print, and said to me personally, "Farce, Peter, is a kind of theatrical elaboration of male fantasies of domination over women." And I have answered, "But Coppélia, Kate is also a farcer" (or *farceuse*, if you want to put it in French properly.) Her verbal and physical energy in resisting humiliation make her the interesting and attractive person that she is. That's why she's so striking in her first two scenes. In her third scene, when she meets Petruchio, it is she who initiates both the physical brawling and the verbal combat. Now, at that point in the play, her behavior has a strain of compulsiveness to it that the male farcers do not have. She has the energy, but her resilience is more stubborn than it is adaptable, and she relies very heavily on the threat of physical violence, or the outright use of physical violence.

But that's precisely the point. Her liberation from raging shrewishness, from compulsiveness and destructiveness, is marked by her growth in farcical range, in range of the activities of farce. What Petruchio teaches her, essentially—or what she learns from Petruchio, because it's really a matter of her observation and picking it up and learning to practice it herself—what he teaches, what she learns, is play. This is the central activity and the dominating metaphor of *The Taming of the Shrew*: play, game, pastime. You remember, the whole thing is a play, literally; the lord's play put on for the entertainment of the tinker, Christopher Sly.

And the play contains a gallery of games. Bianca's suitors put on disguises and play roles in order to woo her. Grumio plays games with Kate's hunger; when they get back to Petruchio's country house, he offers her beef, mustard, and she's so hungry she says, "Both! Either!" And Grumio says, "Well, then, I'll give you the mustard without the beef." Petruchio plays games with words: "I am content. You shall entreat me stay, and yet not stay." That is, I'm content that you're begging me. I'm not going to listen to your begging, but I'm glad that you're doing it. The first courtship is a very elaborate verbal game with some astonishingly filthy metaphors going on; I won't go into them at the moment. The master game is, of course, Petruchio's sustained pretense of being a worse shrew than Kate is. Through this game, he acts a parody of Kate's ill temper. He holds the mirror up to her faults until she realizes what she's been like, what her effect on other people has been.

Now Kate, originally, could not play games. Everything was deadly earnest. For that, she herself was not wholly responsible. Bianca pretends to be meek and humble; Kate sees through that, as a sister will. But everyone else is taken in, so it infuriates Kate that Bianca is getting away with this. Baptista is too biased toward Bianca, and not intelligent enough to think how to cope with Kate. Kate is interested in men; we can tell that from the scene between her and Bianca, where she jealously asks Bianca about her suitors and which of the suitors she, Bianca, favors. But she herself, Kate, hasn't met any man yet who can command her respect, who is intelligent enough to cope, strong enough to stand up to her. So she lives in uncivilized anger, shrewishness. She is "curst." That's an adjective that's used several times in the play as a synonym for shrewish; it means bad-tempered, cantankerous. But it can also mean under a curse, suffering from a curse, the victim of a curse. And a curst, angry person cannot play, and if you can't play, you're not fully human. The ability to play is one of the marks of being human.

Now, she is slowly released from this by the development of her interest in Petruchio. And it's difficult, in Acts II and III, to trace that interest. There is very little given her to say that would mark it, and most actresses do it by looking at Petruchio at odd moments when he's not looking at her. But there are a few things in the lines. When Petruchio, at the end of the courting scene, swiftly arranges the marriage with Baptista, Kate protests, but not very long. Then, when Petruchio is late for the wedding itself, she is not relieved, as she would be if she really disliked him, or had no interest in him. Nor is she immediately angry, as the heroine of the other Elizabethan shrew play is. She's embarrassed, almost as if she were disappointed. In Acts IV and V, however, the development of her mind is quite carefully traced. The first step is compassion, compassion for the victims of Petruchio's temper-tantrums. When Petruchio beats Grumio for being responsible for the horse falling in the mire, she tries to pluck Petruchio off Grumio's back. We don't see that, because you can't put horses and mud on the stage, but we hear about it. But we do see the episode when a servant accidentally spills some water, and Petruchio beats that servant, and Kate tries to intervene there. "Patience, I pray you; 'twas a fault unwilling."

The second step on her part is perplexity, puzzlement, a sense that something is going on she hasn't quite grasped. "I ... am starv'd for meat, giddy for lack of sleep; / With oath kept waking, and with brawling fed; / And that which spites me all than all these wants, / He does it under name of perfect love." What is he doing, what does it mean? So she resorts once more to anger, and to a kind of super common sense, insistence on plain fact: "Hey, look, it's 2:00 p.m. in the afternoon, not 7:00 p.m. in the evening; what are you talking about?" And finally, she sees what is going on, that Petruchio is playing a game, that she has married a gamester who, in his game playing, can revise the whole world. And that is what happens in the key scene of the play, the scene when they are on their way back to Padua for Bianca's wedding.

They're on the road, and Petruchio says

> Come on, i' God's name; once more toward our father's. Good Lord, how bright and goodly shines the moon!"

Kate: The moon? It is not moonlight now. Tis the sun.
Petruchio: I say it is the moon that shines so bright.
Kate: I know it is the sun that shines so bright.
Petruchio: Now by my mother's son, and that's myself,
It shall be moon, or star, or what I list,
Or ere I journey to your father's house.
Always cross'd; nothing but cross'd!

Hortensio tries to intervene and says to Kate, "Say as he does, or we shall never go." And Kate says,

Forward, I pray, since we have come so far,
And be it moon, or sun, or what you will;
An if you please to call it a rush-candle,
Henceforth I vow it shall be so for me.

Now, the key thing is "if you please it to call it a rush-candle." Not only has she agreed to go along with him, but she's kicked the ball into another court. She's exaggerated; a rush-candle is the cheapest kind of candle you can get, a mere piece of rush stuck in some tallow or grease. If you call the glorious sun a rush-candle, you're willing to go along with anything.

Petruchio: I say it is the moon.
Kate: I know it is the moon.
Petruchio: Nay, then you lie; it is the blessed sun.

He's changed the rules again.

Kate: Then, God be bless'd, it is the blessed sun;
But sun it is not, when you say it is not;
And the moon changes even as your mind.

Now she's not only kicking the ball into another court, she's directly mocking him. "The moon changes all the time, your mind changes all the time. You're just a giddy person." She's learned the game. So Petruchio immediately stages another game. In comes a very old man, and Petruchio greets him as if this were a beautiful young woman.

Good-morrow, gentle mistress; where away?
Tell me, Kate, and tell me truly too,
Hast thou beheld a fresher gentlewoman?
Such war of white and red within her cheeks!
What stars do spangle heaven with such beauty
As those two eyes become that heavenly face?
Fair lovely maid, once more good day to thee.
Sweet Kate, embrace her for her beauty's sake.

Now, this is conventional Petrarchan praise. White and red in the cheeks, stars for eyes—this is the way a beautiful woman is talked about in the most conventional possible way. Kate tops him:

Young budding virgin, fresh and fair and sweet,
Whither away, or where is thy abode?
Happy the parents of so fair a child;
Happier the man whom favourable stars
Allots thee for his lovely bed-fellow.

Now it is impossible to say to an old man "young budding virgin" onstage and not get a howl of laughter. She's taken Petruchio's conventional phrase and exaggerated it so greatly, that it becomes wonderful farce. Momentarily, it exhausts her. Her next line, "Whither away, or where is thy abode," isn't very interesting; she's gagging, she's trying to think of what to say next. And then she comes up with it: "The man who marries you is going to be enormously happy, who has thee for his lovely bedfellow." She's taken this old, withered man, and shoved him into bed with some young stud as the perfect plaything. It's gorgeous.

Petruchio: Why, how now, Kate! I hope thou art not mad;
This is a man, old, wrinkled, faded, wither'd,
And not a maiden, as thou sayst he is.

Kate: Pardon, old father, my mistaking eyes,
That have been so bedazzled with the sun—

and any actress worth her salt is going to look back at Petruchio and say, "Is it the sun or the moon at this point. I know your games, I can play them as well as you." She has learned to improvise as well as he does, even better. The game releases her from her compulsiveness, from her anger, from her insistence on literal fact. The game transforms her; game or play has a cathartic effect. In play, human beings can master their circumstances and gain release from bondage to themselves. She can work out her antagonism and thus arrive at love.

That is what really makes it possible, emotionally, for Kate to deliver the final speech on wifely submission to a husband. She has found a man worth submitting to; she takes pleasure in following his directions. Play has brought release and health, and clearly, the whole of *The Taming of the Shrew* is meant to do just that. The anonymous lord who stages *The Taming of the Shrew* with his company of actors for Christopher Sly, the tinker, aims to bring, and this is a quotation from the opening scenes, "mirth and merriment." This frame isn't at all necessary for Shakespeare's play; many productions cut it out altogether, since it's not complete in Shakespeare's text. But it does amplify the story of the shrew by providing a series of game transformations. Christopher Sly is turned into a lord; the lord's pageboy is turned into Christopher Sly's wife. A play is put on, and so we are prepared for the transformation of Kate the shrew into Kate the loving wife in the major play.

All these things allow Shakespeare to reflect on his own great game, which is the theater. The theater is a place where actors play, where they say that the sun is the moon, particularly if they are playing in a London amphitheatre in the 1590s, where the performances take place in the afternoon. But what they are doing is a play, say, called *Romeo and Juliet*, where Juliet appears on a balcony and says, "O swear not by the moon, the inconstant moon, / That monthly changes in her circled orb." The theater is a place where a 13-year-old boy puts on a dress and pretends to be a young, budding virgin called Juliet, or Kate, or Bianca.

And if we accept these games, if we accept that the sun is the moon, and that the boy is Katharina Minola or Juliet Capulet, then we are transformed, at least for the duration of the play, and perhaps for longer than that. But the game must be played well, with precision, with carefully elaborated detail. You can't do that if you're angry; once she stops being angry, Kate becomes a very accomplished farceuse indeed, and she and Petruchio are playing a game in the final scene to dish the nasty relatives and to uphold their honor as a couple at her sister's wedding. They don't ask for the quarrel that starts the bet; it's imposed upon them. But they win it.

Even as Kate and Petruchio elaborate the fantasy of the sun and the moon and the virgin and the old man, the anonymous lord elaborates the details of Christopher Sly's supposed madness, and gives precise directions to the troupe of players. And if all goes well, the play is therapeutic. The play brings health. As Christopher Sly is told, "Your doctors ... thought it good you hear a play, and frame your mind to mirth and merriment, which bars a thousand harms and lengthens life." Mirth and merriment bars harms; it makes you healthier. It extends your life. Comedy brings life; Shakespearean comedy does.

The Merchant of Venice—Courting the Heiress
Lecture 7

Over 50 years ago, a great actor, director, and Shakespearean critic, Harley Granville-Barker, said there was no more reality in Shylock's bond and the Lord of Belmont's will than there is in *Jack and the Beanstalk*, and he spoke wisely.

*T*he Merchant of Venice is a fairy tale. Winning the hand of a princess by a lottery is unrealistic. Borrowing money on collateral of a pound of flesh is unrealistic. Shakespeare frequently used unlikely plots. The purpose of art is not realism. Characters and events may be true to life without being realistic on the surface. Portia's father's will displays a genuine concern of fathers.

The casket plot contrasts the three suitors. The prince of Morocco is a man of heroic exploit and reputation. His rhetoric imitates that of Marlowe's Tamburlaine. His love is merely the desire to have what every other man desires. The prince of Arragon is a snob. He assumes that he deserves Portia. Shakespeare is suspicious of desert, especially in matters of the heart. Like Morocco, Arragon essentially chooses himself rather than Portia.

Bassanio is a problematic hero since the plot does not allow him to do anything heroic. This is a difficulty that recurs in high comedy, which tends to stress not the manly and heroic values of courage and strength, but the more womanly values of wit, grace, and civilized behavior. Thus, the leading protagonists of high comedy tend to be women. Bassanio has been described as a fortune-hunter out to gain Portia's money in order to repay his debts. Shakespeare describes Bassanio as a knight on a romantic quest. He displays generosity in small matters.

The leading protagonists of high comedy tend to be women.

Bassanio's heroism emerges in his choice. The song that precedes his choice distinguishes between desire ("fancy") and love. Bassanio is aware of this distinction. The casket labels reveal the risk in love. Bassanio's great generosity is to leave the choice to Portia. ∎

Essential Reading

Shakespeare, *The Merchant of Venice.*

Supplementary Reading

See BBC-TV videotape of *The Merchant of Venice.*

Barber, *Shakespeare's Festive Comedy*, chapter 7.

Coghill, "The Basis of Shakespearean Comedy."

Danson, *The Harmonies of "The Merchant of Venice."*

Questions to Consider

1. How much do we know about Portia? How does she handle her difficult situation?

2. Compare the suitors with lovers elsewhere in Shakespearean comedy—Orsino, Orlando, Benedick.

The Merchant of Venice—Courting the Heiress
Lecture 7—Transcript

This is the first of two lectures on *The Merchant of Venice*. *The Merchant of Venice* is a fairytale. Over 50 years ago, a great actor, director, and Shakespearean critic, Harley Granville-Barker, said there was no more reality in Shylock's bond and the Lord of Belmont's will than there is in *Jack and the Beanstalk*, and he spoke wisely.

"In Belmont is a lady richly left," and not only is Portia rich, she is also beautiful, wise, virtuous, imminently desirable on all counts. But according to her late father's will, she can only be wooed by lottery. Her suitors must choose, between three caskets of gold, silver, and lead, which contains her picture. And it's a pretty stiff lottery; the contestants must swear, not only to abide by the results of the choice, but if they lose, never to woo a woman in way of marriage again. Choose the right box, and you win the princess and the fortune; choose the wrong one, you go forever without love.

If you take it from Bassanio's point of view, it is a story of outrageous wish-fulfillment. He is a spendthrift; he is head over ears in debt, he persuades his friends to float one more loan for him, with which he buys clothes, presents, a new sports car. He toodles off to Vassar to woo the heiress and she turns out not only to be rich and virtuous and beautiful, but she's madly in love with him. And on top of all that, after winning the lady, he never has to repay his friend for the loan because the old Scrooge from whom they got the money has proved to be so villainous, he doesn't deserve to have his docket back.

The other plot may seem more real. The casket story happens in Belmont, a beautiful mountain, a fairytale place of love and music. The rest of the play happens in Venice, a commercial society and great power, well known to many Elizabethans. Antonio is prosecuted for a large, unpaid debt, imprisoned, brought to trial and to the point of death. But at the heart of this plot, too, there is a fairytale motif—the loan in which the collateral is a pound of the borrower's flesh. It's a grimmer sort of fairytale. In fact, it is the kind of fairytale that was collected in Germany in the nineteenth century by those two folktale-loving brothers named Grimm. In Grimm's fairytales, chopping up people and even eating them occurs fairly frequently. And there are lots of other improbabilities in this plot, too. Antonio loses all his ships at sea—that's why the debt cannot be repaid—and then he gets them all back again. Portia and her maiden, Nerissa, go to Venice and appear in open courtroom disguised as men, and nobody perceives the reality underneath the disguise, even though their husbands are prominent in that courtroom.

Now, Shakespeare was fond of fairytales. He exploited them frequently. The ultimate wicked uncle, for example, is Richard III. King Lear's daughters are a version of Cinderella and her stepsisters. *A Midsummer Night's Dream*— that's a play in which juice distilled from a flower and squeezed into the eyes of a sleeping young man will cause him, when he wakes up, to fall violently in love with someone quite different from the person he formerly adored. And often, my students have asked me, "What is the point of reading all this unrealistic stuff? Why should a rich man leave a will that disposes of his daughter and her fortune by lottery?" Isn't it silly to think that our love depends on magic flower juice? And in the case of King Lear, a very great realistic writer indeed, Tolstoy, complained that it was far too much coincidence to suppose that King Lear had two utterly wicked daughters and one good one. And his best friend, the Earl of Gloucester, had one utterly wicked son and one good one, and they went through the same experiences with those children simultaneously.

To all of which, I respond to my students that the purpose of art is not realism. Realism is one of the techniques that art uses, one of many. It happens to have been the principal technique used by a lot of late nineteenth and early twentieh century art: the novelists like Tolstoy and Galsworthy and Dreiser; the playwrights like Ibsen and early O'Neill. But it is not a favored technique in Asian art, or African, or most medieval art, or modern painting. Shakespeare is occasionally realistic. That is, occasionally, he imitates the surfaces of real life, surface verisimilitude. He will write a scene in prose for characters in a state of casual relaxation. But realism, in that sense, is not a principal artistic technique of Shakespeare's time either, and his characters are not novelistic depictions of real people. They are constructs, they are artifacts, they are embodiments of insights into the human condition.

Thus, they are not realistic on the surface. As I remarked in an earlier lecture, kings of England do not deliver speeches from the throne in blank verse. But they may be something better than realistic; they may be true. They may be true to the inner realities of our lives, the urges and energies of human beings, the forces within our psyches. And the plots are not realistic transcriptions of events, even when they're based on events from history. The plots arrange events artistically in order to reveal truths about human behavior.

To go back to Portia's father's will, no, rich men don't leave documents setting up casket lotteries to dispose of their daughters. But fathers do care about the characters of young men who come courting their daughters, and often try to find out, in one way or another, what the guy is really like. Is he interested in the daughter, or only in the fortune? That is the inner reality that the casket story concerns. That is what Nerissa says to Portia in the first act:

> Your father was ever virtuous, and holy men at their death have good inspirations; therefore the lottery that he hath devised in these three caskets, of gold, silver, and lead... will, no doubt, never be chosen by any rightly but one whom you shall rightly love.

The right chooser will be the right lover. So, let us look at the choosers in this play. The Prince of Morocco is a man of great reputation, proud of his military exploits.

> By this scimitar,
> That slew the Sophy and a Persian prince,
> That won three fields of Sultan Solyman,
> I would outstare the sternest eyes that look,
> Outbrave the heart most daring on the earth,
> Pluck the young sucking cubs from the she-bear,
> Yea, mock the lion when he roars for prey,
> To win thee, lady.

This is the heroical man, the man of hyperbole. This kind of rhetoric is not going to win Portia's hand. It might blow her out of the room. In fact, it's a very particular kind of rhetoric. The style had been invented nine years earlier by Shakespeare's contemporary, Christopher Marlowe, to dramatize the story of Tamberlaine. Tamberlaine is one of those Eastern conquerors with seven-league boots, who crushes kingdoms with every stride and flattens opponents with every speech. Marlowe had a terrific theatrical success with *Tamberlaine*; he had found a new voice for the Elizabethan drama, and for a couple of years afterwards, practically every playwright in London wrote a *Tamberlaine*-type play, trying to cash in on the popularity of the mode. But by the mid-1590s, when Shakespeare is writing *The Merchant of Venice*, the *Tamberlaine* rhetoric had come to seem simpleminded, outdated. When Shakespeare uses it, it marks the limitations of a character, rather than the character's strengths. We'll meet this kind of rant again in Hodspur, the Northern border lord in *Henry IV*, who is indeed a very great warrior, but is totally out of his depth when it comes to politics or women.

For the Prince of Morocco, his choice amongst those caskets is based precisely on this kind of boastful pride, his consciousness of worldly reputation. On the golden casket is written, "Who chooseth me will gain what many men desire," and Morocco says:

> Why, that's the lady! All the world desires her;
> From the four corners of the earth they come,
> To kiss this shrine, this mortal-breathing saint.
> The Hyrcanian deserts and the vasty wilds
> Of wide Arabia are as throughfares now
> For princes to come view fair Portia.
> The watery kingdom, whose ambitious head
> Spits in the face of heaven, is no bar
> To stop the foreign spirits, but they come
> As o'er a brook, to see fair Portia.

Well, that's exciting stuff, ravishing stuff, and in fact, it's a direct imitation of one speech of Tamberlaine's, about how he's going to entertain the woman he loves, "to entertain divine Zenocrate." But listen to the sense of the words, as well as their enthusiasm. From the four corners of the earth they come to view fair Portia; they cross lands, deserts, stormy seas to do so. Portia is desirable to Morocco because everybody else desires her. "She is what men want; therefore, I want her, therefore, I'll gain her." Love, of course, is not simply a matter of seizing what you want.

The second suitor, the Prince of Arragon, is a subtler man. He understands the temptation of gold and rejects it.

> 'Who chooseth me shall gain what many men desire.'
> What many men desire! That 'many' may be meant
> By the fool multitude, that choose by show,
> Not learning more than the fond eye doth teach;
> Which pries not to th' interior, but, like the martlet,
> Builds in the weather on the outward wall,
> Even in the force and road of casualty.
> I will not choose what many men desire,
> Because I will not jump with common spirits
> And rank me with the barbarous multitudes.

Obviously, he's a snob. Now, a snob is a man who places a high value on himself and his own position, in contrast with others, and that is the way Arragon chooses. He reads the label on the silver casket:

> 'Who chooseth me shall get as much as he deserves.'
> And well said too; for who shall go about
> To cozen fortune, and be honourable
> Without the stamp of merit? Let none presume
> To wear an undeserved dignity.
> O, that estates, degrees, and offices,
> Were not deriv'd corruptly, and that clear honour
> Were purchas'd by the merit of the wearer! ...
> How much low peasantry would then be glean'd
> From the true seed of honour! and how much honour
> Pick'd from the chaff and ruin of the times,
> To be new varnish'd! Well, but to my choice.
> 'Who chooseth me shall get as much as he deserves.'
> I will assume desert. Give me a key for this.

And what he finds inside is the picture of a blinking idiot. Now, some readers have thought that there's something modest in Arragon; he'll take no more than he deserves. But Shakespeare finds desert to be a questionable notion. We are all faulty in various ways. Portia, in the famous speech on mercy later in the play, observes that, "In the course of justice, none of us / Should see salvation." We're all damned, unless God gives us grace. Hamlet says the same thing in a snappier way. When Polonius tells Hamlet he will look after the traveling players according to their desert, Hamlet suddenly has a temper-tantrum: "God's bodkins, man, much better! Use every man after his desert, and who would scape whipping?" We all deserve to be thrashed.

To claim desert is very risky, especially in love. A genuine lover, I should think, is delighted, even astonished, that the object of his love returns his affection. We are humble in love. It is a surprise to discover that the person we find wonderful feels the same way about us. Indeed, neither Morocco nor Arragon is really thinking about Portia at all. Essentially, they choose themselves. Morocco chooses his own desire, Arragon his own desert. Bassanio, on the other hand, understands that love is not just desire, and is not desert at all. It involves looking beyond oneself and beyond the surface of other things to a reality that requires commitment.

Now, I can't go straight to Bassanio's choice immediately. I've got to say something more generally about the character first. Shakespeare confronts a difficulty in characterizing Bassanio. He's going to win Portia; Portia is the protagonist of the play, the leading character, the heroine, and I suppose that makes Bassanio *ex officio* the hero. But the nature of the plot does not allow him to be very heroic. The story demands that his friend, Antonio, pledge a pound of flesh for his sake, and that puts Antonio in a position of risky heroism, but lets Bassanio rest as the passive recipient of favors. How can we say that he's an admirable man, the one whom Portia should rightly love?

Now this difficulty is a special case of a recurring trouble that happens in high comedy. High comedy is the realm of wit, of grace, of civilization, and chiefly has been the realm of women. The values of wit and grace and civilized behavior are very well expressed onstage by women. Men, of course, can be witty and graceful too, but in Western convention, men have been thought heroic when they go out and do something that calls for strength and courage, and high comedy doesn't allow much room for that. This certainly is the case for Shakespeare's romantic comedies. They celebrate the values of intelligence and courtesy and love, and Shakespeare gives the leading parts to the women—Portia, Rosalind, Viola, Helena—despite the fact that, in his theater, that means loading the weight of the play on the boy actor, instead of giving it to Burbage, the leading actor of the company, who plays Hamlet and Lear and any king you want. In the histories and tragedies, the lead is always a man. Two women manage to get equal billing, Juliet with Romeo, Cleopatra with Antony, but they never take the lead.

But in the comedies—*As You Like It* and *Twelfth Night* and *The Merchant of Venice* and *All's Well That Ends Well*—the female lead must carry the play. And it's less easy for the writer to demonstrate worth in her lover. It's a problem in dramatic strategy, a problem that Shakespeare went some distance toward solving when he wrote *As You Like It*. In *As You Like It*, he has Orlando win a wrestling match in the first act. That takes care of that; he's okay. And he rescues his brother's life from a lioness in the fourth act offstage, so Rosalind can dominate the rest of the play.

But some readers feel that Shakespeare never solved the problem with Bassanio. In fact, some have been very hard on Bassanio indeed, considering him a fortune-hunter. He wants, and needs, Portia's money to pay his debts. Now, it's quite true that he needs the money, but it isn't the only thing that is true about him. I think it's shortsighted to consider him merely a fortune hunter. "In Belmont is a lady richly left," that is the first thing he says about her, but he goes on: "And she is fair and, fairer than that word, / Of wondrous virtues." She is rich and beautiful and good. That's an incremental progression. To call him merely a fortune-hunter is to ignore how Shakespeare writes about him, and to ignore what he actually does in choosing the leaden casket. Shakespeare writes about him as if he were on a romantic quest, a knight errant out of ancient legend pursuing a glamorous goal. He is compared to the Greek hero Jason, leading the Argonauts in search of the Golden Fleece. Portia's "sunny locks / Hang on her temples like a golden fleece, / Which makes her seat of Belmont Colchas' strand, / And many Jasons come in quest of her." That Jason reference recurs several times in the play; when Bassanio has chosen rightly, his friend Graziano says, "We are the Jasons, we have won the fleece."

And Portia goes a step higher than Jason; she compares Bassanio to the greatest of the Greek heroes, Hercules. In this comparison, she herself is Hesione, the princess of Troy, who was one of those unfortunate maidens left out on a beach to be devoured by a monster because they'd offended the god Neptune. And Bassanio is the Hercules who comes along to rescue her. She says:

> Now he goes,
> With no less presence, but with much more love,
> Than young Alcides—

Alcides is another name for Hercules—

> young Alcides when he did redeem
> The virgin tribute paid by howling Troy
> To the sea-monster. I stand for sacrifice; ...
> Go, Hercules!
> Live thou, I live: with much, much more dismay
> I view the fight than thou that mak'st the fray.

And there's some basis for this extreme comparison. Portia is tied to the casket choice, and all the suitors who have come along so far—not only Morocco and Arragon, but six others whom we don't see, but whom Portia describes—are pretty rotten people. Portia is a rich woman, but being only a woman in a patriarchal society, where women aren't allowed much initiative, she suffers the vulnerability as well as the popularity of an heiress. One of these stupid, arrogant, drunken men might just stumble over the right casket at some point, if only by accident.

So by poetry, Shakespeare makes Bassanio something of a chivalric quester, rescuing a virgin in trouble. But the real heroism of Bassanio lies in the choice itself. That choice is preceded by a song, which I will recite to you:

> Tell me where is fancy bred,
> Or in the heart, or in the head,
> How begot, how nourished?
> Reply, reply.
> It is engend'red in the eyes,
> With gazing fed; and fancy dies
> In the cradle where it lies.

Let us all ring fancy's knell:
I'll begin it—Ding, dong, bell.
Ding dong, bell.

Now, songs in Shakespeare are usually addressed to the audience. They make a thematic statement, a statement about a value that is important to the action that we're witnessing. In this case, the song tells us, there's a mystery about love. Fancy is easily explained; fancy is mere attraction, desire, being turned on by someone you find pretty, sexy. The British still use the word in this sense; "Do you fancy her?" means "Do you want to go to bed with her?" Fancy is based merely on appearance. It's engendered in the eyes, it grows as you gaze on the beautiful person, and when the person ceases to be physically appealing to you, it dies. The implication in all that is that love, something more than fancy, something that lasts, is based not on appearance, not on qualities that can be seen, cannot be explained as a mere mechanism of desire. It's easy enough to see why somebody with movie star looks inspires a lot of lust. No one would dare explain why you fall in love with a particular person. Love involves discontinuity. It involves some kind of leap beyond the external qualities, to some inner reality.

Implicitly, that song I've quoted asks whether Bassanio is merely a fancier, like the other suitors, or a true lover. Bassanio responds to the test with a meditation explicitly distinguishing between reality and the false charms of appearance:

So may the outward shows be least themselves;
The world is still deceiv'd with ornament.
In law, what plea so tainted and corrupt
But, being season'd with a gracious voice,
Obscures the show of evil? In religion,
What damned error, but some sober brow
Will bless it, and approve it with a text,
Hiding the grossness with fair ornament?
There is no vice so simple but assumes
Some mark of virtue on his outward parts.
How many cowards, whose hearts are all as false
As stairs of sand, wear yet upon their chins

> The beards of Hercules and frowning Mars;
> Who, inward search'd, have livers white as milk!

And on that basis, he rejects the appeal of the gold and the silver caskets and chooses meager lead, "Which rather threaten'st than dost promise aught." He rejects mere appearance; he knows you have to go beyond it. He does understand what love is about, as opposed to mere desire. In love, you have to leap. In fact, the nature of the leap is specified in the casket labels.

Gold says, "Who chooses me shall gain what many men desire," but love is not mere desire, not mere chasing after whatever your hormones are excited by. The silver casket says, "Who chooses me shall get as much as he deserves," but love is not merited, deserved. It is bestowed. The lead casket says, "Who chooses me must give and hazard all he hath." In love, you give yourself. Love is a commitment of all you have, and in the age before divorce courts, love is something you cannot do with your fingers crossed. Bassanio is willing to make that commitment. He has the generosity to give himself. Now, the cynic may still respond, "Of course he gives himself. He's going to get Portia and her fortune. He wants that money." And he does, that's true. But the final point is that he doesn't take Portia and her fortune, doesn't take them in any way that would validate the cynic's charge of fortune-hunting, because he has an act of generosity yet to perform in this scene of choice.

The little verse that he finds on the lead casket tells him, "Turn you where your lady is / And claim her with a loving kiss," but he doesn't claim her. Although a few idiotic editors of Shakespeare have inserted the stage direction "kisses her" at that point, the next speech, in fact, Bassanio refuses to do precisely that. He does the opposite of claiming her; he gives the choice back to her:

> Fair lady, by your leave;
> I come by note, to give and to receive.
> Like one of two contending in a prize,
> That thinks he hath done well in people's eyes,
> Hearing applause and universal shout,
> Giddy in spirit, still gazing in a doubt
> Whether those peals of praise be his or no;

> So, thrice-fair lady, stand I even so,
> As doubtful whether what I see be true,
> Until confirm'd, sign'd, ratified by you.

He gives the choice back to Portia. The casket has told him he has won, but he is not claiming the right of victory. He leaves it up to her. Inasmuch as Portia is tied to the caskets, bound to marry whoever chooses right, it is an extraordinarily perceptive and generous thing to do. He has freed the heiress from the lottery, and then left her free. If she doesn't like him, if she doesn't ratify his position, he'll pack up and go away.

That is giving and hazarding all you have, all you have won. This is the generosity of love, giving the one you love her own choice, and that is the significance of this unrealistic fairytale.

The Merchant of Venice—Shylock
Lecture 8

> Shakespeare's England was almost monolithically Christian, so that to be a Jew was defined negatively. It was to be not a Christian, to be one who had rejected the dispensation of love, mercy and salvation that Christianity says is available through Jesus Christ. [Shylock] is an alien, not part of the Christian community of love.

Shylock may be merely a villain, a character contrasting with the generosity of Antonio, Portia, and Bassanio. The character of Shylock is founded on a three-part stereotype. He is a miser. He is a usurer; money lending at interest was officially condemned but tolerated as a necessary evil. He is a Jew at a time when Jews were thought of simply as "other," as non-Christian, as scapegoats.

In England this stereotype had a special purity. Only in England did Jews dominate finance, albeit temporarily. They were a major source of Crown revenue. The belief that the Jews killed Christian children—the "blood libel"—originated in England. Jews were banished from England between 1290 and the 1660s. No real people could be damaged by English anti-Semitism, since very few Jews lived in England during Shakespeare's time. The stereotype of the Jewish usurer and murderer could flourish in the absence of experience.

Shakespeare develops the character beyond stereotype.

Actors have reinterpreted the role of Shylock over time. We do not know how Richard Burbage played Shylock in 1596. In the late seventeenth century, Shylock was a comic villain. In the eighteenth century, Charles Macklin made Shylock a serious villain. In the Romantic period, Edmund Kean made him an honest villain, marked by directness and honesty. In the Victorian period, Henry Irving made him a heroic patriarch, marked by dignity and heroic pride. In 1970, Laurence Olivier made him a banker-aristocrat of the industrial age.

Shakespeare develops the character beyond stereotype. "Hath not a Jew eyes?" is both a cruel piece of exaggerated and vengeful illogic and an overwhelming outpouring of painful feeling. Revenge is not an automatic, physiological reaction, as bleeding is when pricked or laughing is when tickled. Shylock points out that Jews resemble Christians both in their humanity and—at times—their inhumanity. Shylock contains the faults of us all. ■

Essential Reading

Shakespeare, *The Merchant of Venice.*

Supplementary Reading

See BBC-TV videotape of *The Merchant of Venice.*

Gross, *Shylock: Four Hundred Years in the Life of a Legend.*

Shapiro, *Shakespeare and the Jews.*

Questions to Consider

1. Compare Shylock's mode of speech with that of Bassanio or Antonio.

2. Shylock does villainous things and yet we feel enormously sympathetic to him at times. Is Shylock a coherent characterization? Consider especially the passage with Tubal at the end of 3.1.

The Merchant of Venice—Shylock
Lecture 8—Transcript

In the last lecture, I called *The Merchant of Venice* a fairytale. Fairytales require villains: giants, ogres, stepmothers, or wicked uncles. In this context, Shylock is simply and directly a villain, a cruel and vengeful usurer who plots the death of a good man, and the detail of a pound of flesh gives the appropriate scary overtone of cannibalism. In fairytales, we do not usually trouble to explain the villainy of the villain; it's simply there, like the beauty of the heroine and the courage of the hero. James Thurber makes that point very neatly in his modern, sophisticated fairytale, *The Thirteen Clocks*. The villain there is an evil duke. Near the end of the story, when things are going against him, he has a moment of warm self-pity. "Why are they all against me?" he asks. "Everybody has faults. Mine is being wicked."

In *The Merchant of Venice*, Shylock is the wicked man who threatens the life of Antonio, and thus gives Portia a chance to show her strength and intelligence in the courtroom of Venice. And Shylock can be played simply as an ogre; he fits into the thematic pattern I was tracing in the last lecture. I was arguing for Bassanio's gracious generosity. The leading Christian characters, Antonio and Portia, are also generous, outstandingly generous. They have the money to be generous on a scale that Bassanio cannot be. Antonio is willing to extend repeated loans to his friends. He has rescued debtors from Shylock, he is willing to bind his body for Bassanio's success at the start of the play, and binds his soul for Bassanio's fidelity to Portia at the end. Portia is eager to enrich Bassanio, eager to extend hospitality to the wandering lovers, Lorenzo and Jessica, whom she's never met before, and eager to rescue Antonio, even offering to pay his debt thrice over. She's never met him either, but he's her husband's best friend.

This celebration of generosity and friendship and love rises to an explicitly Christian level in Portia's great speech on mercy:

> The quality of mercy is not strain'd;
> It droppeth as the gentle rain from heaven
> Upon the place beneath...
> It is an attribute to God himself.

It even rises to the level of a metaphysical force. In the last act, Lorenzo describes the music of the spheres, the music supposedly made by the stars as they move in their orbits. He is speaking of what Dante called "the love that moved the sun and the other stars," that is, the love that created and sustains the universe.

All this Gentile generosity stands in opposition to Shylock. Antonio and Portia frequently open things, share them; Shylock shuts them. His motto is "Fast bind, fast find—a proverb never stale in thrifty mind." He ties Antonio up in the bond of flesh. He shuts up his house, locks the doors, tells his daughter to shut the windows, lest the music of Venetian merrymaking come in. In the trial scene, he craves not mercy, but the law. All these actions cohere with the basic formula for the character, the stereotype that is the backbone for Shylock. He is a miser, he is a usurer, and he is a Jew.

Now, misers are, of course, unattractive, especially onstage. Usurers are more problematic. In the Renaissance, and for a quite a while before, in the Middle Ages and back to classical times, the lending of money at interest was, in theory, universally condemned. The idea, which turns up in Aristotle, turns up in the Bible, was that moneylenders do not grow crops, or raise animals, or make useful objects out of wood and stone. Those could be considered natural ways of making a living, cooperating with the processes of increase that are inherent in nature. Moneylenders make an income by causing coin to produce more coin, making barren metal breed, and unnatural form of reproduction.

That, of course, was the theory; it was not the practice in the Renaissance. The nascent capitalism of the period depended upon money lending. Queen Elizabeth kept her government going by building up an excellent credit rating on the money market at Antwerp. Shakespeare himself was a speculator. Francis Bacon, in his essay "Of Usury," which is as far as I know the most sensible piece of Elizabethan writing on the subject, concluded that, "to speak of the abolishment of usury is idle. All states have ever had it in one kind or rate or other." The whole paradoxical situation is summed up in the law that governed moneylending in England during Shakespeare's adulthood, the Parliamentary Act of 1571. This act condemned usury as a mortal sin, and made it legal so long as you didn't charge more than 10 percent. Shylock is serving as a scapegoat for a practice that was condemned by both church and state throughout Christendom, a practice that was necessary throughout Christendom.

Shylock is also a Jew. Now here, we have to change our frame of reference from the way we think now. We have Christians, Jews, Muslims, Buddhists, atheists, pantheists, and all matter of things, including witches, and each of them can be defined positively. Shakespeare's England was almost monolithically Christian, so that to be a Jew was defined negatively. It was to be not a Christian, to be one who had rejected the dispensation of love, mercy and salvation that Christianity says is available through Jesus Christ. He is an alien, not part of the Christian community of love. He lives under what Saint Paul called the old law, the law of strict justice, an eye for an eye. In this regard, he is also a scapegoat, for the Christian community of Venice in this play has difficulty living up to its own ideals, as Christian communities always do. The clearest example is the character Gratiano. At the end of the trial scene, he expresses a degree of hatred and vengefulness equal to Shylock's own. Shylock embodies those aspects of Christian society that fail to be fully Christian, and he's punished for it.

This is very painful for us. It is hard to think of Shylock merely as a character; we automatically take him as Shakespeare's representative of all Jews. Therefore, no comedy of Shakespeare causes more discomfort for modern readers and playgoers. Productions will elicit public protests, calls to the producer, editorials in *The New York Times*. Some critics have transformed the play from being the anti-Semitic comedy of *The Merchant of Venice* into the sympathetic tragedy of the Jew of Venice. It is hard for any Jewish person to sit through this play without sensations of fear, or anger, or shame. Any decent Gentile probably shares some of those feelings. It would be grotesque to hold Shakespeare responsible for the Holocaust, but he is certainly handling material that, in other hands, produced uniquely wicked acts. I don't like thinking the greatest writer in English is anti-Semitic. Some explanations are necessary.

So far, I've been talking about a stock figure, a stereotype, a stereotype that existed all over Europe for centuries. But for three reasons, the stereotype had, in England, an almost laboratory purity. First, only in England in the Middle

Ages did Jews actually gain significant leverage in finance. Elsewhere, the notion of the Jew as usurer was a myth, based only on isolated cases. English Jews, however, were the kings' men. They were vassals of a special kind. They were a major source of crown revenue, exempt from regular taxes, subject to special exactions as demanded by the king, operating through a special office attached to the king's household that was explicitly called the "Exchequer of the Jews."

Second, it was in England that a story got started that was to plague Jews right down to the present century. On Good Friday in the year 1144, in the town of Norwich, the dead body of a young apprentice was found. The Jews of that town were accused of having murdered him in mockery of the Passion of Christ. Riots and the murder of Jews followed. Episodes of this sort run through anti-Semitic mythology. The usual form is that Jews murder Christian children in order to incorporate their blood in the unleavened bread of Passover.

Third, in the year 1290, England expelled all its Jews, the first time any European state had done that sort of thing. King Edward I had gotten all the money he could through the Exchequer of the Jews, and thus, without loss, he could bow to religious objections to the Jewish presence in England. And, of course, there were Gentiles who wanted to take over the business. Not until nearly four centuries later, which is 40 years after the death of William Shakespeare, were practicing Jews readmitted to England.

This state of affairs has two important results for the historical understanding of Shakespeare's play. First, in Elizabethan London, anti-Semitism wasn't a social passion capable of doing damage to real people. The audience could not leave the play looking for a Jew to lynch; there weren't any Jews to be lynched. There was a tiny community of about 100 Sephardic Jews living in London, and like everybody else in England, they conformed outwardly to Anglican practice and had their own rituals in private. And there was, a couple of years before this play was written, a scandalous episode involving a Portuguese Jewish doctor who was converted to Christianity, and was accused of plotting to poison the Queen and was executed for that. But the chance of Shakespeare himself, or any single member of his audience, actually knowing a Jew, in a city of 200,000 people, was very slight. That's one result of that lab purity I'm talking about.

The second result is this; in this vacuum of real experience, the myth of the Jewish usurer-murderer could flourish as an exotic stereotype, a foreign bogeyman, the sort of fairytale figure I've been talking about. And flourish it did; Christopher Marlowe created a lurid stage figure in his *Jew of Malta*, using all the stereotypical details. His Jew is a sadist and an evil figure that poisons wells, kills a whole convent of nuns, kills under pretense of administering medicine, and blows up a barracks of soldiers, the whole lot.

But Shakespeare was not Marlowe. The stereotype serves as a backbone, or blueprint, for the characterization of Shylock, and we see it occasionally, as when Shylock is called "faithless," as if Jews didn't have their own faith, or "dog" and "devil;" the objects of prejudice are usually dehumanized. But the characterization of Shylock is more than these things, as we can see if we look at the stage history of the play, where the role of Shylock has been reinterpreted by great actors of successive generations to find quite different things.

I cannot tell you how Richard Burbage played Shylock for Shakespeare in 1596; there is no eyewitness account. The closest we can come is a bit of verse that was penned some 50 years after Burbage and Shakespeare were dead. It goes like this: "His beard was red, his face was made / Not much unlike a witch's, / His habit was a Jewish gown / That would defend all weather, / His chin turned up, his nose turned down, / And both ends met together." Red hair, hooked nose, up-curved chin, and a witch face—this is a grotesque, a comic character to be despised, to be laughed at. A hundred years later, in the eighteenth century, the actor Charles Macklin was, for decades, associated with the part of Shylock. Macklin shifted it from comic villainy into serious villainy. Memoirs of the period say that he gave full vent to the contrasting passions of the part. He displayed a frightening malice. He was, and I quote, "all shade, not a gleam of light, subtle, selfish, fawning, irascible, tyrannical. Sententious gloominess of expression was linked to ferocity and malice by continuous weight and power." And another quote, "The audience seemed to shrink from the character." No longer funny, but very villainous.

The Shylock of Edmund Kean in the Romantic period, at the beginning of the nineteenth century, was also famous. His was a lighter version than Macklin's. For Macklin's sullenness, he substituted family love, racial pride, striated with pain. The distinguishing mark in Kean's performance was apparently directness, not the malice of Macklin, but honesty. The Romantic critic William Hazlitt wrote a famous comment: "Our sympathies are much oftener with Kean's Shylock than with his enemies. He is honest in his vices; they are hypocrites in their virtues." Now, that's a very important statement; something major is shifting in the whole scale of Western feeling, when you praise a villain for being direct and open at the expense of largely virtuous people who occasionally fall down on their virtues. The Romantic critics often sound like youngsters of any generation; they will put up with anything, as long as it's straightforward. The greatest sin is hypocrisy. Better the aggressive Jew than the hypocritical Christians, the Christians who don't make it.

The next great step in the stage reinterpretation of Shylock was to intensify the racial representation of the character, to have him carry all the destiny of the Jews. This is accomplished by Sir Henry Irving, Victorian actor, first actor in England to be given a knighthood for his services to the theater. Irving had all the dignity and heroic pride of a Hebrew patriarch; from the point of view of the anti-Semitic myth, he moved out of the realm of the bad Jews, the murderers, the well-poisoners, and back to the good Jews, the chosen people, Abraham, Elijah, Moses. He was venerable, grieved, lonely, austere; his vengefulness could just be written off as the forgivable result of abuse. One of his famous effects came in the scene of Jessica's elopement. Jessica elopes with Lorenzo in a scene of merrymaking: music, torches, crowds of young people dancing on the bridges over Venetian canals (Victorian production was very lavish indeed.) Then, all those people swept offstage, taking with them the musicians and the torchbearers, so that the light and the color all disappeared, and the stage went shadowy and silent. Then you heard, from way offstage, the tapping of Shylock's stick as he walks slowly home from dinner out at Bassanio's. And he crossed the full width of the stage and knocked on his own door; remember, he's given the keys to Jessica and told her to lock the house. But he gets no response to the knocking, and he turned and looked at the audience, and you could tell from his face that he knew he had lost his last living relative. Now, you cannot do that kind of thing without building enormous sympathy for the character.

The most famous twentieth-century Shylock has been Laurence Olivier, the first English actor to be made a lord. His production, directed by Jonathan Miller for the National Theatre of Great Britain, was set in Victorian times, with black frockcoats on the men, bustles on the women. And Shylock was a banker aristocrat of the industrial age; people lending money are no longer usurers, they are financiers. And Shylock was the Baron de Rothschild, friend of the Prince of Wales, polished, urbane. Olivier used the most complex stage accent I have ever heard. His normal speech was cultivated English, like that of the upper class Gentiles, BBC English, we would think of it as now. Layered on top of that was an attempt at something even more aristocratic, lazy vowels and dropped final G's in words like "speakin'" and "meanin'," the sort of accent I haven't heard for years now but in 1970, when this production was mounted, could still be heard in very elderly dukes and Oxford dons, the sort of accent that you would use to play Lord Peter Wimsey on television. But underneath those two layers, emerging when Shylock was upset or afraid, was Shylock's original native speech, whatever that may have been, a matter of vowels and changes of pitch that were strange to Anglophone ears altogether.

Olivier's most memorable moment was his exit from the trial scene, the moment that Portia said, "The law hath yet another hold on you," and mentioned the penalty of death against an alien who plots against a Venetian. Olivier went absolutely stiff, as if he were wrapped in baling wire. His eyes bulged, his face went red. I was sitting in the fourth row and I was terrified; I thought he was having a heart attack. I thought I was going to be present at a dreadful moment, when the most famous classical actor of the century dies onstage in front of us. Indeed, Olivier had an extraordinary capacity to create a sense of danger, really to scare an audience. He uttered his three remaining speeches staying like that, in strangulated tones, and then when told he could leave, after he had said he would become a Christian, he moved only to make that exit. And as I remember, the one gesture he made was to grab a stair railing to support himself; he was not going to break in front of these people. And he got himself offstage, and then you heard a crash. He had fallen, and it was followed by a great keening wail, not sobs, but a big, chest-heaving, throat-ripping sob that seemed to go on forever.

Shylock does not appear again in the play. But at the end of the last act, Jessica, his daughter, was left alone onstage, clearly regretting her choice to leave her father for these Christians, and we heard again, from offstage, a voice, this time chanting the Kaddish, and I thought it meant Shylock had died. I was told later that Jews sometimes chant Kaddish for a child who marries a Christian, because that child is dead to the family. Whichever way you interpret it, it meant that the play ended in death, not in the happiness normal for comedy.

Now, any Shakespearean scholar has opinions about what should or shouldn't be done onstage. I must object to some of the things I described. Irving's full-stage cross and knock on the door is not in Shakespeare's text, and it contradicts what's in Shakespeare's text, a speech about "my daughter and my ducats," that indicates a quite different response to Jessica's elopement. He doesn't know whether he regrets the loss of the woman or the money more. And coming on with the Kaddish at the end is very heavy; it kills the wonder, the open-ended question "What does happen to Shylock?" after he loses and is forced to turn Christian. But in general, the liberty and depth of interpretation that I have been describing from these actors seems to me to be justified. Kean and Irving and Olivier were responding, of course, to their own times, to changing circumstances, to changing feelings about the treatment of minorities. But even if they take imaginative shortcuts, revising details in the play, there is room in the play for them to do so. The richness of Shakespeare's imagination has produced a Shylock who not only fulfills the stereotype, but does something more important; tells us what it's like to be inside the stereotype.

I'd like to work that out in many details, but in a lecture of only 30 minutes, I must go directly to the big speech, the most famous speech in the play. Shylock has been grieving the loss of his daughter and his ducats. He's also just found out that Antonio has lost all his money and cannot repay the loan. He plans to extract the collateral, a pound of flesh. Antonio's friends object: "Why, I am sure, if he forfeit, thou wilt not take his flesh. What's that good for?"

And Shylock responds:

> To bait fish withal: if it will feed nothing else, it will feed my revenge. He hath disgrac'd me and hind'red me half a million; laugh'd at my losses, mock'd at my gains, scorned my nation, thwarted my bargains, cooled my friends, heated mine enemies; and what's his reason? I am a Jew. Hath not a Jew eyes? Hath not a Jew hands, organs, dimensions, senses, affections, passions? fed with the same food, hurt with the same weapons, subject to the same diseases, healed by the same means, warmed and cooled by the same winter and summer, as a Christian is? If you prick us, do we not bleed? If you tickle us, do we not laugh? If you poison us, do we not die? And if you wrong us, shall we not revenge? If we are like you in the rest, we shall be like you in that. If a Jew wrong a Christian, what is his humility? Revenge. If a Christian wrong a Jew, what should his sufferance be by Christian example? Why, revenge. The villainy you teach me, I will execute; and it will go hard but that I better the example.

One could describe that as a villainous speech, unjust and illogical. Whatever Antonio has done to Shylock, he has not done him mortal injury, so to respond with a plot of death is overkill. As for the logic, well, we have no choice when we are pricked but to bleed, when we are tickled but to laugh, when we are poisoned but to die. Those are physiological responses. But when we are wronged, we have choices. Revenge is not a knee-jerk reaction; it's a chosen response. And to represent it as if it were a knee-jerk reaction is to forgo the humanity of making choices, making decisions. The speech works like a trap; we're led into sympathy with Shylock, and then appalled by his conclusion.

I think that that comment is perfectly sound. It is also insufficient. It responds to the intellectual argument of the speech, but not to the power of the writing. It neglects the enormous range of feeling expressed, its hurried and compelling range of sensation and emotion, from food and laughter to poison and disease, from bargains and organs to summer and winter, and on to revenge. The release of crowded energy, the pouring forth of passion, is overwhelming. Further, the speech is not just a plea for sympathy, a direct piece of pathos asking us to have pity on the oppressed because they too are human. It's also an accusation. If Jews and Christians are alike, in that they both are human, they are alike in that they both are inhuman. That is, I can sum up the speech in either direction. I can say, "I am a Jew, and Jews resemble Christians in laughing, bleeding, dying and the rest," or "I am a Jew, and Christians resemble Jews. You too are Jews, in your villainies and revenges, not to mention your concern with money. You are like this stereotype Jew, whom you believe me to be." That is, Shylock is part of us all. If we hold ourselves aloof from this cruel and revengeful man, we do not know ourselves. If he is strange, outrageous and variable, so are we. None of us can fully live up to the law. We all need mercy, forgiveness, and grace. Portia remarks, "In the course of justice, none of us / Should see salvation."

Shakespeare begins with a couple of old stories, a well-known stereotype, a set of moral oppositions between generosity and hard bargaining. But these things are the framework of the play, not the experience of it. Shakespeare took the stereotypes of common life and the allegorical frameworks of the old medieval drama. They are very useful structures to build on, but he expressed within them the realities of feeling that they merely label abstractly. That is the achievement of Shakespeare at his particular moment in the development of English playwriting. He can fill the abstract patterns with something like the pulse of life itself. That is the abundance of Shakespeare.

Measure for Measure—Sex in Society
Lecture 9

In this case, the plot is intricate, and unusual, and Shakespeare made some key changes in the sources from which he inherited it.

Like other Shakespearean comedies, *Measure for Measure* ends with four couples on the point of marriage, but the means by which they arrive at this point are unusual. The play derives from an old folktale ("the unjust judge") in which a woman tries to save a man (her husband or brother or father) from execution by begging the judge for a pardon. There are various endings to this scenario.

In this case, the judge, Angelo, acting for the absent duke of Vienna, offers to pardon the young fornicator, Claudio, only if his religious sister, Isabella, will sleep with him (Angelo). When Claudio begs Isabella to comply with Angelo's demand, she rejects his plea. But the disguised duke intervenes, arranging an assignation in which Angelo's rejected fiancée Mariana will substitute for Isabella in Angelo's bed. Although he believes he had slept with Isabella, Angelo nonetheless orders the execution of Claudio. When Angelo is accused of injustice in the last act, after many confusions and revelations, the play can end happily with four unions: Claudio and Julietta, Angelo and Mariana, Lucio and Kate Keepdown, the duke and Isabella.

Unusually for Shakespeare, the play deals extensively with a brothel and with syphilis.

The play differs from standard Shakespearean romantic comedy in many ways other than its peculiar plot. The characters cannot be romantic or lighthearted: they are far too troubled by the power of lust, the abuse of authority, and the threat of dishonor and death. The actions occur in stifling and claustrophobic places, and the jokes are gallows humor.

Instead of being a source of life and pleasure, sex is a source of death and pain. It brings people to hatred of themselves and lack of charity to others. Unusually for Shakespeare, the play deals extensively with a brothel and with syphilis. At 1.2.108–110, Claudio compares the workings of sexual desire to those of rat poison. At 3.1.137–148, the threat to Isabella's chastity leads her to denounce her brother Claudio as a bastard. In his soliloquy at the end of 2.2, in one of Shakespeare's great speeches of personal awareness, deserving of a close reading, Angelo is filled with self-loathing upon the discovery of sexual desire. ■

Essential Reading

Shakespeare, *Measure for Measure.*

Questions to Consider

1. Trace the motif of "fairness" in the play as covered in this lecture. Is the duke fair to Angelo by placing him in a position of tempting power? Is Angelo fair to Claudio—both at the beginning and the end of the play? Is Claudio fair to Isabella? Is Isabella fair to Claudio? What other endings could you envision for this play?

2. Compare Shakespeare's treatment of sex in this play to any of the other comedies covered in this course of lectures. What reasons can you adduce for the negative "spin" he puts on sexual desire in *Measure for Measure*?

Measure for Measure—Sex in Society
Lecture 9—Transcript

With *Measure for Measure*, I must begin with the plot. The next few minutes will sound rather like plot summary, something I try to avoid in these lectures, and something I certainly discourage in student papers. In this case, the plot is intricate, and unusual, and Shakespeare made some key changes in the sources from which he inherited it. It does derive from an old story, a folktale. The people who study these things call it the "tale of the unjust judge." A man is condemned to death on some legitimate cause. A woman, deeply attached to him, sometimes his daughter, sometimes his wife, sometimes his sister, goes to the judge and begs for mercy, asks for a pardon. The judge finds himself lusting after the woman, and therefore offers a bargain; you satisfy my desire, I'll issue the pardon. The magistrate then proceeds to welch on the deal. He takes the woman, but in the morning after, orders the execution to proceed nonetheless. There are various endings, depending on which version of the story you encounter. The woman merely grieves, or she curses the judge, or she contrives her revenge, or some higher authority intervenes to punish the judge.

It is, as I say, an old story, many times retold, and receiving literary treatment from both Italian and English writers in the Renaissance, before Shakespeare took it up. The French essayist Montaigne spoke of it in one essay, and spoke of it as an historical story, that women had saved their men from execution on certain known occasions. The story goes on being retold. Some 25 years ago, the American songwriter Bob Dylan composed a version of this, a song called "Seven Curses," which sets this tale in the American Wild West. The crime for which the man is originally arrested and condemned in that version is horse-stealing.

In Shakespeare's version, in *Measure for Measure*, the condemned man is young Claudio, guilty of fornication, which, in Vienna, is a capital crime. The sister, Isabella, is an enthusiastically religious young woman who is on the verge of entering a convent. She is, in fact, dressed in the robes of a novice, or postulant, throughout the play. But she is persuaded to go to the judge, Angelo, and beg pardon for her brother. Now, Angelo is not only a magistrate, he is also, temporarily, the supreme authority in the city of

Vienna. The ruling duke has gone on sabbatical; where, nobody knows. This all-powerful deputy has hitherto lived up to his angelic name. He had been just and upright; he has been so virtuous, that some people think he's got ice in his veins instead of blood and the other bodily fluids. But he does develop a violent lust for Isabella, and after two terrific interviews with her, proposes the bargain—your chastity for your brother's life.

Isabella is torn by the moral dilemma, and further torn when her brother wavers between respect for his sister's honor, and his own desire to live. That's where Shakespeare really starts making changes in the story. Isabella does not yield to the judge, as had happened in all previous versions that we know of this story. Instead, she decides, "More than our brother is our chastity." Shakespeare also has the duke intervene at this point, disguised as a friar. This duke-friar persuades Isabella to agree to a midnight meeting with Angelo, and also persuades a second young woman, called Mariana, who was once Angelo's fiancée, and is still in love with him, to fulfill the assignation on Isabella's behalf. This plot device of substituting one woman for another in a midnight assignation has been called the "bed trick." Angelo then believes he has deflowered Isabella; in the dark, all cats are gray, particularly for a man with such little sexual experience as Angelo has. Then, for fear that Claudio will eventually take revenge for his sister's loss of honor, he orders the execution to proceed nonetheless. When the duke finally returns to Vienna in his own identity, Isabella and Mariana publicly denounce Angelo as a murderer, a hypocrite and a virgin-violator.

Well, it all works out happily at the end with four marriages. Claudio is not dead after all; with the help of a kindly prison officer, the duke manages to deceive Angelo about that. Instead of sending him Claudio's severed head, they send him the head of a notorious criminal who just happens to have died the night before in prison. This is called the "head trick." Claudio can, therefore, marry the young woman he has slept with. Angelo faces death for his crimes, but the duke requires first that he marry Mariana in order to legitimize her position. And she, thereupon, begs mercy for her new husband, on the ground that he is her husband, and she does still love him, and he hasn't really violated Isabella. A witty young wastrel called Lucio, who has an important role as go-between in the plot, is obliged to marry a prostitute who he has impregnated. And in an unexpected final move, the duke himself proposes marriage to young Isabella.

All this looks like the standard conclusion of a comedy; four couples get married. It's like the end of *As You Like It* or *Twelfth Night*, except that this is not a standard comedy. The play is far too charged with the power of lust, with the abuse of authority, with the real threat of dishonor and death. The characters cannot be lighthearted about life, as they usually are in Shakespearean comedy. Romantic love is conspicuous by its absence from this play. Much of the action occurs in uncomfortably enclosed places; we get a claustrophobic feeling as we watch or read this play. There are scenes in prisons, scenes in brothels, scenes in the judgment chambers of Angelo and his colleagues. There is humor; there are places to laugh in *Measure for Measure*. But it's a wild, jagged humor, a sort of gallows humor. One of the sources of it is a pimp named Pompey. This pimp is eventually plucked out of his brothel, forced to reform. He's given a new job as assistant executioner. From pimp to executioner, from helping people into bed to helping people onto the scaffold; it seems to me a dubious improvement.

Measure for Measure differs from other Shakespearean comedies, especially in its treatment of sex. Now, sex in Shakespeare is usually the source of pleasure and, of course, the source of life. Young lovers look forward, with frank delight, to the consummation of their passions, usually after they have been properly married to one another. There are lots of sexual jokes in Shakespeare, and they're usually good-natured ones. Sex is a force of life. Young people prance out into the green fields and sing, "Hey, nonny, nonny!" on a May morning. But in *Measure for Measure*, sex is, by and large, a raunchy and unattractive source of death.

Out of Shakespeare's 38 surviving plays, there are only two that have scenes in brothels. This is one of them; the other is *Pericles*. Now, houses of ill repute were certainly a familiar part of the London scene of Shakespeare's time. In fact, they were a very familiar part of the London theatrical scene. The brothels were located in the same district of London as the theaters, the South Bank, the other side of the Thames, in order to be out of the strict regulation within the city walls of London proper, governed by the Lord Mayor and the Board of Aldermen. Brothels were right next to theaters. Yet

Shakespeare seldom uses them in his plays. He does use them in *Measure for Measure*. In fact, we meet the staff of a brothel. We meet Mistress Overdone, the madam. "She hath had nine husbands, overdone by the last;" the pun, I think, is fairly obvious, and it sums up the sense of squalor and excess associated with these brothels. We meet Pompey, the pimp. His full name is Pompey Bum; his bum is the greatest thing about him. And he gets arrested several times, in fact; the first time on the complaint of a constable, whose wife, a respectable woman, somehow ended up in the brothel being insulted, being taken by one of the customers in the brothel for one of the workers within the brothel.

This respectable woman, Mistress Elbow, went there merely because she was pregnant and had one of those odd cravings for a particular food that pregnant women often have. In her case, it was prunes that she wanted, and she saw a dish of prunes on the windowsill of the brothel. Actually, that's a rather interesting joke because prunes were believed by some people to prevent you from getting syphilis. If you ate prunes, you were less likely to contract the disease. Therefore, brothels often had prunes available, and to put a dish of prunes on the windowsill, well, there are jokes that this is the way that brothels advertised themselves. It is a way of saying, "This is a bawdy house, gentlemen may come in, if that is what they're looking for." It's a literary joke; I don't know whether people actually believed it or not.

Syphilis; the whole subject of sex is introduced, in this play, by a series of jokes about syphilis. Now that isn't the most attractive way to talk about sex. It's as if we should write a modern play now, a play about sex, and begin it with a series of jokes about AIDS. Well, syphilis wasn't quite as bad as AIDS. Its fatality rate wasn't as high, it wasn't so terribly serious a disease, but it was the worst sexually transmitted disease they knew in the sixteenth century. And it was new in the sixteenth century; the first great outbreak in Europe had happened at the end of the fifteenth century. It came into European culture, either through some kind of transmutation of a germ that had been previously harmless, or it was brought back into Europe by Columbus's sailors. It was an infection that was here in America, to which the Native Americans were immune, but against which the Europeans had no defense. There was no adequate treatment for it. Everybody blamed it on everybody else. The English called it the French disease; the French called it the Neapolitan bone-ache, because the first great epidemic of it happened in Naples. And it turned one of the major pleasures of life into a source of pain, disfigurement, and death. That's the kind of sexual world we're working with in Mistress Overdone's brothels. And the world is not only a matter of unattractive scenes and possible diseases; it's a world where the unattractiveness works into the way people feel about themselves and each other.

I want to talk about three speeches in particular. Claudio, our young hero, is an upper class young man who has slept with his girlfriend, Julietta, and gotten her pregnant. Now, this is not an enormous sexual sin; this couple is in love. She consented to their sleeping together; she insists, "Our offense was most mutually committed." They consider themselves married to each other, and they say, indeed, they would be married if it were not for some problem about a dowry, which is so trivial that Shakespeare doesn't even bother to specify what it is. He is arrested because there is a law against fornication in Vienna, and Angelo, who is in charge of the city, does want to crack down on sexual offenses. And he himself, Claudio, feels overcome with guilt, even though his offense is not very great, as sexual offenses run.

He describes human sexuality, in fact, as being inherently self-destructive. When his friend Lucio asks why he's being taken to prison, what has he done, what is his cause, he says: "Liberty, my dear Lucio; too much liberty. … Our natures do pursue, / Like rats that raven down their proper bane, / A thirsty evil; and when we drink we die." We are like rats, we are like rodents, we are like vermin. We eagerly seek the poison, the ratsbane, that will kill us. The metaphor is drawn from the real action of ratsbane. Many compounds that kill rats that are used for that purpose, do not directly kill the rat. What they do is make the rate very thirsty, so the rat goes in search of water, which he drinks eagerly, and it's the water that activates the chemical compound that kills the rat. The rat dies from drinking what he most desires. We die from the sexual consummation that our bodies yearn for. This is a man caught in the guilt that comes from satisfying his own desires.

His sister, Isabella, has not involved herself in any sexual offense, so rather than feeling guilty, she expresses herself by distancing herself from sex as much as possible. When she tells Claudio that she can save his life if she agrees to Angelo's bargain, Claudio at first says, "You shall not do it." But then he breaks down, and the terror of death overcomes him, and he begs, "Sweet sister, let me live." And she responds with outrage and horror:

> O you beast!
> O faithless coward! O dishonest wretch!
> Wilt thou be made a man out of my vice?
> Is't not a kind of incest, to take life
> From thine own sister's shame? What should I think?
> Heaven shield my mother play'd my father fair!
> For such a warped slip of wilderness
> Ne'er issu'd from his blood. Take my defiance!
> Die; perish! Might but my bending down
> Reprieve thee from thy fate, it should proceed.
> I'll pray a thousand prayers for thy death,
> No word to save thee.

She calls him a beast; he's not a human being. She calls him a faithless coward; he is faithless, he's not Christian, and he's a coward, he's not brave. She regards any sexual possibility as the worst kind. It would be a kind of incest for her to sleep with Angelo in order to give her brother life. Montaigne, who I mentioned earlier, speaking of women saving their brothers' or their husbands' or their fathers' lives by this means, considered it heroic behavior to surrender their honor in this fashion, but she thinks it's utterly vile. She, in fact, completely disclaims all relationship with her brother. "Heaven shield my mother play'd my father fair! / For such a warped slip of wilderness / Ne'er issu'd from his blood." You're not my brother; you can't be my brother, you're not my father's son if you beg this of me. It leads her into a complete want of charity, a denial of their common human condition, their relationship. She completes that speech by wanting him to die: "Die, perish. No word to save thee."

And my third example, Angelo. The judge, Angelo, is an upright man, and has lived so. But he has a 25-line soliloquy at the end of his first scene with Isabella, where he discovers the lust into which he is falling. In this soliloquy, he moves from being an upright judge and careful administrator to an acknowledgment of a sexual desire whose strength, whose very presence astonishes him, a lust that will lead him into seduction under gross pressure, into what amounts to rape, and on into judicial murder and all sorts of hypocrisy. It is one of the great soliloquies in Shakespeare, one of the great speeches of self-discovery that he learned to write for his major characters. I want to deliver it, and then I want to talk about details of it.

> What's this, what's this? Is this her fault or mine?
> The tempter or the tempted, who sins most?
> Ha!
> Not she; nor doth she tempt; but it is I
> That, lying by the violet in the sun,
> Do as the carrion does, not as the flow'r,
> Corrupt with virtuous season.

Let me pause there and comment on those lines. He is astonished at first, and he is so unused to what's going on that he doesn't know where it comes from. Is this coming from inside him, or from her? Is she tempting him? That may be part of a normal male projection; this isn't me, "the woman tempted me, and I ate." The woman was provocative. But, in fact, Angelo is a pretty smart guy, and he sees instantly that Isabella hasn't tempted him. "Not she, nor doth she tempt; but it is I / That, lying by the violet in the sun, / Do as the carrion does, not as the flow'r, / Corrupt with virtuous season." It is I. And Shakespeare emphasizes the "I" by repeating the vowel sound; "it is I / That, lying by the violet in the sun"—that assonance, that repeated "I, as he dwells on the self that astonishes him. In the sun, she is a flower, she is a violet, she will blossom, she will give forth a sweet odor. But I am like carrion; I am like meat, dead meat. I will stink, in contrast to the sweet smell of the flower. He goes on:

> Can it be
> That modesty may more betray our sense
> Than woman's lightness? Having waste ground enough,
> Shall we desire to raze the sanctuary,
> And pitch our evils there?

He's really surprised to find that this woman, who is dressed as a novice, who is dressed in sober religious clothes, can tempt him in the way a harlot, a strumpet, dressed in the clothes of her trade, would not. Woman's modesty is betraying his sense, his sensual nature. And he suspects some kind of bizarre thing going on in himself. Yeah, there are brothels, there is waste-ground, there are trash heaps. But what this involves, this situation between his feelings for Isabella, is that he desires to raze the sanctuary, to knock down the church and pitch his evils there, to build a brothel on the sanctified spot.

> O, fie, fie, fie!
> What dost thou, or what art thou, Angelo?

Now that's the key move in the speech, Angelo's growth of self-perception. First he's disgusted, "O, fie, fie, fie," then the move from "What dost thou?" to "What art thou?" That's a big move to make. We can do many things without defining ourselves in terms of those things. "Oh, I did this, I accidentally did that; I drove too fast at night, but I'm not habitually a reckless driver, I don't define myself that way." But Angelo sees that he has discovered some fundamental part of his identity, so that his doing this, his lusting after Isabella, tells him something about who he really is. He isn't going to blame circumstances, to blame an accidental thing for his current state. He knows it's in him.

He goes on:

> Dost thou desire her foully for those things
> That make her good?

You want to exert your lust on someone who is good? It is the virtue itself that is tempting?

> O, let her brother live!
> Thieves for their robbery have authority
> When judges steal themselves.

He's a very smart guy. He immediately sees the paradox he's gotten into. Here he is, lusting after the girl while condemning her brother for committing fornication. Then he thinks, for one moment, that this might be an innocent feeling. He says,

> What, do I love her,
> That I desire to hear her speak again,
> And feast upon her eyes?

For that one moment, he thinks, possibly this is love, and I could court her, woo her in the ordinary way; to see her again, to feast upon her eyes, to court her, and so forth, carry on as any young man might with a young woman. But no, he sees that as not the case.

> What is't I dream on?
> O cunning enemy, that, to catch a saint,
> With saints dost bait thy hook!

He sees that what he wants is sin, that the devil is working in him, that he doesn't desire to court, to woo, to marry her. He desires to have her; it is the sin itself he wants.

He goes on,

> Most dangerous
> Is that temptation that doth goad us on
> To sin in loving virtue.

The enemy is very cunning, the devil is; he adjusts our temptations to what we are, and he has given Angelo a most dangerous temptation. Angelo's own love of virtue is being used to lead him into vice. The novice, the pious young girl is being used to provide him with a temptation that he hadn't felt before. He goes on:

> Never could the strumpet,
> With all her double vigour, art and nature,
> Once stir my temper; but this virtuous maid
> Subdues me quite. Ever till now,
> When men were fond, I smil'd and wond'red how.

He thought he was different from other men, and indeed, he was different from other men. "The strumpet, / With all her double vigour, art and nature," that is, the whore with her natural beauty heightened by cosmetics and dress and so forth, could never stir his temper. He was never in the least moved to sleep with a loose woman, "but this virtuous maid / Subdues me quite." He discovers he's not better than other men; he's worse than other men. He is moved into lust, and the form of lust that he's moved in is a kind of desecration, to violate the nun rather than to use the whore for the purpose for which the whore is presumably willing.

And he ends with rejecting his own vanity: "Ever till now, / When men were fond, I smil'd and wond'red how." I went about thinking, how can these guys be so foolish as to follow the whores back to their brothels? They are fond, they are silly; how can they do that? But now I've discovered something like it in myself, something even worse.

This, as I say, is one of the great soliloquies in Shakespeare. It is one of those great statements of identity. It's like Henry V saying, "I am a king. Let find thee, and I know," Henry working out what it means to be a king. Or King Lear saying, "I am a very foolish, fond old man." I'm not a king at all; I'm just a silly old geezer. These are speeches running through Shakespeare, to which I will come back. In this particular case, it's part of a whole pattern throughout *Measure for Measure*. Claudio said that sexual desire is like ratsbane. Isabella sent Claudio off to execution, "I'll pray a thousand prayers for thy death." Angelo says he's like carrion next to the flower of Isabella. That is, sexuality leads to death, and on the road to death, we go through self-hatred, and a complete lack of charity to others.

Measure for Measure was not a popular play in the nineteenth century. The Victorian period did not like to discuss sexual matters of this kind on the stage. But at the turn of the century, critics began to take a fresh interest in the play, and differentiated it from Shakespeare's other comedies by calling it a "problem play," or "problem comedy"—that is, a play dealing with social problems.

Measure for Measure deals with some weighty problems: sin, mercy, law, sexual probity (or lack thereof) and more. It is also a play about authority and the problems of authority. This lecture will explore these issues and will consider, at the end, the "problem" of the genre of dramatic quality against which this play strains.

The title of the play recalls a passage in the Sermon on the Mount (The Gospel according to Matthew, chapter 7). In this Gospel account, Jesus warns his followers that people will be judged by the standards by which they themselves judge others. Isabella points out to Angelo at 2.2.113–126 that human beings are inclined to abuse authority and judgment.

The particular law central to the plot makes fornication a capital crime. It is normal in Shakespearean comedy for law to form an obstacle to the happiness of young lovers. In *A Midsummer Night's Dream*, a young woman must marry the man her father selects, or die or enter a convent. In *The Merchant of Venice*, Portia must marry the man who correctly solves the lottery devised in her late father's will. Such laws are not realistic but they set up revealing dramatic situations. The fornication law in *Measure for Measure*, however, although not historically accurate, is nonetheless realistic. Concerned people in Shakespeare's London seriously advocated the death penalty for fornication.

The play explores the way in which various authority figures attempt to cope with the teeming and often gross sexuality of Vienna. Although authority may err, the play never doubts that authority is necessary. Angelo's prescription is "repress," a Puritan formula that allows little room for the urges and weakness of human nature. Isabella's prescription is "withdraw," a monastic formula that may work for gifted individuals but not for society at large. The duke's prescription is "forgive and marry," a formula that leads him into disguise and manipulation of other people's lives.

> **Although authority may err, the play never doubts that authority is necessary.**

The final problem of this problem comedy is that comedy itself may be a problem. Patterns of comedy may not be adequate to the stresses of the human condition. Some of the marriages at the end of the play seem contrived and unpromising. *Measure for Measure* is a provocative experiment testing whether standard theatrical patterns can satisfactorily contain the difficulties of the human condition. ∎

Essential Reading

Shakespeare, *Measure for Measure*.

Supplementary Reading

Dollimore, "Transgression and Surveillance in *Measure for Measure*."

Hunter, *Shakespeare and the Comedy of Forgiveness*, chapter 6.

Questions to Consider

1. Compare and contrast Angelo and Isabella in matters of justice and mercy, life and death.

2. Is the ending of the play satisfactory? By what standard?

Measure for Measure—Justice and Comedy
Lecture 10—Transcript

In the previous lecture, I was speaking about the ways in which *Measure for Measure* differs from other Shakespearean comedies: that it is unromantic, that it is claustrophobic, that it treats sex as painful and death-dealing. It is unusual also in its title. Shakespearean plays are usually named after the principal characters—*Hamlet*; *Romeo and Juliet*—or they're named after some principal event in the play—*The Tempest*, *The Taming of the Shrew*. Some of Shakespeare's titles are pure whimsy—*As You Like It*; *Twelfth Night, or What You Will*.

But in this case, the title directly names a thematic concern. The title of this play is drawn from the Gospel According to Matthew, the Sermon on the Mount, Chapter 7: "Judge not, that ye be not judged, for with what judgment ye judge, ye shall be judged, and with what measure ye mete, it shall be measured to you again." That is, Jesus warned his followers not to judge one another, for we are all sinners, and therefore we risk judgment by the same standards we apply to others. Now, this title is obviously appropriate to Angelo; he falls into the same sin for which he condemns Claudio. And, in fact, the lines about "measure for measure" are quoted by the duke in the last scene of the play, when he is judging Angelo.

But the Christian principle is, in fact, very difficult to apply. If we dispense with judgment, how can we maintain an orderly, civil society? It's very well to say that we should personally forgive others, but how do we maintain domestic order on a larger scale in a city such as Vienna? Central to the large difference between *Measure for Measure* and the standard Shakespearean romantic comedies, is the law that brings Claudio to the chopping block. Fornication, that is, sexual intercourse outside of marriage, is, in Vienna, a capital crime.

Now, it is characteristic of Shakespearean comedy that the characters must deal with some law or decree, some arbitrary ukase, that serves as an obstacle toward their happiness. In *A Midsummer Night's Dream*, for example, ancient Athens has a law that says a young woman must marry the man her father picks out for her. If she does not, then she dies the death or enters a convent, perpetual chastity. In *The Merchant of Venice*, Portia, according to her father's will, must marry the man who correctly gathers the answer to a difficult riddle that he has set. Now, in those two cases, both of those plot premises are realistic only to this extent, that they reflect the authority of fathers in a patriarchal society. But they are not realistic in themselves; they are absurd exaggerations of that authority. The Elizabethans had a patriarchal society, but there are patriarchies and patriarchies, and they certainly didn't allow fathers to exert such arbitrary, total and whimsical tyranny, as a girl must marry the man her father picks out or her head gets cut off. In other words, what these laws do in standard Shakespearean comedy is set up a revealing dramatic situation. Characters have to respond to them, and thus the plot gets going. Once they've done the work, then those laws can be set aside. In *A Midsummer Night's Dream*, the duke benevolently waives the law about paternal authority once the lovers have sorted out their own arrangements for themselves. In *The Merchant of Venice*, Bassanio's intelligence can solve the riddle of Portia's father's casket.

But the case is different in *Measure for Measure*. The fornication law is realistic. Not historically accurate; I must make a distinction here. The Elizabethans were not quite as severe as to say that anybody who committed fornication should die the death. They used the death penalty for more crimes than we do, but the only sexual acts punishable by death in Shakespeare's London were forcible rape and the seduction of children under 10 years old. Lesser offenses, such as fornication, were punishable by fines and by public shame. Nonetheless, this law that Shakespeare invents for his Vienna is not whimsical. An eager moral minority of his time did argue for stronger penalties in sexual matters. There was a Puritan contemporary of Shakespeare's named Stubbs, who wrote a book called *The Anatomy of Abuses*, in which he urged that the death penalty should be imposed upon people who committed fornication or incest, and adultery as well. Some thoughtful people, in other words, hoped that such laws would be passed; other thoughtful people argued against them. The situation is as it might be now, if an American playwright wrote a play whose premise was, there is a law imposing very severe penalties on both the doctor and the woman in all cases of abortion, whatever the reason for the abortion. That isn't the law now, but some people want it to be the law. If a playwright wrote such a play now, we would consider it as a realistic possibility.

Now, like much severe legislation, this "capital punishment for fornication in Vienna" business has not been enforced very strictly for years before the action of the play. But *Measure for Measure* develops the sexual life of Vienna in such a way as to make the audience feel that some such laws are necessary. Early in the play, the duke himself observes that we have "strict statutes and most biting laws," and they've been allowed to lapse, and the result is obscene disorders, the proliferation of brothels, and a general contempt for law itself, so that some kind of cleanup is necessary. And he's selected Angelo to be his deputy because he thinks that Angelo can carry out that cleanup. Angelo's first proclamation is that all the brothels in the town shall be plucked out, and it is done. We first meet Mistress Overdone when she has suffered the loss of her place of work. Of course, the brothels spring up in new places right away. Mistress Overdone gets back to work with a new house, lightly disguised as a tavern.

Sex, then, presents civil authority with grave problems. It is this confrontation of sex and civil authority that has made *Measure for Measure* so compelling for our time. *Measure for Measure* was not a popular play in the nineteenth century. The Victorian period did not like to discuss sexual matters of this kind on the stage. But at the turn of the century, critics began to take a fresh interest in the play, and differentiated it from Shakespeare's other comedies by calling it a "problem play," or "problem comedy"—that is, a play dealing with social problems in the manner of the new social drama written by Ibsen and Shaw at the turn of the century. And in the twentieth century, *Measure for Measure* has gained very great popularity; it has become an important play in the Shakespearean canon. It suits our post-Victorian frankness about sex, and it suits our worries about the regulation of sex.

A lot of our public discourse these days is about sex. What's on our public agenda? Of course, there are non-sexual issues as well; we worry about race and drugs and about violence and education, and a number of things. But we also worry about the equality of women, about the status of a family at a time when single parenthood and divorce and cohabitation without marriage are common. We worry about the rights of gay and lesbian people. We worry about the relation of public authority to abortion, pornography, the spread of sexually transmitted diseases, and most spectacularly, with business executives and Supreme Court justices and presidents, we worry about the sexual harassment of women by men who have authority over them. In the past two decades, audiences of *Measure for Measure* have found that productions of this play speak directly to our present concerns. So, let us look at the ways in which authority tries to cope with the teeming sexuality of Vienna in this play. Specifically, I shall look at three authority figures: Angelo, Isabella, and the duke.

Angelo's formulation for dealing with our sexual urges is repression. Each person should exert continuous self-control, self-discipline. Run around the block, take a cold shower, just say no. The first part of that was a formula for individuals; for society at large, use the law to back up Christian ethics. Define sexual sins as legal crimes, and punish the sinners. Execute these criminals. This is the Puritan response, urged by some of Shakespeare's own contemporaries, such as the man named Stubbs I mentioned before. Purify yourself, and purify the commonwealth. It's a beautifully clear solution, and like most clear solutions to social problems, terribly drastic. It allows very little room for human nature.

This point is made to Angelo early in the play. A more lenient colleague of his, Escalus by name, suggests to him that many people give way to sexual urges, and that, under the right circumstances, or you might call them the wrong circumstances, Angelo himself might fall. Now, Angelo responds to that, but not in the way that Escalus wants him to. He doesn't say, "Since I too am human and might fall, I will behave mercifully toward Claudio." What he says is the converse of that. He says, "If I too fall, then punish me just as severely." Not the answer Escalus wants, but he means it, and he acts on that principle. He would submit to strict justice; he really is quite consistent, Angelo is, until he double-crosses Isabella by ordering the execution. When his deeds are all revealed at the end, he returns to that consistency. He does not beg for mercy himself in the final scene of the play, he prays for execution. "No longer session hold upon my shame, / But let my trial be mine own confession; / Immediate sentence then, and sequent death, / Is all the grace I beg." That he is finally spared is entirely the idea of Mariana and, eventually, Isabella and the duke too.

Angelo has never been a very sympathetic character, a popular character, but Shakespeare is sufficiently sympathetic with him to help us to understand him. My students tend to think of Angelo as a kind of middle-aged authoritarian, a corrupt old judge who just takes advantage of his position to get a nice young girl into his bed. But I find the play works better if Angelo is played as a somewhat younger character. I've seen him convincingly played as a man in his late 20s or thereabouts, a studious and ambitious fellow who has ignored the idle pleasures of his contemporaries and devoted himself to religion and politics and government, who has worked hard and therefore earned quick promotion in the authority of Vienna, earned high office. He's eager to put his ideas to work for the benefit of society. That is, a young zealot who is quite sincere, but has never taken the time to inquire deeply into his own nature, who is seriously inexperienced in some aspects of human life. His own fall into desire, of course, reveals the flaw in his Puritan ideals, but I think he does demand our sympathy. His condition is part of the human condition. I've seen far too many young Puritans myself, both on the religious right and the non-religious left, eager to reform society in one way or another, to deny them a part in the complexion of human abundance.

Isabella looks quite different. She does not appear to be condemnatory. In her first scene with Angelo, indeed, she speaks some of the most eloquent pleas for mercy ever written for a dramatic character; she equals Portia in *The Merchant of Venice*. As a postulant nun, she derives those pleas directly from Christian doctrine. We are all sinful; we all require mercy. God, Who might have punished us, found out the remedy for our sinfulness. He Himself took the punishment, died for us, and therefore made mercy available to us. Likewise, we must be merciful, if we are to get mercy ourselves. That is in the formula of the Lord's Prayer, "Forgive us our trespasses, as we forgive those who trespass against ourselves." Or, as she says, and to Angelo:

> Go to your bosom,
> Knock there, and ask your heart what it doth know
> That's like my brother's fault. If it confess
> A natural guiltiness such as is his,
> Let it not sound a thought upon your tongue
> Against my brother's life.

If there's anything in your heart that's like my brother's heart, issue the pardon for him. In society, we must forgive one another. In personal life, in personal relationships, Isabella plans to withdraw. Where Angelo's formula is repress, hers is retreat, retreat from the squalor of Vienna, from the temptations of the world, and from being one of the world's temptations. She has chosen to enter a convent. She has chosen, in fact, to enter the order called Poor Clares, and the rule of that order, as is explained in her first scene, is very strict indeed. If a nun speaks to a man, she may not show her face as she does so, and if she shows her face, she may not speak. You must not present too much temptation to anybody. Now, this, of course, is the monastic solution to the problem of sex in society, the radical Roman Catholic position of Shakespeare's day, the extreme right of the political spectrum, as the Puritan position was the extreme left.

Shakespeare criticizes Isabella much less severely than he does Angelo, for hers, by and large, is a private solution. To retreat into a convent, into a monastery, is honorable and heroic for those who have a gift in that direction, for those who are supported by the grace of God a theologian would say. And the monastic solution does not usually try to impose itself on populations as a whole. It doesn't impose its values upon other people. But I have said that Isabella is a figure of authority nonetheless, because in the middle of the play, she does climb into the judgment seat. When Claudio succumbs to the fear of death—"Ay, but to die, and go we know not where;/ To lie in cold obstruction, and to rot...'Tis too horrible" to think of—when he has a frightened outcry of that kind, she responds with the hysterical abuse that I quoted in the last lecture, "O you beast, you faithless coward... Die, perish!" Now this is difficult for her, and it is difficult for us to judge her. Twice, she declares that she'd die herself, that she'd rather die, that she would be willing to die for Claudio. And I think she means that; she is the kind of heroic person who could undergo death in order to save her brother's life. Unfortunately, that's not what's been asked of her. It is one thing to say "Death before dishonor," it is another thing to say "Your death before my dishonor." Does anybody ever have a right to say that? I don't think so. Yet it is hard to condemn her altogether. Some of my students, mostly men, conclude that she's prudish, frigid, terrified of sex. And that seems harsh to me. She's a young woman in an age that sheltered young women, and that valued physical chastity much more than we do in the twentieth century. She wants to join a convent, where chastity, of course, carries a very high value indeed.

Other of my students, and these are mostly women, are outraged on Isabella's behalf, that these men, such as Angelo and Claudio, should be trading in her sexuality, and they condemn not only Angelo, but Claudio too. I think that's also harsh. The heart of her problem, I think, doesn't have to do with chastity. It has to do with charity, with her failure to sympathize with her brother when he succumbs to the terror of execution. She has a youthful enthusiasm, but like Angelo, she is also inexperienced. Her enthusiasm momentarily turns her into a judgmental zealot.

Now, out third authority figure is the duke, who is directly or indirectly in charge of the plot, and he exerts that control to ensure that Claudio does not die, that Isabella is not violated, and at the end, all facts are revealed and everybody is brought to judgment. And the judgments are finally merciful. Most extraordinarily, he gets Isabella to plead for mercy for Angelo, even before she knows her brother is still alive. Isabella recognizes that she herself is part of the sinful human condition, and she says:

> Most bounteous sir,
> Look, if it please you, on this man condemn'd,
> As if my brother liv'd. I partly think
> A due sincerity govern'd his deeds
> Till he did look on me; since it is so,
> Let him not die.

Now, it isn't her fault that Angelo fell; she isn't taking the blame, but she is involved in it nonetheless. "Sincerity govern'd his deeds / Till he did look on me;" she was an occasion of sin, however unconsciously. She is part of the human condition, the sinful human condition. She joins the human race.

That plea, and much else, comes about at the end of the play because of the duke's disguises and manipulations of the plot. The bed trick and the head trick make a comic conclusion possible for *Measure for Measure*, and those are not the least of his devices. His initial abdication of authority, leaving Angelo in power, charging him with cleaning up the city, follows precisely a bit of advice given by Machiavelli; if a prince has some onerous task to carry out in the city, go away. Appoint some deputy to do the job. He'll get all the odium, then you'll come back and hear everybody moaning and say, "Oh, he went beyond the charge. We'll get rid of him." The job is done, and your reputation isn't stained.

Throughout the play, the duke tests theories of life and death, techniques of rule, the characters of men and women. And out of his experimentation, he devises a sort of solution for the problems of Vienna; to put it in a nutshell, that solution is "Forgive and get them married." Forgive the sinners, since we all require forgiveness, and get them married, since we require some defined space in order to work out our sexual urges, fulfill our sexual desires. That recipe responds to the extreme solutions of Angelo and Isabella. Where Angelo says, "punish," the duke says, "forgive." Where Isabella says, "withdraw," the duke proposes, "marry."

Now the duke's supervening knowledge and control, together with his disguise as a friar and his highly Christian solution to the problems of the play, have suggested to some readers and theatrical producers that he is, in some way or other, an embodiment of God himself. He seems to have providential status, and one speech of Angelo's in the final scene of the play does attribute to him a divine power, or compare him with a divine power. If that were the case, it would accord with contemporary political theory, which after all did grant divine right to kings. But many other readers find that the duke's solutions are less than wholly satisfactory for the problems of Vienna. Lives are saved, and marriages are arranged, but nothing is done about the fornication law, with which the problem started. Nothing is done about Pompey, the pimp turned into executioner. Mistress Overdone is arrested, but the brothels are still around. And a number of minor characters whom the duke encounters prove quite recalcitrant to his plans. The play never questions the necessity of earthly authority, but it does acknowledge that earthly authority is often mistaken or inadequate, even well-meaning authorities like the duke.

I can put these problems sharply if I return to the marriages that happen at the end of the play, the marriages that I stressed at the opening of the first lecture. Claudio is to marry Julietta; that's right and proper in every way. Mariana marries Angelo; that legitimizes her position and she's still in love with him, so that's fine for her. Or is it? Not all frogs turn into princes. Is he going to be a good husband to her? Lucio, the young wastrel go-between, is required to marry a prostitute, upon whom he's fathered a child. Well, he certainly ought to take responsibility for the results of his actions, but the marriage isn't imposed upon him for that reason; it's imposed upon him because he slandered the duke. This is a punishment for royal calumny, and the prostitute's wishes are not consulted about the matter; she's not an onstage character.

And the duke's proposal of marriage to Isabella comes as a complete surprise to the audience. We have heard no word of their being romantically interested in one another. The proposal may come as a complete surprise to Isabella herself. Shakespeare gives Isabella no speech in response to the duke's proposal of marriage. It is left up entirely to us in the audience, or to the director and actress in a production, how she does respond. I have seen an Isabella who shyly and movingly stretched out her hand to this man, whom she has learned to admire and trust. I have also seen an Isabella who shrieked with horror at this idea and fainted dead away at one more manipulation from this duke. The point I am making is this; the four weddings at the end of the play look very much like naked comic formula. This is the way comedies are supposed to end, and that's fine if it really suits the characters' desires. But what if it doesn't? And it very well may not in this unromantic Vienna.

The final problem about this problem comedy is that comedy itself may be a problem. The patterns of comedy may not be adequate to the facts of human nature. Judged as a comedy, *Measure for Measure* has much to say about sin and mercy and law and the necessity for forgiveness, but there is something contrived about its close. Judged, on the other hand, as a play that bursts the limits of comedy, that asks whether standard dramatic patterns can contain the variety and perverseness of human nature, *Measure for Measure* is a deeply engrossing, highly provocative theatrical experiment.

Richard III—Shakespearean History
Lecture 11

Now there was a flood of historical writing at this period, in the 1590s. Shakespeare drew his information especially from two enormous books, one compiled by Edward Hall, called *The Union of the Two Noble and Illustrious Families of Lancaster and York*, and one by Raphael Holinshed called *The Chronicles of England, Ireland, Scotland.*

History is not a usual term for a dramatic genre like "comedy" and "tragedy." The First Folio uses it as a category, but it was not a consistent Elizabethan usage. Shakespeare took liberties with facts, but within limits. He seeks to reflect accurately the conditions of the time of which he writes. Thus major events, such as the outcomes of significant battles, must not be altered. The boundaries of genre that distinguish Shakespeare's plays are porous. For instance, many of his tragedies have

Richard III, King of England.

historical subject matter. Shakespeare's histories are defined as such by the nature of their subject matter.

There was much historical writing in Shakespeare's England. There were historical works in prose, narrative poems, and plays. (We know of some seventy historical plays, of which some thirty-five are extant.) History was patriotic. Patriotism was felt especially intensely by Elizabethan Englishmen in the wake of the repulse of the Spanish Armada in 1588. History could carry lessons. It provided heroes and villains to be upheld as either positive or negative models of behavior. History was a resource for playwrights in need of new plots.

Shakespeare's work in historical drama was unusual. He rewrote plays of the Queen's men. He wrote eight plays on a continuous stretch of English history (the years between 1399 and 1485), though not in chronological order. These plays examine the decline and fall of the House of Plantagenet. The "Lancastrian Tetralogy" consists of *Richard II, Henry IV 1-2*, and *Henry V*, and the "Yorkist Tetralogy" consists of *Henry VI 1-3* and *Richard III*. Other Elizabethan playwrights

Shakespeare's plays stressed both public events and private passions.

examined historical topics. Christopher Marlowe wrote one English history play. Ben Jonson wrote several plays based on Roman history, but they lack Shakespeare's sense of the variety of character and the fullness of human experience. Shakespeare's plays stressed both public events and private passions. His history plays were vital preparation for his tragedies.

Richard III carries especial historical weight. It is the final play of the cycle considered in historical order. It is concerned to get in as much historical detail as possible. Shakespeare wants to give the play historical weight and fullness, to "get it right." It leads into the Tudor era, in which Shakespeare was writing. ■

Essential Reading

Saccio, *Shakespeare's English Kings*, chapter 1, appendix, genealogies.

Shakespeare, *Richard III*.

Supplementary Reading

See a video of *Richard III*, preferably the Olivier film.

Lindenberger, *Historical Drama*.

Questions to Consider

1. Discuss the value of modern plays and films based on historical fact; e.g., Bolt's *A Man for All Seasons*, the BBC-TV series on various English monarchs, Christopher Burns' TV documentaries on American history.

2. How much, and in what ways, does it matter that the facts be correct in a historical play?

Richard III—Shakespearean History
Lecture 11—Transcript

Shakespeare wrote ten plays named after English kings, and it was John Hemmings and Henry Condell, Shakespeare's partners in the Lord Chamberlain's Men, who decided that we would call these plays of Shakespeare his "histories." When, seven years after Shakespeare's death, they published 36 of his plays in a single volume, they called the book *Master William Shakespeare's Comedies, Histories, and Tragedies*—the Elizabethans didn't mind cumbersome book titles; we now refer to the book more briskly as the *First Folio*—and Hemmings and Condell arranged the book in corresponding categories, first comedies, and then the 10 histories, then the tragedies.

There are some problems about this word "history." Shakespeare's plays on ancient Roman subjects treat equally historic matter, sometimes with greater fidelity to the sources he used. But Hemmings and Condell put those plays into the tragedy section. His plays on British subject matter before the Norman conquest—*King Lear, Cymbaline, Macbeth*—although they handle legendary events display in them some historical concern. Shakespeare could use the word "history" very freely; all the Elizabethans could use the word "history" very freely at times, sometimes meaning no more than a story. It is sometimes used on the title page of comedies and tragedies that are purely fictional works.

It is difficult, in fact, to discern any formal principle distinguishing the ten plays on English kings as examples of a single genre. Some focus on the king named in the title, as *Richard III* does. Some do not; Henry IV is only a supporting character in the two plays named after him. Some end happily for the king; some do not. They are structured in different ways. As used in the Folio, "history" seems to be a category defined by subject matter. A history play is a play that dramatizes major events from the reign of an English king, a reign sufficiently recent so that the events were known in some detail. The playwright may, to some degree, rearrange the events, develop characters, invent or omit incidents. That is, he may take historical liberties out of artistic necessity, so long as the result is felt to reflect the received conception of the times in question.

In Shakespeare's *Richard III*, for example, Richard courts the lady Anne over the corpse of her father-in-law. He wins her hand in marriage, and the marriage proves to be a barren one. But, in fact, Shakespeare's sources gave him no information about how Richard courted Anne, and the marriage produced at least one son, who died before he came to adulthood. The courtship scene is a splendidly theatrical invention displaying Richard's mesmerizing power over other people, and that is an important thing to get onstage, even if you have to invent an incident to do it. And the birth of a child who didn't survive long enough to be of any dynastic significance can safely be ignored in favor of a larger truth about how sterile Richard's reign was as a whole. What Shakespeare could not have changed was, say, the outcome of the Battle of Bosworth, by which Henry Tudor displaced Richard on the English throne. Now, Shakespeare was perfectly willing to change the outcome of a major battle when he was dealing with a more legendary story, with the story of King Lear, for example. But if you have Richard III win at Bosworth, you have sacrificed your claim to historical authority. Writing a play like that would be like the Monty Python sketch in which an Italian Renaissance painter paints the Last Supper with 27 disciples and three Christs. Everybody knows how many people were present at that meal.

Now there was a flood of historical writing at this period, in the 1590s. Shakespeare drew his information especially from two enormous books, one compiled by Edward Hall, called *The Union of the Two Noble and Illustrious Families of Lancaster and York*, and one by Raphael Holinshed called *The Chronicles of England, Ireland, Scotland*. There were many other historians, and there were poets who write long, historical narratives in verse. And English history enjoyed a particular vogue on the stage. Every English monarch, from William the Conqueror to Elizabeth herself, was put on the stage during the 1590s, some of them more than once. We know the titles of at least 70 English history plays that came out over a stretch of about 15 years, between the Armada in 1588 and the death of the Queen herself in 1603. We only have the text of about 35 of those plays. We know the titles of the other 35 because they appear in the records of one theatrical entrepreneur, the only theatrical entrepreneur whose records we have. If we had access to the records of other theatrical companies, presumably, we would know about a lot more history plays.

Now this is a remarkable number of plays to be drawn from a nation's own history, and offered as public entertainment. We may get an occasional history play on Broadway now, but you don't expect to have plays about every president, from Washington to Bush, over a period of a decade or 15 years. History obviously exerted a particular appeal for the Elizabethans. For one thing, it appealed to patriotic impulses. Patriotism was an especially powerful feeling for Protestant Englishmen in the years immediately after the defeat of the Spanish Armada. England was a small, relatively under-populated island nation, and it had withstood an attempt at invasion by the greatest power in Europe, backed by all the gold of the New World. Some Elizabethans were convinced, also, that history was instructive. It provided heroes and villains that the present generation could use as models. It provided patterns of events that could serve as warnings, for they were inclined to believe that history repeated itself. Generally, this works out negatively. Since history is largely a record of disasters, anyway, past disasters can serve as warnings to the present. Don't do this, don't do that, look what happened to so-and-so when they tried it.

In the 1590s, most of the English history plays concerned disputes over the crown; royal persons squabble over who should be next to inherit the kingdom. Now that issue was of major importance in the 1590s. Queen Elizabeth was in her sixties. She had never married; she had outlived all her close relatives. It was not at all clear who her heir would be, and her death could not be far off. Now no mere playwright would have dared to say, "So-and-so should be declared heir to the throne." That would really be interfering with high affairs; in fact, the Queen rebuked Parliament itself for talking about that. But a playwright or an historian could at least warn of the dangers of a disputed succession, could say, in effect, "Agree on the identity of the next monarch; do not let disagreement drive this country into civil war. Look what happened the last time. The Wars of the Roses went on for decades, ending in the reign of the diabolical Richard III. Terrible time. We don't want that to happen again."

It also seems clear that there was a practical reason for this outburst of history-play writing in the 1590s: a theatrical hunger. The theaters had become popular at the end of the 80s and on through the 90s, but a standard public theater held as many as two or three thousand people. London was a city of only 200,000, by no means all of whom went to the theater. Even a successful play would exhaust its appeal quickly. The playwrights were under pressure to provide scripts for stages that ate them up very fast. All this historical material, available in Hall and Holinshed and the other chroniclers and the poets, served as a stockpot: a pantry of plots and characters for playwrights seeking new subjects.

I can imagine a conversation backstage at the Rose or the Swan: "Hey, we need a new play. Has anybody done anything about Henry II? He had a bitch of a Queen. He had some sons who fought against him; we could get a couple of plays out of that. Get somebody to write that up." There was even a considerable amount of recycling. For example, the most successful theatrical company of the 1580s was a group called the Queen's Men. It was formed in 1583; it dominated the scene for the rest of the 80s. It was driven out of London when a plague closed the theaters for a long stretch in 1593-4. It is possible—this is sheer speculation—but it is possible that Shakespeare started his career working in the theater with the Queen's Men. We're very uncertain about what his theatrical affiliations were in his first couple of years in London, the years before he became one of the founding members of the Lord Chamberlain's Men in '94.

At any rate, in the repertory of the Queen's Men, there was a play called *The True Tragedy of Richard III*. Shakespeare certainly drew on that play when he wrote a much better play that he called *Richard III* in '93. The Queen's Men also had a play called *The Troublesome Reign of King John*; Shakespeare rewrote that as *King John* around '95. They had a very successful play called *The Famous Victories of Henry V*, which concerns not only Henry's achievements as king conquering France, but also his madcap youth in his father's reign. Shakespeare seized that piece toward the end of the 1590s and greatly expanded its scope, and got out of it three plays: *Henry IV, Part I, Henry IV, Part II*, and *Henry V*.

Shakespeare was doing more than ripping off and improving his predecessors. Eight of his ten plays on English kings deal with a continuous stretch of time; English politics from the deposition of Richard II in the year 1399 to the establishment of the new dynasty of Tudor in 1485. Collectively, these eight plays dramatize the decline and fall of the House of Plantagenet, the reigns of the last seven Plantagenet kings of England. As far as we know, no other playwright attempted to create this sort of superdrama, a stage chronicle going on for 40 acts, covering nearly a century of historical material.

Elsewhere in the courses taped by The Teaching Company, in a set of lectures entitled *Shakespeare: The Word and the Action*, I have lectured on the overall patterns that may be discerned in that large endeavor, and I will not repeat now what I said in that lecture. Indeed, my purpose is not to emphasize the architecture of the whole series, not now. My theme now is the richness of the individual plays, and it is a striking thing that whatever coherence the series of eight possesses as a whole, Shakespeare's intention to write upon such a scale was formed only gradually. If he had started with the idea that he was going to cover a century of history in eight plays, he presumably would have composed them in chronological order—begun with *Richard II*, gone on to *Henry IV*, *Henry V*, *Henry VI*, and then on to *Richard III*. But he didn't; he started with the last half of the story, with the Wars of the Roses, with the Henry VI plays. There are three plays named after Henry VI, and it isn't even clear that he wrote them in chronological order or that he was the sole author of them. This is his prentice work, and he may have been revising the work of others, or he may have been a novice playwright collaborating with others.

He then went on to *Richard III*, which concludes the whole series historically. And those four, the three plays on Henry VI and *Richard III*, I will refer to as the Yorkist Tetralogy, the four plays on the Yorkist group of the Plantagenet dynasty, because their central story is the rise of the Yorkists to the throne, and their eventual loss of the throne to the Tudors. Then Shakespeare moved back in historical time to write the Lancastrian Tetralogy: how Richard II was displaced on the throne by his cousin, Henry of Lancaster, in the play called *Richard II*, then Henry's own reign in the two plays named after Henry IV, and his son's reign as Henry V. Each of these plays, in its own right, explores dynastic, political, and military affairs with great richness.

Now Shakespeare's achievement in history stands out if we compare him to other playwrights of his time. One of my regrets about this course is I don't get to talk about the other Elizabethan playwrights. They're really very good; some of them could write comedies and tragedies that can stand perfectly well by Shakespeare, and we ought to pay them more attention than we do. We shouldn't let Shakespeare just be the sun that eclipses all the other stars. But he really beat them in histories, hands down. They restricted their sights when they wrote history. Marlowe wrote only one English history play, *Edward II*. It's a good play, and it's something of a model for Shakespeare's *Richard II*; both are plays about weak kings who are deposed by their lords and then murdered in prison. But Marlowe's play is largely a tale of personal passions. We gain from it very little of what Shakespeare regularly gives us, the sense of the welfare of the kingdom as a whole, what it was like to be ruled by these Plantagenets.

Ben Jonson provides the other side of the coin. He avoided English history; he went for Roman history, which came to him much better digested. The Roman historians are much more orderly than those vast, untidy English chronicles written by Hall and Holinshed. And from the Roman historians, he wrote a play called *Sejanus* and a play called *Cataline*, and these are very fine accounts of political intrigue during the late Republic and the early Empire of Rome, very good political plays. But Jonson lacks Shakespeare's sense of variety of character, the fullness of human experience. Shakespeare's histories grasp both the personal and the public, individual people wrestling with the issues of power and caught in the web of time.

One final generalization before I turn to *Richard III*. All but one of Shakespeare's king plays are in the first decade of his writing career, the decade that begins at the end of the 1580s and runs through to 1599. They represent just about half of his effort in his first ten years of writing. The other half is mostly comedies. You can see that clearly if you consult the chart that accompanies these lectures. From 1599 on, after he'd finished the series on the Plantagenets, then he started the major tragedies: *Julius Caesar*, *Hamlet*, *Macbeth*, *King Lear*. The history plays are not only good in themselves, they are also vital preparation for the tragedies. Through his continuous exploration of historical material, he discovered, and learned to work out, intimate connections between private decisions and public actions. In the history plays, there is a growing two-way traffic between the private world of the individual psyche, and the public world of national politics. And it's that two-way traffic that later gives the tragedies their extraordinary depth and range. This is the way in which Shakespeare developed the ability that serves him so well in *Hamlet*, the ability not only to depict a remarkable protagonist in his own mind, but to set the career of that protagonist within the fate of a rotten Denmark, a corrupted nation. It is this ability that enables him to write a tragedy where he can convincingly depict the hero, Coriolanus, changing the fate of Rome because of something his mother says to him. The histories are, in themselves, remarkable examples of Shakespeare's abundance; in the overall arc of his career, they are the source for even greater plenty.

Let me turn to *Richard III*. It is certainly abundant. It's a long play, more lines than anything else in Shakespeare except for *Hamlet*. It has an enormous cast: 38 named characters, some unnamed extras, and 11 ghosts. More important, since it dramatizes the end of the Plantagenet dynastic struggle, it carries more sheer historical weight than any of the other histories. All the wrongs of the Wars of the Roses funnel into this play. Characters are repeatedly grieving for their losses and crying out against the atrocities that others have perpetrated. Indeed, so frequent are the references to dead members of the royal house, and to their royal adherents, that reading the play for the first time can be heavy going for people who are not familiar with English medieval history and don't have a genealogical chart to consult.

In other words, Shakespeare is determined to get it all in. It's a bit like reading the battle scenes in *The Iliad*. I remember how Homer will tell you, when he gets a soldier into fighting, he'll stop to tell you what city he comes from, who his father was, and perhaps some little story about him. Then he's speared two lines later, and you never hear anything more about him, or his father, or his city, or that story. But you've got to have it. Whether or not Shakespeare had a clear idea at the time he wrote *Richard III* that he was going to go back and fill in the whole beginning of this series, he certainly knew he was concluding this large four-play achievement on the Yorkist section of the fifteenth century. He wants to give the play weight and fullness. He wants to get it right.

By the way, I am not asserting that his account would be accepted by modern historians. There's been much dispute over the real character of Richard III. Shakespeare's sources were Tudor sources. He had no reason to reject them, and he clearly thinks it's important to get it right, according to them. There's a bit of dialogue precisely on this matter in the middle of *Richard III*.

The boy king, Edward V, is about 12 years old, is talking with the Duke of Buckingham about the Tower of London, and he asks whether Julius Caesar built the tower. Buckingham responds, "Indeed, that is the case, Caesar built it." The boy king questions more closely, "Is it upon record, or else reported / Successively from age to age, he built it?" That is, is there documentary evidence on the point, or is this mere word of mouth?

Buckingham answers, "Upon record, my lord," and the boy responds, "But say, my lord, it were not regist'red, / Methinks the truth should live from age to age, / As 'twere retail'd to all posterity, / Even to the general all-ending day." It is an accidental irony, presumably not known to Shakespeare, but the fact in question is false. The Tower of London was not built by the Romans; it was built by the Normans. But it is important to Shakespeare that the truth should live from age to age, whether upon record, as the professional historians like it, or by word of mouth, as it is in the theater, for the history dramatized in the play of *Richard III* leads straight into the political establishment that governs England as Shakespeare is writing the play. It leads into the reign of Queen Elizabeth. It is her grandfather, Henry Tudor, Earl of Richmond, who wins the Battle of Bosworth and establishes his own dynasty, the dynasty of Tudor. It is her grandfather, Henry of Richmond, who closes the play with the final speech. He strengthens his own rather indirect Lancastrian claim to the throne by marrying Elizabeth of York, the eldest daughter of Edward IV, the surviving sister of the murdered little Edward V. She is the first princess on the throne of England to hold the magical name, the all-important name of Elizabeth.

In the final speech of the play, Henry of Richmond constructs an avenue, leading from the events on the stage that have been enacted—the Wars of the Roses—straight into the audience, the present time in Shakespeare's London, when the play was first performed. Shakespeare has Richard [sic Richmond] issue the orders that close the battle scene:

> Inter their bodies as becomes their births:
> Proclaim a pardon to the soldiers fled
> That in submission will return to us.
> And then, as we have ta'en the sacrament,
> We will unite the white rose and the red:

Smile heaven upon this fair conjunction,
That long have frown'd upon their enmity!
What traitor hears me, and cries not Amen?
England hath long been mad, and scarr'd herself;
The brother blindly shed the brother's blood,
The father rashly slaughter'd his own son,
The son, compell'd, been butcher to the sire;
All this divided York and Lancaster,
Divided in their dire division,
O, now let Richmond and Elizabeth,
The true succeeders of each royal house,
By God's fair ordinance conjoin together!
And let their heirs, God, if thy will be so,
Enrich the time to come with smooth-fac'd peace,
With smiling plenty, and fair prosperous days! ...
Now civil wounds are stopp'd, peace lives again-
That she may long live here, God say Amen!

Richard III—The Villain's Career

Lecture 12

Lengthy and detailed though the play is, it is built with iron girders.

This lecture considers the shape of Richard's career and the play. Despite the length and detail of the play, Shakespeare builds a firm structure from fifteen years of medieval history, 1471 to 1485. The play opens with the victory of Richard's oldest brother, Edward IV, and his firm establishment upon the throne of England in 1471. It then compresses the events of some dozen years into a few scenes, arriving quickly at Edward's death in 1483. The short reign of the boy-king Edward V is dramatized in greater detail. The final two acts cover the reign of Richard III. The chief actions during the play are the conspiracy of Richard and his allies, and the lamentations of those whom he displaces and leaves bereft.

> **The structural firmness of *Richard III* is evident in its symmetrical balancing of scenes and in its pattern of retribution.**

The structural firmness of *Richard III* is evident in its symmetrical balancing of scenes and in its pattern of retribution. The two courting scenes (Richard's courtship of Anne, and his later courtship of Elizabeth Woodbridge for the hand of his niece, Elizabeth of York) parallel each other, the second having been invented out of the first. The first courtship marks Richard's extraordinary power and skill, especially in twisting Anne's words back against her. The second courtship marks his loss of skill. This time Elizabeth assumes rhetorical dominance over Richard. The scene shows how thoroughly Richard has lost his control over other people.

The two nightmare scenes parallel each other, the second (Richard's nightmare before the battle of Bosworth) being invented out of the first (Clarence's nightmare in the Tower the night before his death). The first establishes the ultimate frame of moral reference for the play. The second brings that frame to bear on Richard. Shakespeare turns the scenes that advance the story into a moral structure. There is a second, more rigid form of structural firmness in the play: a pattern of retribution. The curses of Queen Margaret of Anjou in Act 1 are balanced by her gloating in Act 4.

Richard is a star part of great audience appeal. We enjoy his role-playing, his wit, and his histrionic skill. He attains the crown by playing a series of parts, thereby deceiving and entangling the other characters. Often he warns the audience of what role he will play, then comments in soliloquy upon his performance afterward.

He confides in us, so that we share his triumphs over others. In Shakespeare's later plays, soliloquy becomes a more internalized, more subjective monologue of self-exploration. In *Richard III*, however, soliloquy is a means by which Richard describes and presents himself directly to the audience. We admire his intelligence and cunning, and we become in a sense co-conspirators with him. He may act out for us desires (such as brother-hatred) to which we ourselves would dare not yield.

Richard eventually loses his hold over us. We cannot tolerate his murder of the two innocent princes, though we might be less outraged by his murder of his brother, the guilty Clarence. His blunt announcement of Anne's death and, late in the play, his odious silencing of his mother's rebukes likewise win him no sympathy. It is a testimony to Shakespeare's richness that he can evoke in us several different emotional responses to Richard during the course of the play.

Shakespeare tries to give Richard an interior self in his nightmare speech. He develops a conscience and acknowledges himself as a murderer. In this soliloquy, Richard unveils for the first time the inner workings of the self, rather than simply to present already formulated ideas and plans to us. ∎

Essential Reading

Saccio, *Shakespeare's English Kings*, chapter 7.

Shakespeare, *Richard III*.

Supplementary Reading

Hammond, Introduction to *Richard III* (Arden edition).

Sher, *The Year of the King*.

Questions to Consider

1. At what moment do our feelings change about Richard? Consider closely his treatment of the princes, his treatment of Buckingham, and his treatment of the women in 4.4.

2. Compare the different handling of Richard in Olivier's film, Ian McKellan's film, and the BBC-TV version.

Richard III—The Villain's Career
Lecture 12—Transcript

In another lecture in a series called *Shakespeare: the Word and the Action*, I have already discussed the ways in which Shakespeare constructed the villainy of Richard III. I analyzed closely his first great soliloquy, which occurs not in the play called *Richard III*, but in the play immediately previous in the series, *Henry VI Part 3*. And in that lecture, I placed his villainy within the context of certain leading Renaissance ideas. In today's lecture, I will be concerned with the artistic structure by which Shakespeare dramatized the whole career in the play that is called *Richard III*, Richard's career as usurper and as king. I will focus first on the pattern of events in the play, and then proceed to talk about the ways in which Shakespeare relates his villainous Richard to other characters in the play and to us in the audience.

The play begins with an event that historically took place in 1471, the victory of Richard's oldest brother, Edward IV, first Yorkist King of England, his firm establishment upon the throne of England. He then compresses the events of some dozen years into half a dozen scenes, arriving quickly at the death of Edward IV, from natural causes, in 1483. Then, Shakespeare dramatizes more closely the three-month nominal reign of the boy king, Edward V, during which Richard of Gloucester maneuvers for his nephew's crown. The last two acts cover Richard's own reign, a two-year reign cut short at the Battle of Bosworth. The chief actions during the play are conspiracy on Richard's side, and lamentation from those he displaces and leaves bereft. It is almost exclusively a court play, a play dealing with intrigues and secret murders. Not until the final act do we reach a battlefield.

Lengthy and detailed though the play is, it is built with iron girders. The structural firmness of *Richard III* appears especially in two features, a symmetrical balancing of scenes and a pattern of retribution. With each Shakespeare uses material from his sources, of course, but with each he works a brilliant variation on the historical material available to him. Shakespeare's sources told him that, late in Richard's reign, after his wife Anne had died, Richard courted his sister-in-law, the dowager Queen Elizabeth Woodville, for the hand of her daughter, his niece, Elizabeth of York, to strengthen his own hold on the throne, and to prevent his rival

Henry Tudor, from marrying the girl. This outrageous courtship, proposing what, in fact, is an incestuous union, uncle with niece, provides Shakespeare with a major scene in Act IV of *Richard III*. His sources were mute about Richard's earlier courtship, his courtship of Anne, before he seizes the throne. Well, he takes a cue from the later courting of the dowager Queen, and invents Richard's zestfully macabre wooing of the Lady Anne over the corpse of her father-in-law in Act I of the play.

The obvious parallelism of the two courting scenes makes a point about the curve of Richard's career. He is spectacularly successful with Anne; he manages to persuade a woman, whose husband and whose father-in-law he himself has killed, to marry him. Now some of my undergraduate students are very upset about this, particularly the women, that Anne should yield to Richard, that any woman would consent to so detestable a match. Did Shakespeare suppose that women are so weak that they will marry any murderer who asks them? Well, the scene is meant to be disturbing, but not to show a general conclusion about the weakness of women.

Richard himself concludes that he has done something perfectly extraordinary. "Was ever woman in this manner woo'd? / Was ever woman in this manner won?" It's meant to show how extraordinary Richard's abilities are. He is crafty; he picks a time when Anne is extremely vulnerable. Her political position is weak to the point of nonexistence; she is a Lancastrian widow, when all the Lancastrian lords are dead. She's distraught with grief; she is in the act of burying her father-in-law. She's vigorous enough to curse him, but her cursing is a simple emotional outpouring. She hasn't got Queen Margaret's age or expertise in cursing people, and she doesn't have Queen Elizabeth's skill in court intrigue, in verbal in-fighting.

Above all, Richard is good at this kind of thing. She's quarreling with a man who's undisturbed by emotion, who has no scruples, and who thinks faster than she does. He uses her curses against her. His rhetorical technique is to let her commit herself to some shrill denunciation, and then to twist her own words back on her. This happens in Act I, Scene II, and she says, "O, he"— meaning the King—"was gentle, mild, and virtuous!"

> *Richard:* The fitter for the King of Heaven, that hath him.
> *Anne:* He is in heaven, where thou shalt never come.
> *Richard:* Let him thank me, that holp to send him thither;
> For he was fitter for that place than earth.
> *Anne:* And thou unfit for any place but hell.
> *Richard:* Yes, one place else, if you will hear me name it.
> *Anne:* Some dungeon.
> *Richard:* Your bed-chamber.
> *Anne:* Ill rest betide the chamber where thou liest!
> *Richard:* So will it, madam, till I lie with thee.

He keeps responding to her one-liners until she feels emotionally cornered trapped. Then he gives her his sword, and bares his bosom to her, saying "If you feel that way about me, go ahead, kill me." Well, very few of us can actually take a sword and drive it into somebody in cold blood, particularly a woman who is not trained in the use of arms. Richard could, but he knows that Anne can't.

But the situation is different three acts later, when he comes to court the dowager Queen for the hand of her daughter. He's lost his knack, his skill at keeping the upper hand. When Richard seeks to swear that he truly loves her daughter and treat her well as wife and Queen, she knocks everything down that he tries to swear by.

> *Richard:* Now, by my George, my garter, and my crown—
> *Elizabeth:* Profan'd, dishonour'd, and the third usurp'd....
> *Richard:* Then, by my self—
> *Elizabeth:* Thyself is self misusest.
> *Richard:* Now, by the world
> *Elizabeth:* 'Tis full of thy foul wrongs.
> *Richard:* My father's death—
> *Elizabeth:* Thy life hath it dishonour'd.
> *Richard:* Why, then, by God—
> *Elizabeth:* God's wrong is worst of all.

The roles are reversed. She is in the answering position; she is on top rhetorically. And she's even more skillful than he had been with Anne. She's faster; she tops him in half lines instead of in whole lines. More importantly, she wins. She fools him completely. She leaves the stage, promising that she will, indeed, woo her daughter on his behalf, and he's completely taken in. He mocks at her after she is gone, "Relenting fool, and shallow, changing woman!" But, in fact, what she does is go straight out and write a letter promising her daughter's hand to Henry Tudor. He is fooled so completely, he doesn't even know he's fooled, and it's the first time that's happened in the play. The contrast of those two courting scenes in Act I and Act IV mark how thoroughly he's lost his all-important control over the other characters in the play.

There's another pair of balanced scenes, and again, the earlier one in the play is Shakespeare's own invention, suggested to him by the material that gave him the later one. The sources told him that the night before the Battle of Bosworth, Richard had a horrible nightmare, and we see that happen in a soliloquy, which I'll return to a bit later in this lecture. Well, early in the play, his brother Clarence suffers a nightmare in the Tower of London, just before Richard's hired thugs come to murder him. Well, the sources had told Shakespeare that Clarence certainly died in the tower, and probably by means that Richard had arranged, but they said nothing about nightmares or anything about Clarence's moral or emotional state at the time he died. Shakespeare invents for him a terrific dream speech too, in which he dies, goes to hell, and is denounced by the ghosts of the men he had betrayed and killed in the Wars of the Roses. And Clarence's speech describing the dark monarchy of hell is a very important speech in the moral structure of the whole play. It happens in Act I, Scene IV. Well, Act I, Scene I is Richard in soliloquy; Act I, Scene II, Richard courting Anne; Act I, Scene III is Richard dealing with the Queen and her relatives and old Queen Margaret. Then we get to Clarence.

It's as if the stage got wider as we go through the first act. We begin with a narrow, closed world of Richard's egotism in soliloquy. Then we have him conquer a woman, then we have him take on something that's even more difficult—the whole batch of wrangling royal relatives, and Margaret is particularly difficult to handle, because she's very experienced at this type of thing. Then, finally, there is the scene of Clarence's death. Now, Richard himself does not actually appear in that scene. He remains offstage;

it's his hired thugs who work for him. But the nightmare expands our moral horizons.

There are more things than the earthly going on in this play. It isn't just the self, or the woman, or the royal family. There are also heaven and hell, death and judgment, the ultimate metaphysical religious scale of things. That wide perspective that is achieved in the scene of Clarence's death returns with Richard's nightmare the night before Bosworth. And once again, we have ghosts, including the ghost of Clarence, and this time, we don't just hear a speech about them, describing what they look like and what they said. We see the ghosts ourselves. We hear them ourselves as they damn Richard and pray for Henry Richmond. That is Shakespeare's way of taking ideas from his sources and turning them into scenes that advance the story, and also into a moral structure that is, as I say, as firm as a set of welded girders.

As I mentioned before, there's a second form of structural firmness in this play, one that is even more rigid than those balancing scenes I've been talking about: a pattern of retribution. Here, Shakespeare takes a liberty with history, in order to portray history more vividly. Unhistorically, and quite unrealistically, he brings back old Queen Margaret into the action for two scenes, one in the first act, one in the fourth. Now, Margaret of Anjou was the widow of King Henry VI, and after the Yorkists triumphed over King Henry, and got rid of the Lancastrians, that allowed Margaret's French relatives to ransom her and send her back to France, where she died before Richard III came to the crown. That is, she really has nothing to do with the events of this play at all. But she makes a fine voice for the past because she's been through all the past, all the atrocities of the Wars of the Roses that the reign of Richard wraps up.

So Shakespeare brings her back, has her lurk about the palace, half woman, half witch, a kind of personified cry for vengeance. In the first act, she curses all the Yorkists for their part in destroying her family and her happiness, and then, in Act IV, she gloats over the misery of the Yorkists, as her curses come true. And the curses do all come true, and are underscored over and over again. Queen Elizabeth, Grey, Rivers, Buckingham, Hastings all remember what Margaret has said when they come to meet their dooms.

So firm a structure, made up of repetitions, parallel scenes, fulfilled curses, accurate predictions from ghosts, may make the play seem a bit like an algebraic equation. Everything that's done on one side has to be done on the other, and the result might seem, from the mere description, a little dull. But *Richard III* is not in the least bit dull. In the theater, it has proved to be one of the most popular and enduring of Shakespeare's plays. Quarrelsome royalty, cursing ghosts, vengeful hags—it's marvelous fun. But the major attraction of the play is Richard himself, and every actor worth his salt wants to play the role—Shakespeare's first star part of lasting appeal, and the only leading part in Shakespeare who gets to open the play with a soliloquy. Despite his villainy, he really is an attractive creature, a person of wit, of intelligence, and above all, of histrionic skill. He is Shakespeare's first player-king. Aside from killing all the other royal heirs, his chief method of plotting his way to the crown is playing a series of roles, parts, parts that deceive and entangle people, even the people who are suspicious of him at first.

He plays the loyal brother to Clarence. He plays the humble suitor, sick with love, to Anne. He plays, when faced with the court, the Queen's relatives, the blunt and straightforward royal veteran who just can't bear these upstarts around the palace. In the scene where Buckingham publicly persuades him to be king, he is playing a pious Christian involved in prayers; he appears on a balcony between two bishops, and he doesn't want to be distracted from his devotions. "Why would you bother me with worldly things?" Often he warns the audience beforehand of what role he will play, and then comments on his own performance in soliloquy afterwards. That is, he is not only an expert actor, but he writes his own scripts, and he writes the review afterwards—a complete man of the theater. And this, too, is Shakespeare's heightening of the material history had given him. The Tudor accounts of Richard, of course, do stress how deceitful and scheming he was. But they do not say that his villainy had this particular theatrical cast to it, that he was capable of mesmerizing performance. That's Shakespeare's addition; that's the addition of a man of the theater himself.

His histrionic ability gives the character a special relationship to us in the audience. He has a large number of soliloquies and asides, more, in fact, than Hamlet does. He's frequently down on the edge of the stage, talking to us as directly as I am talking to you right now, talking to us about them, and what he's going to do to them. That is, he is our mediator between them and us. He can get us on his side, as it were. We can't speak back to him; that's convenient, we don't have to actually agree to it. We can be silent co-conspirators. "Look, I'm going to marry her. Isn't this going to be fun? Just watch me do it. Didn't I do that nicely? I'm going to make him very unhappy; in fact, I'm going to have his head chopped off. My, my, did you see that? That was good."

And that's what a soliloquy is for Shakespeare early in this point I his career; it is direct speech to the audience. It isn't a man pondering something through, deep within his psyche, and we just happen to overhear it. Shakespeare will get to that later in his career, and I'll talk about it in a later lecture. Here, a soliloquy is direct address. Richard is not exploring himself; he is describing himself. "This is what I am. Here are my plots. Here are my jokes." Because he's clever, because he's witty, because he's playing tricks on other people, we begin to enjoy him. We become, as it were, co-conspirators. Superior intelligence and cunning are usually attractive on the stage, especially when we are made to feel that we share it, which, of course, we do, since he lets us into the plot and those other people aren't. We feel part of the one-up-manship because he has told us that it is coming.

Richard may even appeal to darker instincts inside us. We may enjoy some of his crimes as crimes. Yes, he murders his brother, and we know it's bad to hate and murder your brother. In fact, it's the primal crime, Cain killing Abel. But most of us do hate our brothers a little bit; certainly little girls and boys in the nursery fight very frequently, and they have to be told by their parents, "No, no, no, that's wrong, that's unnatural, you love your brother." If the instruction takes hold, we internalize that lesson, and we come to think that brother-hatred is unnatural. In fact, Richard is called unnatural very frequently in the course of the play. But there's a good deal of that resentment still left in us, no matter how old we get. And a character like Richard plays on it. He acts out our submerged feelings. This may be one of the uses of the theater in civilized life; it provides a release for feelings that we do not allow ourselves to indulge, a release in a harmless context. "Oh God, that was fun, that's just the way I feel about my brother. I'm glad he did it," and then you can go back, and have a nice drink with your brother, and forget about the matter.

The alliance between Richard and the audience lasts for much of the play, but not for all of it. Eventually, he loses us. His crimes become too much. Let me compare some of the crimes. Killing his brother Clarence, and killing the little boy king and his brother, are both crimes of murder. I suppose that in the books of the recording angel, the marks are equally black for both of them. But we feel differently about them, in our semi-rotten earthly hearts. Clarence was grown up, guilty of quite a number of crimes himself, and there's some comedy about the way he gets polished off. He's plunged into a vat of wine. But killing a couple of innocent and helpless boys is no fun at all. Courting Lady Anne is rather fun, at least for men, in a macabre and chauvinist sort of way, especially since Anne starts the scene with shrill cursing. When Richard, in Act IV, comes to announce her death, however, "Anne, my wife, hath bid this world goodnight," that fails to amuse me altogether. Insulting and baiting the Queen's relatives for their upstart pretensions is giving them, more or less, what they deserve. When, however, late in the play, Richard's mother rebukes him, and he orders drums to be beaten and trumpets to be blown merely to drown out her voice, I find him simply odious, and not in the least bit subtle.

Shakespeare manipulates our responses brilliantly. It's part of his richness that he can invite us to feel in a variety of ways about this criminal. We can enjoy him for about two-thirds of the play, then Richard loses control over events, loses control over other characters, and loses control over us. Then Shakespeare tries one more thing. He tries to get inside Richard. The night before the Battle of Bosworth, Richard dreams that the ghosts of his victims all tell him to despair and die, and he awakes in terror:

> What do I fear? Myself? There's none else by.
> Richard loves Richard; that is, I am I.
> Is there a murderer here? No. Yes, I am.
> Then fly. What, from myself? Great reason why:
> Lest I revenge. What, myself upon myself!
> Alack, I love myself. Wherefore? For any good
> That I myself have done unto myself?
> O, no! Alas, I rather hate myself
> For hateful deeds committed by myself!

Under the supernatural pressure of those ghosts, Richard develops a conscience and perceives himself as a murderer. Furthermore, Richard, who had thought that he could live perfectly well without loving anyone, realizes that, to exist, one must, to some extent, love oneself. And yet, he finds himself quite unlovable.

In this speech, Shakespeare begins to write something that might be called a genuine internal monologue. Richard is not simply presenting already formulated ideas and plans to us; he is thinking, feeling out something for the first time. Shakespeare begins to depict the inner working of the self. At this point in Shakespeare's career, his method of writing that kind of thing is still rather primitive. The speech I've just been quoting is much less sophisticated than the speech of Angelo's that I discussed in a lecture on *Measure for Measure*, let alone what Shakespeare can do with Macbeth's musing late in his career. I'll get to *Macbeth* near the end of this course.

Shakespeare simply gives Richard two voices: the villain we're used to, and the newly awakened conscience. "Is there a murderer here? No. Yes, I am... I love myself... Alas, I hate myself." Read on the page, that's rather unconvincing, especially since there's been nothing earlier in the play that shows that Richard has any conscience whatever. However, the simple contradictions don't sound much like the twisty operations of a truly divided mind. A good actor, of course, can make them work. The great eighteenth-century actor, David Garrick, was famous for this moment, and had himself painted by Hogarth in this speech.

But Shakespeare does not try to sustain the moment, does not transform the character for the remainder of the play. It's only a moment. Richard goes forth to battle with all his old dramatic exuberance and black humor, delighting in evil for its own sake. "March on, join bravely, let us to it pell-mell; / If not to heaven, then hand in hand to hell."

Richard II—The Theory of Kingship
Lecture 13

In our century, readers and playgoers are likely to regard *Richard II* as a lyrical tragedy about a beautiful and eloquent man who happens to have been born king, but who lacks the talents necessary for the job. Its interest is chiefly personal, psychological. ... In its own time, *Richard II* was perhaps the most political play Shakespeare wrote.

A performance of *Richard II* was commissioned in 1601 by a supporter of the attempt by the earl of Essex to take over Elizabeth I's government. The Lord Chamberlain's Men were exonerated of conscious complicity in Essex's treason. They denied that the play would motivate any listener to engage in political action. The play shows the spectacle of a divinely anointed king deposed by his subjects, and those subjects' justifying their action as proper. This action raises questions not at issue with obviously illegitimate kings such as Richard III.

It was common doctrine, propagated in sermons, that kings were divinely appointed to rule, and that disobedience and rebellion against kings were therefore wicked. St Paul argues that "the powers that be are ordained of God" (Rom. 13:1). A rebel is led into committing all seven deadly sins and breaking all Ten Commandments.

It was common doctrine, propagated in sermons, that kings were divinely appointed to rule, and that disobedience and rebellion against kings were therefore wicked.

This homiletic doctrine of obedience asserts the king's authority; it does not necessarily assert that the king is always right. Hence the royal uncles in the play, Gaunt and York, choose at crucial moments loyalty to the crown over loyalty to their own sons. Hence York's vehemence in denouncing Bolingbroke's return to England against Richard's decree of exile, and Carlisle's vehemence in predicting disasters to follow if Richard is deposed.

On the other hand, the doctrine of royal authority does not explain the whole of *Richard II*. We are also invited to compare the political virtues and defects of Richard and Bolingbroke. Shakespeare's abundance frequently entails such an invitation to compare different characters in similar situations. Richard and Bolingbroke must each deal with angry quarrels among their nobles. Richard's decisions in Act 1, although defensible, are flawed in various ways. Bolingbroke, in Act 4, retains more royal control.

Richard and Bolingbroke must each confront rebellion. Richard in Act 3 does little in response, relying on his divinely sanctioned authority. He takes little constructive action to impede Bolingbroke. Bolingbroke is swift and efficient in practical action to foil the plot to restore Richard. Since Bolingbroke's effective rule follows Richard's mistakes, the play suggests that (despite the illegality of Bolingbroke's seizure of power) the kingdom is better off in his hands.

The visual and verbal pattern of vertical movement contributes to the political content of the play. The chief action of the play may be diagrammed as an X, with Richard as the descending line, Bolingbroke as the ascending line. Richard is aloft at Coventry in Act 1, but he is "on the ground" when he returns from Ireland in Act 3. Later, Bolingbroke stands amid the kneeling Yorks in Act 5. Their paths cross in the scene at Flint Castle in Act 3, when Bolingbroke and his army catch up with Richard. Linguistically, the many verbal references in the play to "up" and "down" focus when Richard describes his descent from the Flint Castle walls to the "base court" as the fall of Phaeton. The vertical patterns of the play, both visual and verbal, suggest not that Bolingbroke is at fault for rebelling, but that Richard is at fault for ruling so poorly that he must be overthrown.

The play, in depicting a conflict between a political theory proclaiming the supervening authority of the king and practical facts displaying the superior abilities of a usurper, presents a perfect political dilemma. Bolingbroke can rid the realm of a damaging king only by further damaging the realm, leaving it open to civil war and kinstrife. In consequence, the actual removal of Richard is a politically ambiguous event. York considers it a resignation, Northumberland wants an impeachment, Richard handles it as a de-coronation that sacrilegiously reverses the ceremonies of anointment and investiture. The event remains open to interpretation and violent dispute for a century to come. ∎

Essential Reading

Saccio, *Shakespeare's English Kings*, chapter 2.

Shakespeare, *Richard II*.

Supplementary Reading

See BBC-TV videotape of *Richard II*.

Barkan, "The Theatrical Consistency of Richard II."

Gurr, Introduction to *Richard II* (New Cambridge edition).

Kastan, "Proud Majesty Made a Subject: Shakespeare and the Spectacle of Rule."

Questions to Consider

1. The American constitution provides a legal way to remove an unsatisfactory president from office: impeachment. The English Parliament had in fact discovered and developed powers of impeachment just before and during Richard's reign, but it used them only to eliminate unsatisfactory ministers of the crown, not the king himself. Would the political issues posed by Richard's rule be better solved by legally impeaching him?

2. The garden scene (3.4) allegorically represents the powers of government by analogy to the tasks of gardeners. Is the analogy useful? Does it satisfactorily suggest what Richard should have been doing as king? Does it satisfactorily suggest what should be done about Richard?

Richard II—The Theory of Kingship
Lecture 13—Transcript

In our century, readers and playgoers are likely to regard *Richard II* as a
lyrical tragedy about a beautiful and eloquent man who happens to have
been born king, but who lacks the talents necessary for the job. Its interest is
chiefly personal, psychological; we watch this willful and unfortunate man
come to awareness of the realities of his position. Before I talk about those
emotional things, I must talk about politics. In its own time, *Richard II* was
perhaps the most political play Shakespeare wrote. As far as we know, it was
the only play of his used in its own time for a direct political purpose. In
1601, some six years after Shakespeare had written it, the Earl of Essex—
Queen Elizabeth's last favorite, who had disappointed and angered her by
mishandling an expedition to quell rebels in Ireland—attempted a coup to
take over Elizabeth's government. The day before Essex's rising, one of his
noble supporters had the Lord Chamberlain's Men put on a performance
of Richard II, evidently hoping that this historical example of the armed
insurrection against a crowned head of the English state would inspire
Londoners to repeat history.

In the event, the rising was easily crushed. Essex himself was quickly tried
and sent to the chopping block, and the Lord Chamberlain's Men were
interrogated for their apparent complicity in an act of open treason. They
claimed that they knew nothing about these high matters. They were just
actors, they thought they were satisfying a nobleman's whim to see an old
play. They said the play itself was so out of fashion, they would not have
revived it had they not been paid a fee to do so. The play itself was no longer
able to attract an audience. I think what they were trying to imply when they
said that was that the play really wouldn't inspire anyone to do anything.
At any rate, the Lord Chamberlain's Men were exonerated of any blame in
the treason.

There is certainly enough in Shakespeare's play to make a conspirator hope
that it could have an effect on an audience. It does display a king being
overthrown by his subjects, and shows those subjects arguing that this,
indeed, is a proper thing to do. I have found that my students' interest in the
play shifts from the personal to the political when we study it, in times when

the public life of our own time is turning toward the thought of overthrowing our rulers. Students got very interested in this as a political play during Watergate with President Nixon. They are again interested in it now, during the troubles of President Clinton. There is certainly plenty of argument in *Richard II* to respond to that kind of political interest.

Of all Shakespeare's history plays, *Richard II* most sharply opposes the Elizabethan theory of royal rule to practical facts about the man who happens to be the king. Richard is, unquestionably, the legitimate occupant of the throne, supported by the divine right of kings. Yet he acts in a way that damages the kingdom. When, if ever, does it become appropriate to remove such a king? This is a question that does not arise with *Richard III*; Richard III is a usurper, a tyrant, and a murderer—clearly a bad king; clearly you want to get rid of him as soon as you safely can. There's no political problem, no constitutional problem, that that brings up. But with a king like Richard II, who has, unquestionably, inherited the right to rule, there is a constitutional problem, and no constitutional solution.

I just said that Richard is supported by the divine right of kings. As a matter of fact, that phrase is slightly anachronistic; Shakespeare doesn't use it. It didn't come into use until a few years after his time. But, although he didn't have the phrase, he is certainly writing about the thing—the doctrine that kings are ordained by God, and their subjects are thereby obligated to obey them. The best source in which to find this doctrine, as it would be understood by ordinary Elizabethans in a theater audience, is in the sermons of the time.

The government of Elizabeth I published a volume containing 33 sermons, or homilies, appointed to be read in churches. You must remember that the Church of England is a state church. Elizabeth was the head of the church as well as the state, and the book was officially intended to provide sermons for clergy who were not talented at writing their own. The government conveniently gave them these sermons so that the general population would understand Christian doctrine in the most appropriate way, which, of course, was likely to be a way that was convenient also to the secular interests of the government. The last homily in this book of sermons, the last and by far the longest—it is five parts long, so presumably it took five Sundays to deliver the whole thing—concerns the virtue of obedience. And obedience is interpreted almost exclusively in a political context. That is, for five successive Sundays, John Q. Elizabethan was lectured at on the wickedness of rebellion. The Biblical text from which the homily starts is Paul's "Epistle to the Romans," Paul to the Romans, Chapter 13, Verse 1: "Let every soul be subject unto the higher powers. For there is no power but of God: and the powers that be are ordained of God." That is, the king is God's deputy, to use the phrase that Shakespeare puts into King Richard's mouth, "the deputy elected by the Lord."

Kings and queens are appointed by God to rule his faithful people. Such subjects as are disobedient or rebellious unto their princes disobey God and pursue their own damnation. That is, rebellion is a sin as well as a crime, a mortal sin, a deadly sin. The homilist goes so far as to say that it's the worst of all sins. It is certainly the first of all sins; Lucifer's rebellion in Heaven started the whole history of sin, and Adam's disobedience in the Garden of Eden continued it. Even weak and wicked kings are said in the sermon to be ordained by God. If God sends his people a bad king, it's because that's a sinful people who deserve some punishment.

Let me give you one more taste of the rhetoric that the Elizabethans could hear on a Sunday morning: "How horrible a sin against God and man rebellion is cannot possibly be expressed according to the wickedness thereof. For he that nameth rebellion nameth not a singular or one-only sin, as is theft, robbery, murder and suchlike. He nameth the whole puddle and sink of all sins against God and man, against his prince, his country, his countrymen, his parents, his children, his kinsfolk, his friends, against all men universally, all sins heaped together." Sounds like fun.

Let me try to head off a possible confusion here. The homiletic doctrine of obedience is fundamentally a doctrine about authority, not a doctrine about infallibility. It does not say, "The king can do no wrong;" it specifies the divine source of the king's authority and the wickedness of attempting to withstand or overthrow him. In a rough analogy, we could say that our democratically elected presidents derive their authority from a majority vote, but that does not mean the majority of voters would approve of every single thing the president does. It's a rough analogy, because we can get rid of a bad president by voting him out of office in the next election, or, in extreme cases, by impeaching him, whereas a divinely appointed king is king for life. That's precisely the problem about a weak king like Richard, that he has divine authority, and that is why a number of people in the play make decisions that go against their natural instinct or natural loyalty. It is why Old Gaunt, early in the play, agrees with the council to banish his own son, Bolingbroke. He is bowing to the authority of the crown, instead of loyalty to his son. That sort of point is doubled because, at the end of the play, Old York does exactly the same thing—denounces his son, Aumerle, for treason to the new king, because loyalty to the crown is more important than loyalty to his son.

The importance of loyalty to the crown also explains why York is so horrified when Bolingbroke breaks exile against the king's command and returns to England. It explains why the Bishop of Carlisle predicts, with such vehemence, that the deposition of Richard II will be followed by a series of catastrophes—civil war, the slaughter of men by their own kin, a land soaked in blood. Of course, the audience knew he was right; it did lead to the Wars of the Roses, to nearly a century of turmoil. This homiletic doctrine of the king's authority explains, at least in part, why Richard believes that he can rely on God's aid, on armies of angels that will come to his assistance when Bolingbroke rises in rebellion. This is the sort of thing that was the official view of the government in Shakespeare's time. It was the sort of thing that was believed, certainly by some of Shakespeare's fellow countrymen, and it incorporates the view in some of the characters, some of the speeches of the play.

The play is a play; it is not a sermon, and it simply does not reiterate "The king is the king is the king, and that's all there is to it." That view is in the play, expressed occasionally with fervor and splendor, but there are certain facts in the play that do not accord with it. You might say having a bad king like Richard III is something a sinful population might merit for a time. In fact, there's a minor character in *Richard III* who says exactly that. But that doesn't seem to be the case with Richard II. No previous sins have been brought to our attention, for which Richard's mistakes of rule might be the adequate punishment. In fact, Gaunt, York, and others frequently point out that England has had a noble and heroic past up until the time of Richard II, and it is Richard himself who is damaging the realm.

Moreover, if we simply adopt the homilists' view that rebels are utterly wicked, we have to say that Bolingbroke, in this play, is a complete villain. We may have different views about Bolingbroke; some like him more than others do. But there's no doubt that he is able, that he can be just and merciful, and that he is popular amongst the common folk. Indeed, the way Shakespeare builds the play—he leads us to measure the virtues and faults of Bolingbroke against those of Richard in some quite deliberate comparisons. This is a most important aspect of the abundance of Shakespeare. In the large scope of his five-act play, he has room to set up parallel situations, to see different people handling similar situations, so that they serve as foil and contrast to each other.

In *Richard II*, there are two kings: for the first three acts, Richard, until Richard collapses; thereafter, Bolingbroke. In those two chunks of the play, they have to deal with very similar problems. Richard faces a bitter quarrel between Bolingbroke and Mowbray at the start. When he cannot appease them, he banishes them. It is a reasonable move; his counsel concurs, even including Gaunt. They all want to avoid civil disturbance. But Richard also makes some mistakes in those scenes, I think. Since nothing has been settled about the charges raised by Bolingbroke and Mowbray against each other, it is manifestly unfair to banish one of them for life and the other for only ten years, later reduced to six. That arbitrary gesture is part of a larger frivolity on Richard's part. He first calls the trial by combat between them, setting a date some months away. Then he lets the trial by combat all be set up, and gets to the point of just engaging combat; and then he throws his warden down and stops the whole thing and issues the sentences of banishment.

It looks like Richard is showing off, self-indulgently displaying the power of the king at the expense of these nobles who are quarreling with each other. When I saw Michael Pennington play the part, he was, in effect, saying through all those opening scenes, "Boy, I just love being king, You can do that, and everyone will stop," and it made the point very clearly. Above all, amongst Richard's mistakes here at the beginning is a matter of fault. The major issue at odds between the quarreling lords is, who is responsible for the death of Thomas of Woodstock, Duke of Gloucester, and it is made pretty clear that, somehow or other, Richard himself is. Some kind of political cover-up for a royal murder is going on.

Bolingbroke, once he takes over, faces the same quarrel, who killed the Duke of Gloucester, at the beginning of Act IV. Angry nobles are once again blaming each other, throwing down their gloves, challenging one another. In fact, the situation is potentially worse this time around, because there are at least six lords involved this time around, not just two. But, if you read through that short scene carefully, you will see that Bolingbroke handles the matter much more neatly than Richard had. Bolingbroke doesn't argue, or reason, or plead. He doesn't make any dramatic gestures, interrupting a duel. He gives terse orders; he finds out where each of them stands. He then tells them, "Your differences shall all rest under gage / Till we assign you to your days of trial," which sounds official and clear. But what it really means is, "Don't you do a thing about this until I tell you to." We never find out exactly what happens in this matter, but the scene leaves us with the impression that whatever did happen, it wasn't likely to leave Bolingbroke's control.

On a larger scale, both of these kings face rebellion, and the way each responds is revelatory. Richard, in effect, does nothing. He produces those magnificent speeches relying on the power of God, about his divinely bestowed authority. But he does not take constructive steps to oppose Bolingbroke's march across England. Shakespeare carefully underscores this shortcoming. He has the Bishop of Carlisle and the Duke of Aumerle, who are loyal to Richard, staying at Richard's side, he has them say to Richard, "The means that Heaven yields must be embraced." That is, God will supply the means, you must supply the initiative. Or, as we say more bluntly these days, God helps those who help themselves. In the last act, Bolingbroke faces a rebellion to restore Richard, led by Carlisle, Aumerle, and various others. When York breaks the bad news to Bolingbroke; Bolingbroke's response is to say, "Tell us how near is danger, / And we will arm us to encounter it." His sword is out of its fabric already. There's not a moment spent in sorrow, or shock, or astonishment, or annoyance about this news; let's just cope with it. And he continues to act with directness and efficiency. The special circumstances of Carlisle and Aumerle entitle them to mercy; other heads roll. That's it.

I've mentioned that these parallels occur at opposite ends of the play. It's not like, in *King Lear*, the story of Gloucester and Lear running beside each other all the way through the play; these are frame pieces, Richard facing a quarrel in Act I, Bolingbroke facing the same quarrel in Act IV. Richard facing rebellion in III, Bolingbroke facing the rebellion in V. That placement causes the parallelism to make quite a specific point, that Bolingbroke's a better king. The kingdom is in safer hands at the end of the play, despite the illegality of Bolingbroke's crown; despite his rebellion, the kingdom is safer, better off. He's better at the job of being king.

There's another pattern crucial to this play, relevant to kingship. This is a pattern of vertical movement. You can diagram the major pattern of this play like the letter X. The descending shaft of the X is Richard. He is on high at the beginning, in control; at the end, he is fallen and dead. The ascending shaft is Bolingbroke; his starts being exiled, being banished, he ends up as king. Now, such a diagram is not merely an intellectual or abstract matter. It is visual on stage during the course of the play, visible in the positions of characters onstage. They are in high or low positions, literally. At the start of the play, at the scene of the lists at Coventry, when Richard is arranging the trial by combat, Richard is on a raised platform. He specifically says that before the combat begins, he will descend for a moment—he uses the word "descend"—to receive the homage of the two lords. The he goes back up into his place to judge the combat and of course to stop it. In the middle of the play, when Richard has come back from Ireland and is losing against the rebellion of Bolingbroke, he starts talking about being low:

> For God's sake, let us sit upon the ground
> And tell sad stories of the deaths of kings:
> How some have been depos'd, some slain in war,
> Some haunted by the ghosts they have depos'd,
> Some poison'd by their wives, some sleeping kill'd,
> All murder'd: for within the hollow crown
> That rounds the mortal temples of a king
> Keeps Death his court.

In other words, this business of the fall of a king isn't simply a metaphor. It sounds like that, but when the play is staged, it becomes real. The king really does fall to a lower position. At the end of the play, Bolingbroke is aloft, and there is a scene when all three members of the York family are kneeling to him: the Duke of York, the Duchess, and their son Aumerle, all on the ground. It's very marked, because the Duke and Duchess are elderly people and have trouble getting down into a kneeling position. The king, Bolingbroke now, is standing amongst them, and he now has the all-powerful word to say who will live and who will die.

In this pattern, the crossing point of the X, the intersection of the two trajectories, can be marked with precision. It is the scene at Flint Castle, when Bolingbroke and his army catch up with Richard. Richard starts that scene up on the castle walls. Bolingbroke and Northumberland and the army come in on the main stage. He is aloft, they are below. They tell him, however, to come down. They would have conference with him in the courtyard, as they call it, the base court. And so he comes down:

> "Down, down I come, like glist'ring Phæthon,
> Wanting the manage of unruly jades.
> In the base court? Base court, where kings grow base,
> To come at traitors' calls, and do them grace."

He is both physically descending on the stage and using the folding imagery in the language. The poetry and the action come together; this is what poetic drama is about. A poetic drama is not just a play that happens to be written in verse; it's where the symbolism of the physical action and the symbolism of the language coincide. This is the reason for writing poetic drama. Here, they come together, in Richard's action and his words. He is falling, and this makes clear that he is responsible for the fall. He is like Phæthon, wanting to manage unruly jades—the boy who begged the Sun God to let him ride the chariot of the Sun, but was unable to control the horses, and had to be knocked off the chariot by Zeus himself, by a thunderbolt, before he destroyed the Earth. All that rising and falling imagery condenses at that moment to point the responsibility for what happens in England on Richard's side, not on Bolingbroke's.

We have a paradox here, a complete conflict between political theory and practical facts. The political theory enjoins obedience to God's ordained king. If you depose him, hideous disaster will follow for the realm. The practical facts say that Bolingbroke is the better king, and Richard is responsible for the wrong that is done to the realm. The play depicts a perfect political dilemma. There is no way, under the constitutional circumstances that prevail in this play, for this set of circumstances to be solved. What does happen, then, in *Richard II*? What happens when Richard hands over the crown to his cousin Bolingbroke? That is a scene that is dramatized in Act IV, a scene so inflammatory that it was censored out of the first printings of *Richard II*, and it's a very interesting scene, because the men in it cannot find the right word to describe what it is that they're doing.

The Duke of York wants to stage an abdication. Richard is "to do that office of thine own good will / Which tired majesty did make thee offer, / The resignation of thy state and crown." Resignation, a smooth, easy, voluntary retirement. Northumberland, on the other hand, wants to conduct an impeachment, or a trial, the central action of which will be the reading of a list of Richard's misdeeds and Richard's assent to that list, charges that will, in his phrase, satisfy the commons, please Parliament. Richard himself wants a real deposition, a decoronation, the reverse of the coronation ceremony, sort of like a Black Mass, where you say the Lord's Prayer backward and put the cross upside down. In this case, it's a matter of washing off the balm of anointment, handing over the crown in a way that will make clear his enemy's deliberate violation of sanctified political order.

Each of these three men—York, Northumberland, and Richard, in other words—tries to put a label on this: abdication, impeachment, decoronation, a label that will define the event. None of them fully succeeds. Richard leaves the scene, still proclaiming himself a true king. The subject becomes a matter for argument for the rest of the series of history plays. What really did happen there? How can we describe it? How can we set it right? Interpretation will rage through the remaining history plays, both in words and in battles.

Richard II—The Fall of the King
Lecture 14

Bolingbroke is successful in taking Richard's kingdom, whether or not he intended to, because Richard, in effect, throws it away.

This lecture considers the personal aspects of the leading characters of *Richard II*. Bolingbroke is an opaque character, forceful but not fully revealed to the audience. Although normally talkative, he is silent at key moments. Neither in public utterance nor in soliloquy does he tell us at what moment he decides to reach for the crown itself instead of merely the restoration of his stolen inheritance. As a consequence of Bolingbroke's opacity, an actor or a reader may interpret him either as secretly ambitious from the start or as a wholly accidental king.

Also as a consequence, the psychological interest of the play is focused on Richard. Richard forfeits his moral authority through his complicity in his uncle's death. He forfeits his economic power because of his extravagance. He forfeits his legal power by illegally seizing Bolingbroke's estates, thereby upsetting the natural order of society.

> **Richard forfeits his moral authority through his complicity in his uncle's death.**

Richard's character appears in the power of his language. His language may be powerful for extrinsic reasons: he is king. The scene at the Coventry lists (1.3) demonstrates repeatedly his royal ability to translate his wishes into reality. Richard's language is also powerful intrinsically. The Barkloughly Castle scene (3.2) shows his expressiveness in a variety of emotional modes: parental concern for the land of England, inspiring vigor in comparing himself to the sun, noble melancholy in resigning himself to misfortune, piercing grief on the fate of kings.

The power of Richard's language may cause conflicting responses of sympathy and impatience. We may be moved by its beauty and pathos. We may be irritated by its excess, and by Richard's reliance on talk when action is necessary.

Richard uses language largely to construct roles for himself. Greeting the English earth, he plays parental guardian of the land. Invoking the analogy of king to sun, he assumes the splendor and glamour of the sun. The fantasy of becoming a pilgrim (3.3.147–171) shows fully the detailed elaboration, the self-deception, and the double effect of these verbal self-portraits. His favorite role is Jesus Christ. The analogy is justified: the king is God's deputy. The analogy is unjustified: it is presumptuous and inaccurate.

In the prison scene (5.5), Richard starts to use language for self-exploration rather than self-dramatization. His language is halting, tested, and considerate, rather than fluent and easily elaborated. He arrives at *anagnorisis*, a realization of what he is and how his own actions have contributed to his downfall. ∎

Essential Reading

Shakespeare, *Richard II*.

Supplementary Reading

See BBC-TV videotape of *Richard II*.

Altick, "Symphonic Imagery in *Richard II*."

Calderwood, "*Richard II* and the Fall of Speech."

Questions to Consider

1. Read what Henry IV says about his usurpation of Richard's crown in *Henry IV*, Part 1, 3. 2, and *Henry IV*, Part 2, 3.1 and 4.4, and compare that to his actions, speeches, and silences as Bolingbroke in Richard II. How much can we conclude about his intentions and motives?

2. What may we infer about Richard II's character from his treatment of the dying Gaunt in 2.1? From his dialogue with the groom in 5.5? Richard's queen at the time of his deposition was actually a child, a French princess whom he married for diplomatic reasons. It was Shakespeare's decision to make her a mature woman. What does he gain thereby? What is Richard's relationship with his wife?

Richard II—The Fall of the King
Lecture 14—Transcript

I've talked about the politics of *Richard II*. I'd like to go on and talk about the characters, about Bolingbroke and about Richard himself. Actually, I'll talk about Bolingbroke only briefly. It is hard to say much more about him than in the political lecture that I've already given; he's rather an opaque character. I don't mean as a bad piece of characterization, thin or cardboard; in fact, I find him very solid, very forceful. But he's not a very exposed character. In the deposition scene, Richard calls Bolingbroke a "silent king," and although that description is not literally true—he's quite talkative, in fact he's got the longest role in the play except for Richard himself—but he is silent at key moments in the play. He's talkative at the beginning when he's challenging Mowbray; he's talkative near the end when he's king. But at the crucial moments of the transition of power, in the middle of the play in Acts III and IV, he restricts himself to official statements. He doesn't tell us at what moment he decides to reach for the Crown itself, instead of the restoration of his stolen estates. He does not reveal to us his ambitions. In fact, this is quite unusual; he is the only usurper in Shakespeare—and Shakespeare has a lot of usurpers—who has no soliloquy and no private conversation with friends to reveal to the audience what his intentions, his motives, his desires are.

The mind of the usurper is not open to us, and thus it is possible to have a wide range of interpretations. Some critics have suspected that he secretly yearns to be king from the very beginning of the play, and have mined the opening speeches for some hint of that. This is a notion that fits in with our current political ideas that everybody in politics has a secret agenda, they're all up to something. There's a middle kind of possibility, that he's the kind of politician that doesn't allow himself to have a formulated ambition until it's already half-fulfilled, until he's already pretty sure that he can get what he wants. There's another possibility, which, at the moment, I think is the most interesting. At least, I've seen it very interestingly played. It's always easy to play Richard II; it's a demanding role, but there have been many fine Richards. One doesn't often hear of people speaking of fine Bolingbrokes, but I have seen one. Several years ago, at the Oregon Shakespeare Festival in Ashland, an actor named Derrick Lee Weeden did a brilliant Bolingbroke, who clearly was sincere about wanting only the restoration of his stolen inheritance, and was utterly astonished when Richard collapsed in front of him in the confrontation at Flint Castle in Act III. A look of amazement passed over his face. "What is it that I have done? I've pushed for this, and he's altogether collapsed"—you expect people in power to hang on to as much power as possible—"now *I've* got to take over?"

You saw a very interesting hardening in Wheaton, as Bolingbroke, for the rest of the play as he realized, one step after another, what he had to do. He's the only one who can be king; the king must do this, the king must do that, until he ends up indirectly commanding the murder of Richard. It was a most interesting performance. That, too, is a possibility for Bolingbroke, that he didn't know where what he was doing might lead, and didn't intend to go that far. One effect of this opacity in Bolingbroke, however, is quite clear. If we can't get into the mind of the usurper, most of the psychological interest of the play falls on Richard. He is really the center of our attention; so let me turn to Richard.

How does Richard fall? In essence, almost of his own accord. Bolingbroke is successful in taking Richard's kingdom, whether or not he intended to, because Richard, in effect, throws it away. He throws away his power, or weakens it until it slips out of his grasp. He throws away his moral power by his complicity in the death of his uncle, the Duke of Gloucester. It is very dangerous for kings to kill people, particularly people up at their level of social placement, their royal relatives. It suggests that people can be killed, gives other people ideas. If you murder, you reveal that you, yourself, are murder-able. It is interesting about this play that it begins and ends in the same way. It begins with a king who, somehow or other, has royal blood on his hands, Richard being somehow responsible for Gloucester's death. It ends with a king, Bolingbroke, who somehow or other brought about the death of Richard. It's an aspect of this being a history play, rather than a tragedy, there is no complete catharsis; we've returned to the same situation again.

He throws away his moral power; he also throws away his economic power by his extravagance. Gaunt and York, the royal uncles, both rebuke him for his rash, fierce blaze of unrestrained living and partying. He's driven to the desperate expedient of financing the expedition to Ireland by farming the realm—that is, by selling to somebody else the right to tax his own subjects. The waste of money would have been very plain, I think, to the Elizabethan audience, because Elizabeth herself was notably frugal about running the government. Richard also throws away his legal power by seizing his cousin Bolingbroke's estates, seizing the dukedom of Lancaster when his uncle Gaunt dies. That is the really fatal move that interferes with the whole order of medieval society, if you take somebody's direct inheritance. As York points out, "How art thou a king / But by fair sequence and succession?"

I want to investigate this weakening of power, to go beyond the history and see it reflected in the character that Shakespeare creates, especially in the language that Shakespeare gives Richard. The power of the king, or the lack thereof, is particularly reflected in the power of his words. This is a play in which words, in which language as such, is very important. Take the scene early in the play at the Coventry lists, where there's supposed to be a trial by combat. The first 117 lines of that scene consist of an extended series of challenges, recognitions and orders, all leading up to what will be a decisive deed; the two knights will charge each other and have a fight. At the last moment, Richard throws his warder down, and doom is pronounced, instead of being worked out in action. Words take the place of deeds. What was supposed to be settled with swords is settled with a sentence. Words take on the power that deeds normally have.

The stress on the importance of words continues in the scene. After Mowbray is banished for life and leaves the stage, Richard reduces the length of Bolingbroke's exile from 10 years to six, and Bolingbroke specifically says: "How long a time lies in one little word! / Four lagging winters and four wanton springs / End in a word: such is the breath of kings." The king can say something and it will change four whole years of Bolingbroke's life. The king can say it very frivolously. When Derek Jacobi played this role, he had Richard pluck the word "four" out of the air, as it were. He's talking to Gaunt, "Thy sad aspect / Hath from the number of his banish'd years / Pluck'd four away." He could have said five, he could have said six. It means a tremendous amount to the people involved, but Richard can be utterly frivolous about what word he chooses. Because he's king, it makes it reality. After all, if a bunch of fraternity guys are sitting around a fraternity, and one of them says, "Bring on the dancing girls," the other will probably laugh at him. If they're sitting around having beer with a king, and the king says, "Bring on the dancing girls," lo, there will be dancing girls. Someone in the king's entourage will be familiar with the fact that the king likes to have dancing girls when he drinks beer, and they will be on tap, as it were. The king's word has a special power. It corresponds to reality more closely than the words of the rest of us. It can make reality. That is what Bolingbroke is saying, "Such is the breath of kings."

Richard's fall, his loss of power, is played out in words. There are no battles in this play. Everything hinges on what is said. Most especially, Richard's own realization of his loss of power slowly comes to him in the loss of the power of the king's word. That power is extrinsic to himself as a man; people did things, not because he said it, but because he was the king. Once he ceases to be a king, his words lose that extrinsic power. In the deposition scene in Act IV, toward the end of the scene, he asks for a mirror: "If my word be sterling yet in England, / Let it command a mirror hither straight," but nothing happens. His word is not sterling yet in England; it isn't worth pounds sterling (that money metaphor is important). It wouldn't persuade anybody to do anything that that person didn't choose. Bolingbroke has to endorse the request before somebody goes off and gets a mirror: "Go, one of you, and fetch a looking glass," says the new king, and it happens.

Richard is bankrupt of the special external power of the word, but only that external power. Intrinsically, he's anything but a verbal bankrupt. The inherent power of words, Richard possesses in abundance. This man can talk. His tongue is golden, and particularly in the third act. He takes off on gorgeous flights of rhetoric, images of unforgettable power and beauty. When Richard II has said something, it has been definitely said. I still remember the first time I read this play, when I was 14, and I got to Act III. I started into those big speeches he has, and it was as if the top of my head were lifted off. I didn't know people could talk that gorgeously. I didn't understand it all; I was only 14, after all. But I loved it, and I quickly memorized it the way a kid can. I would go around talking about "the hollow crown / that rounds the mortal temples of a king" on all occasions, appropriate and inappropriate. At 14, in school, there are few appropriate occasions to talk about such things, and my classmates soon laughed it out of me. It is remarkable stuff. Shakespeare has managed to come up with a character who really can speak, a position that all playwrights would love to be in. So he keeps giving him more and more to say, adding aria after aria to Richard's part. In that scene, which takes place at Barkloughly Castle as he's landed, coming back from Ireland to get back home, he starts with 23 moving lines on the king as parental guardian of the land, caressing the earth and greeting it. Then he goes on to 27 stirring lines about the likeness of the king, the sun, rising in his throne, the east banishing the creatures of the night. Then, he has 11 noble lines of resignation to mutability and misfortune. He has 35 absolutely unforgettable lines about the deaths of kings and the hollow crown that rounds the mortal temples of the king. He's only just gotten started. We're only halfway through the play; he's got 2½ acts more to go.

Some people have wondered if Shakespeare had gotten a little bit self-indulgent here. He's discovered a splendid new aspect of his talent, and he can't help just going on, writing more and more in this vein. Possibly he did feel a little that way. If I had just sat down and written out the speech about the death of kings and the hollow crown, I think I'd sit back for a moment and say, "I'm on a roll this afternoon! It's terrific!" But, I think the excess here is deliberately calculated. It works to create a complex response in us, in the audience. It creates in us a curious mixture of sympathy and impatience. We're sympathetic because Richard is suffering, because he can tell us so fully all about his suffering, so accurately and sensitively about every quiver of his pain. At the same time, he goes on and on, ever finding new images for his sorrow, graves and worms and epitaphs, buckets of water in a well, burial in the king's highway. There comes a point—it may be a different point for each one of us, depending upon our tolerance for other people's self-pity—when most of us will want to say, "For heaven's sakes, shut up and do something."

It's right that we should want to say that. This combination of pity and exasperation is right. We must feel compassion for his grief; he is suffering. At the same time, we must see and feel the concern of the men who are causing him that grief. We identify their impatience about having a king like him, and their regret that they are obliged to hurt him in order to save the kingdom. Shakespeare is evoking in us a complex emotional state in order to do justice to the complexity of the political problem that I was describing in the last lecture. You don't like having a king like this, and yet you don't like the damage you have to do to get rid of him. Shakespeare's technique is well calculated, in giving us this gorgeous rhetoric in excess when action is called for.

Let me carry this a bit further. What does Richard use this intrinsic power of the word for? What's he doing in these long, gorgeous speeches? Chiefly, he's constructing roles of himself, roles to play, pictures of himself. He's an actor; these are dramatic parts. When he's caressing the earth, he's playing the king as parental guardian of the land. That's a recognized role of the king, except that it's only a role in his case. He's made it an actor's gesture; really to be guardian of the land would take sensible military policies, well- thought-out fiscal plans. He's making it simply a symbolic gesture of caressing the soil. When he's exploiting the traditional comparison of the king to the sun, he's taking to himself all the splendor of that analogy, without doing the work that it implies, the economic management, the administrative action it calls for—really to get rid of the clouds and the creatures of the night.

Richard's a player-king, like Richard III, only Richard III was a very calculating player-king. His roles were deliberate political performances with practical ends to be gained. Richard II devises roles to satisfy his own ego, to give dignity to his situation. He's the kind of actor who isn't interested in finding the truth of the character. He's the kind of actor who likes simply having the wonderful costume and being stage center in the spotlight. Let me give you another example. At Flint Castle, when he's thinking of coming down and submitting to Bolingbroke and Northumberland:

> What must the king do now? Must he submit?
> The king shall do it. Must he be depos'd?
> The king shall be contented. Must he lose
> The name of king? O' God's name, let it go.
> I'll give my jewels for a set of beads,
> My gorgeous palace for a hermitage,
> My gay apparel for an almsman's gown,
> My figur'd goblets for a dish of wood,
> My sceptre for a palmer's walking staff,"

He's working out all the props. He's going to give up the props that are associated with kingship and become a monk or a hermit. A set of beads, that's a rosary; a hermitage, a dish of wood, a pilgrim's walking staff. Turn in this costume and get a new one, with its associated properties. Only it's all a fantasy. He's not going to be a monk or a hermit; he's going to be a prisoner. Perhaps he'll be dead. He goes on with that for quite some time, and finally says to Aumerle, who's standing there next to him, "Aumerle, thou weep'st, my tender-hearted cousin! / We'll make foul weather with despised tears". He goes on with an elaborated image of how they will dig their graves with their own tears. This goes on for about eight lines, and then he says, "Well, well, I see / I talk but idly, and you laugh at me." There's the double reaction. "Aumerle, thou weep'st… I talk but idly, and you laugh at me." What he's doing inspires both our sympathies and, to some degree, our contempt.

I suppose his favorite role is the role of Jesus Christ. When he thinks that his favorites, Bushy, Bagot and Greene, have gone over to Bolingbroke's side, he condemns them as Judases. Only he's worse off than Christ was; he calls them "three Judases, each one thrice worse than Judas." I suppose that makes him nine times worse than Christ was on Good Friday. He comes back to that comparison in the deposition scene. When he thinks that everybody has deserted him, he says:

> I … remember
> The favours of these men. Were they not mine?
> Did they not sometime cry "All hail!" to me?
> So Judas did to Christ; but he, in twelve,
> Found truth in all but one; I, in twelve thousand, none.

He's upped the ante there. Now he's 12,000 times worse off than Christ was on Good Friday. It's not only offensive that any believing Christian should compare himself directly to Jesus Christ in this fashion; in his case, it's also grossly inaccurate. It's just not truth. It's not true that Richard has [sic not] found truth in all but one; Aumerle has stuck by him. The Bishop of Carlisle, at that moment, has just been arrested for arguing against the deposition. The comparison is just too much, and yet, there is a grain of truth here. He is God's representative; that is the political theory, and they are telling him,

"You're not a king," which is what the Romans and the Jews said to Christ on Good Friday. They are giving him great pain, and they will kill him.

The role-playing goes on and on. It doesn't really cease until Richard is in prison in his final scene in the play. It's not the final scene, because we return to Bolingbroke on the throne to close the play, but it is the next to last, Act V, Scene V. His mode of speech at last changes. He is no longer using words for self-dramatization, to glamorize himself, to find a role to play to get through this. He's using words for the more difficult and painful task of self-exploration.

> I have been studying how I may compare
> This prison where I live unto the world
> And, for because the world is populous
> And here is not a creature but myself,
> I cannot do it; yet I'll hammer it out.
> My brain I'll prove the female to my soul,
> My soul the father; and these two beget
> A generation of still-breeding thoughts.

Richard II has not spoken that way before. The words no longer flow easily; he is no longer a fountain of metaphors that come forth overflowing. He's got to hammer things out. Every thought he has, in a soliloquy that lasts for 66 lines, he contradicts. He thinks of things divine; he tries to console himself with a quotation from the Bible. Then he remembers there are contradictions in the Bible. The Bible says different things. He thinks of ambition; maybe there's a way he can get out and get the throne back. Then he thinks, how foolish to think that, when you're in a dungeon of a medieval castle. Through all those thoughts, he ends up with this very difficult one:

> But whate'er I be,
> Nor I, nor any man that but man is
> With nothing shall be pleas'd, till he be eas'd
> With being nothing.

That may mean, simply, we're never content. Content is not a possible human condition, so we'll always be restless with whatever we achieve until we finally die. It may mean something that goes a little deeper, however. Not until we have faced our own inner nothingness, can we be said really to know ourselves. That seems to me to be an important statement, at least for an actor like Richard. If you finally know that you've been playing roles, that everything was surface, that there was a nothingness inside that you were covering over with these glamorous roles, then you have achieved something in the way of self-knowledge. You have come to some self-recognition, what Aristotle called *anagnorisis*.

It's the most useful word I find in Aristotle for talking about Shakespearean tragedy: *anagnorisis*. Aristotle probably meant by it, at first, just recognition of a fact, recognition "this man in disguise is really Orestes." But it has come to mean, in the discussion of tragedy, recognition of who one is and what one has done, a much deeper kind of recognition. Not until Richard faces that nothingness can he thank whomever it is that plays the music for him there in prison. At that point, a humble groom comes in to offer him love, to offer love to a Richard who, no longer being king, has no way to reward love, except to be grateful for it, for what it is, the love of a fellow human being. For that, he does thank the groom. He has achieved something in self-recognition. He has achieved something in recognition of his own fault in losing the crown—"I wasted time, and now doth time waste me"— so Shakespeare finally gives him action. He fights for his own life. The assassins come in; he kills three of them before he himself goes down. He can die fighting for a self that finally does exist. Perhaps the real tragedy of Richard II is that he starts living truly in the moment that he dies.

Henry IV—All the King's Men
Lecture 15

With *Henry IV*, we reach the heart of the histories. The two plays named after this king constitutes the most diverse, entertaining and profound accomplishment by any playwright I know of in the dramatic rendition of history.

The political narrative of *Henry IV Part 1* and *Henry IV Part 2* hinges on the legitimacy of Henry IV's crown. Anyone dissatisfied with his rule can claim that he ought not to be king anyway. The Percy family, led by the fiery young Hotspur, helped to put Henry on the throne, and it feels under-rewarded. Edmund Mortimer, a Percy in-law, was a closer heir by blood to Richard II. The archbishop of York, kin to the Percys, rises in arms to settle grievances.

The central role is Henry IV's eldest son, nicknamed Hal, whom legend had made a madcap prince, a prodigal son who haunts taverns with his friend Falstaff. Shakespeare makes him a self-conscious prodigal, deliberately courting a bad reputation in order to astonish England with his real excellence when he comes to the crown. Accordingly, although each play ends with Hal's historical deeds as prince of Wales, most of his scenes concern his private dealings with his tavern cronies and his father. The plays alternate public events with scenes not only in taverns but also in rural locations with artisans, servants, and farmers.

Organizing this rich diversity is the principle of contrast among three main groups: the king and his advisers, Falstaff and the tavern crew, and Hotspur and the rebels. One of the things that distinguishes these three groups is their attitude toward time. The court group, focused on the king, regards time as a linear chain of necessity, full of dangers, requiring constant calculation. The tavern crew, focusing on Falstaff, lives for entertainment and pleasure, disregarding time. It seeks to evade or defuse emergencies rather than to meet them. The rebels, led by Hotspur, regard time as the opportunity for chivalric exploits. Hal has significant resemblances to each group, but no one sees his overall plans. Each group underestimates him.

In this world, any sense of the divine right of kings has gone underground Kingship has no aura or mystique in this play. Henry IV never speaks of the glory of the crown as Richard II had. He exploits the trappings of majesty purely as political tools. He is disappointed with Hal because Hal seems to have no political awareness.

Kingship has no aura or mystique in this play.

Hal is in fact highly political; his tactics differ greatly from his father's. His soliloquy in 1.2 outlines his scenario, hinging entirely on the principle of foil or contrast between his current lax behavior and his intended reformation. He believes that he can handle all contingencies. We may wonder to what extent he is rationalizing mere self-indulgence. Like Saint Augustine, Hal seeks to postpone his reformation. He does publicly earn acclaim for traditional royal virtues at the end of each play: valor and military honor at the end of Part 1, justice and good rule at the end of Part 2. ∎

Essential Reading

Saccio, *Shakespeare's English Kings*, chapter 3.

Shakespeare, *Henry IV, Parts 1 and 2*.

Supplementary Reading

See BBC-TV videotapes of *1 and 2 Henry IV*.

Bevington, *Introduction to 1 Henry IV* (Oxford edition).

Greenblatt, "Invisible Bullets: Renaissance Authority and Its Subversion, *Henry IV* and *Henry V*."

Kernan, "The Henriad: Shakespeare's Major History Plays."

Melchiori, *Introduction to 2 Henry IV* (New Cambridge edition).

1. The historical Hotspur was two years older than King Henry IV: Shakespeare makes him a young man of Hal's age. Why? Discuss in detail the personality of Hotspur and the way Shakespeare uses him in Part 1.

2. What is Hal's conception of kingship? What is the relevance of personal characteristics—and the reputation a person in public life has for private behavior—to his or her capacity to lead or rule? Do the *Henry IV* plays throw any light on public debates such as those America has had about the behavior of President Clinton?

Henry IV—All the King's Men
Lecture 15—Transcript

With *Henry IV*, we reach the heart of the histories. The two plays named after this king constitutes the most diverse, entertaining and profound accomplishment by any playwright I know of in the dramatic rendition of history. The heart of this achievement lies in its richness. Several plotlines, numerous striking characters, various sharply evoked moods of life thrive in a capacious dramatic structure that highlights both their virtues and their contrasts. Its scenes throw into juxtaposition values that are, in the long run, incompatible, but do so in a way that invites the audience to identify and sympathize with each one. A minor character remarks, "Homo"—that is, the Latin word for man—"Homo is a common name to all men." We're all the same underneath. *Henry IV Part 1 and 2* dramatizes, with both fullness and precision, the great variety of common and uncommon men who are caught up in the web of history, all the king's men, and the king himself.

The political narrative enacts what Edward Hall called the "unquiet time" of *Henry IV*. Having snatched the crown from his ineffective cousin Richard II, Henry is a king with obvious liabilities: a questionable title, blood on his hands, and debts in his pocket. The Percy family, led by the fiery young Hotspur, who had helped to crown Henry, becomes dissatisfied with his rule. One of the family's complaints originates in Henry's refusal to ransom Hotspur's brother-in-law, Edmund Mortimer, Earl of March, who is a member of the royal family. In fact, he is by blood more closely connected with Richard II and therefore technically might be considered the right heir to the throne, rather than King Henry himself.

The Scots cause trouble in the North. A revered ecclesiastic, the Archbishop of York, who is kin both to the Percys and to a man who is executed by Henry in the course of the deposition of Richard, rises in arms to settle grievances that he attributes to Henry's government. All these persons I have mentioned can claim Henry's dubious right to the crown of England and the murder of Richard II as a justification for rebellion. Henry's struggle to hold the throne constitutes the chief historical narrative of the play, of both plays Parts 1 and 2.

The leading role, however, is not the king; the king is but a supporting part. The leading role belongs to Henry's eldest son, Prince Hal, who becomes Henry V in the last act of Part 2. By Shakespeare's time, a wealth of anecdotes had accumulated around the figure of this medieval hero, anecdotes best known to Elizabethan theatergoers from an anonymous play I mentioned in an earlier lecture, *The Famous Victories of Henry V*. These legends make Hal a prodigal son, a madcap, a highway robber who prefers spending time drinking in taverns to his princely duties as Prince of Wales. In Shakespeare's rendering, his drinking buddies and fellow thieves become the crew of the Boar's-Head Tavern, and chief among them is Shakespeare's most remarkable comic invention, the fat knight Sir John Falstaff. I will devote the whole next lecture to Falstaff; he will come in only from time to time to the present one. An equally remarkable Shakespearean invention, however, lies in recasting the prince. Shakespeare's Hal is not just a prodigal. He's a prodigal with a plan, a self-conscious prodigal, a political prince who designs a wasteful career as an appropriate training ground to be king, and as an effective manipulation of his public image, in order to gain maximum advantage when he comes to the crown. Accordingly, in many scenes of both parts, Hal engages not in the military and administrative activities assigned to him by history, but in a series of private encounters invented by Shakespeare, private encounters with his cronies in Eastcheap, and with his anxious father.

In following Hal and Falstaff, the two plays depict a panorama of English life, not only at the court and in the taverns of London, but also in rural locations, populated by artisans and the servants and the lesser gentry, a broad swathe of the population. In Part 1, this wealth of character and incident is organized on the structural principle of contrast. Contrast is the principle you really have to grasp to read these plays well, or to produce them well. There are three major groups: the king and his advisors at court, Falstaff and the crew in the Tavern, and Hotspur and the rebels out in the battlefield. They are juxtaposed in similar activities that display their contrasting attitudes toward life. To take it on a big scale, the rebels are out to steal the kingdom from the king. Falstaff and the tavern crew just practice highway robbery on the road to Canterbury in order to finance their drinking. The king, of course, has stolen the whole kingdom and is trying to hang on to it. They are in analogous positions.

These contrasts occur in all sorts of matters, large and small, obvious and subtle. In order to have one that can be reasonably discussed in a short period, let me talk about their view of time. Each of them conceives of time in a different way. The king is burdened with the liabilities of his past and threatened with disloyalty from every quarter, so he's become a careful calculator, an administrator who squeezes every possibility out of each moment. For him, time is an extended linear chain of events, consequences from the past, provisions for the future. It's crowded with dangers, and he responds with a series of contingency plans, meeting and manipulating every emergency. He's the kind of king, you feel, has got a file back there, with folder on every possibility. If a messenger ran in and said, "My lord, we're at war with the Pope," he would have a folder on three ways to invade the Vatican, and decide which one's the best way to employ this time. I don't make him sound like a very attractive character, I'm afraid. But I will tell you, I developed an enormous sympathy for Henry IV when I became chair of the Dartmouth English Department, and my life, or at least my day, could be made hell by any one of 40 people at any time. I liked him a lot, and as a matter of fact, I went on to play the part in a production at Dartmouth that happened in the summer that I ceased to be chair. Everything that I learned in the four years as chair, I poured into playing that part.

Falstaff has nothing to do with such measured clock-time and its requirements, its forethought. For him, there are no appointments, there are no necessities. Time is a vast meadow in which to wallow, an unending, repeatable cycle of those wonderful pleasures that do repeat: food, drink, entertainment, jesting, sex and sleep. Emergencies are not to be met, but to be defused, evaded if possible. Worldly concerns like political order, social values like honor, simply do not matter to him. "What's honour? A word, a breath. Who hath it? He that died o' Wednesday."

For Hotspur, the Northern border lord, time is opportunity. It consists of the immediate moment, the moment that will provide a chance for a great exploit, the moment when one can "pluck bright honour from the pale-fac'd moon." He also has a view of history, but his view of history simply consists of those moments. It's a record of great exploits, of knightly honor, enormous achievements. He's impulsive, he's loyal to family, he's enamored of military fame, he's free of guile and suspicion. He's the sort of young warlord upon whom a primitive civilization absolutely depends. This is the guy you need to defend you against the enemies. The audience likes him a lot, too. He's also anarchic and quite out of his depth when it comes to the politics of late Plantagenet England. He doesn't really understand what politics are at all, wouldn't begin to penetrate the deviousness of a man like Henry IV.

Each of these figures—the king, Falstaff and Hotspur—is admirable: Henry for his laborious responsibility; Falstaff for his jollity and his shrewdness for seeing through the pretensions of great people; Hotspur for his forthrightness, his charismatic courage. Each provides a model for Hal, and Hal, in turn, resembles each one of them. In the long run, he is as astute as his father, he is nearly as witty as Falstaff, and he becomes as brave and heroic on the battlefield as Hotspur. Each of them also underestimates Hal with appropriate emotional responses. Each of them sees only in Hal the apparent wastrel. They are ignorant of the far-seeing calculation with which Hal prepares to pay the debt he never promised—that is, to assume the kingship with the astonished applause of the whole kingdom.

I am back to kingship again. In this play, kingship does not seem to have any particular mystical value. Kingship may be God's ordinance for his rule of his faithful people, but any sense of divine right has retreated into the remote background. Henry's own usurpation has drastically weakened any sense of that right, of the king being a divinely enshrouded post. It's more a world of Machiavellian politics. Kingship is a human construct, a contraption, a fiction, invented by human beings to hold society together. It's Henry's job to make that contraption work, make that fiction work. He doesn't talk, King Henry, about the glory of the crown, the glamour that Richard II liked exploiting. When he invokes anything close to divine royalty, it's usually just as a tool to accomplish something. He has a terrible quarrel with Hotspur's uncle, the Earl of Worcester, and finally says to him, "Majesty might never yet endure / The moody frontier of a servant brow." "Majesty might not endure" sounds as if it could be a semi-mystical statement about the glory of the position, but he's just saying it to get rid of Worcester. He's saying, "Watch out! I'm not going to put up with your behavior." He means power, not glory.

More frequently, he doesn't even bother with statements that sound like an evocation of the awe of kingship. He talks about the tactics necessary to maintain authority. He has a long scene with his son, rebuking his son for his wild behavior his wasting of opportunities. In it, he compares himself to Richard II and talks about how Richard II was a skipping king, who idled away his time with foolish companions and "enfeoff'd himself to popularity." He had too many friends, whereas he, Henry, Bolingbroke, carefully rationed his public image so that he never got stale in the eyes of the public, and the public was always eager to see him. On his deathbed, he sums up his whole reign in terms of fiction, saying, "All my reign hath been but as a scene / Acting that argument." It's all a play, it's all drama; I've been playing a role. That's the only way we can do it; that's the only way we can hang on to a crown.

The Percys' function in this part of the contrast is to challenge the position of the king. "Who does he think he is up there, king or something? We put him up there; we can get him down again." Hotspur says things like, "I am whipp'd and scourg'd with rods, / Nettled and stung with pismires when I hear / Of this vile politician, Bolingbroke." Vile politician, Bolingbroke— he won't call him King Henry IV; he calls him by his earlier name, Henry Bolingbroke, and he's a mere politician, not a king. Politician was, for the Elizabethans, a rather nasty word. Law was a good thing, but policy was simply manipulation. Falstaff's role is to mock the pretensions of everybody, whether they're in Westminster Palace or out in the field.

If kingship is a fiction, it is nonetheless a necessary fiction. Prince Hal may postpone acting royally; he cannot avoid it in the long run. At some moment, he must choose to take it up. Henry, in the long scene I've mentioned, the long father-son scene, gives Hal a thorough scolding. This is in the middle of Part I; he accuses Hal of lacking all political sense.

> Thy place in Council thou hast rudely lost ...
> And art almost an alien to the hearts
> Of all the court and princes of my blood.
> The hope and expectation of thy time
> Is ruin'd, and the soul of every man
> Prophetically doth forethink thy fall. ...
> Thou hast lost thy princely privilege
> with vile participation;

that is, with bad companions, with base associations, those Eastcheap taverns. It is one of the great father-son scenes in drama, and really a terrible scene, not terrible in the sense of tragic, but terrible in the sense of having the real pain of a father and a son who cannot communicate with each other. I've mentioned that I played the role of the king, and I worked with a young man playing Hal. Very hard on us, it turned out to be extraordinarily difficult to do, and we found it was extremely difficult because we would never look at each other. They've each got long speeches to each other, and they keep talking past each other, so every time I'd try to fix him in the eye, he would look aside. If he looked back at me, I was so angry with him, that I would turn away.

We finally figured out that that was supposed to be the chemistry of the scene, the continual glancing off each other. Each is talking from his own point of view, and they can't make the leap to each other's. The extraordinary thing, personally, for me as I played this scene, my parents, my own parents came to see it. They were then in their late 70s. My mother is a very shrewd woman, and after the performance she took me aside and said, "You were quite remarkable in that scene when you were rebuking your son. You were behaving exactly like your father, and exactly in the way that you have always objected to your father behaving when you've had fights with him. No wonder that poor young man couldn't look at you." As I say, it's one of the great scenes of father and son not connecting.

Hal, as a matter of fact, is highly political. He just has a scenario that is quite different from his father's. One of the king's faults is the fault of many successful men: having been successful in one particular way, he's insisting that his son should be successful in the same way. That's the way to success; he cannot see the possibility of alternatives. But Hal himself exposes his own plan to us in the audience; he has a soliloquy early on. It goes like this; he's just been talking with Falstaff and Poins, and he's talking in general about his association with that tavern crew:

> I know you all, and will awhile uphold
> The unyok'd humour of your idleness.
> Yet herein will I imitate the sun,
> Which doth permit the base contagious clouds

> To smother up his beauty from the world,
> That, when he please again to be himself,
> Being wanted, he may be more wond'red at
> By breaking through the foul and ugly mists
> Of vapours that did seem to strangle him.
> If all the year were playing holidays,
> To sport would be as tedious as to work;
> But when they seldom come, they wish'd for come,
> And nothing pleaseth but rare accidents.
> So, when this loose behaviour I throw off
> And pay the debt I never promised,
> By how much better than my word I am,
> By so much shall I falsify men's hopes;
> And, like bright metal on a sullen ground,
> My reformation, glitt'ring o'er my fault,
> Shall show more goodly and attract more eyes
> Than that which hath no foil to set it off.
> I'll so offend to make offence a skill,
> Redeeming time when men think least I will.

That's his plan; that is his reformation, and it will glitter over his fault like a foil glitters behind a jewel. It's interesting that Shakespeare himself uses the foil-jewel metaphor, which we have picked up from him to use as a critical tool to understand Shakespeare. He is very aware of this business of contrast that he's doing, that heightens the qualities of each individual thing by showing similar things in different contexts. In this case, in the case of Hal's speech, the contrast is between his present behavior as an apparent ne'er-do-well, as a prodigal son, with his future behavior, when he becomes king. Everybody, gathering from his present behavior such low expectations of him, such grim hopes of what's going to happen when he becomes king, will be delighted when he turns out to be an excellent king. He will get all the more applause. He will get all the more obedience. That, at least, is his scheme, and it may indeed work.

He seems to think that everything within his control. He compares himself to the sun; that is, of course, the traditional comparison, the king and the sun. And he's, of course, the king's son as well, so it's a kind of triple pun.

The sun permits the clouds to smother up his beauty from the world, and then disperses him when it chooses, when the sun chooses. He seems to think it's all within his power, which may be a dangerous assumption for any human being to make, but nonetheless Hal makes it. The part of the speech that makes me most suspicious, most inclined to suspect a measure of rationalization, is the argument about holidays. "If all the year were playing holidays, / To sport would be as tedious as to work; / But when they seldom come, they wish'd for come." I'll agree with that as a general statement. That's true; Saturday we enjoy if we have worked hard all week. If we haven't worked, if we've been lazy and done nothing, then Saturday is no special treat. In fact, we're all the more bored and the weekend means nothing in particular. It isn't a rare accident. I agree with the general truth; I just don't think it's relevant to Hal's situation, because he isn't taking a rare holiday. Every day for him is a holiday; it's all Saturday.

We don't see when he's working at all, so this may be something of a rationalization, putting off the evil time when he must pay attention to his duty. It's understandable; it's much more fun, after all, being a Falstaff in the tavern, joking and drinking. That's much more fun than being in a palace with a gloomy, guilt-ridden, usurping father. But I am reminded of other people who have postponed doing their duty. The most famous example is Saint Augustine, who had trouble in his youth with lust, with lechery, and is famous for having prayed, "O Lord, make me chaste, but not yet. I want to have some more fun first."

At any rate, he is going to reform, and Dr. Johnson, the great critic of the eighteenth century, considered this speech to be remarkably reassuring for the audience. It tells the audience, yes, this is fundamentally a good man, and he will come to attention to his duty. The twentieth-century reaction is generally in the other direction. We're not so worried about the politics here. We're more worried about the sense of personal disloyalty. He's using Falstaff, using that friendship as part of his scheme of public image. Therefore, it isn't really a friendship, and some of my students dislike Hal for this cold calculation in what should be a human relationship. Nonetheless, there it is. This is his scenario, from which he will not deviate, and he does not.

In fact, he does reform twice. Here, the fact that Shakespeare is writing a two-part play contributed enormously to his scope in dealing with such a reformation—*Henry IV, Part I*; *Henry IV, Part II*. An effective king must have a variety of strengths, and Hal achieves some of them at the end of Part I, and others at the end of Part II. Part I occurs largely in a military context. Hal emerges from his apparent laziness and blazes across the Battle of Shrewsbury, where he saves his father's life, defeats and kills Hotspur, and wins military honor. Placed between Hotspur on the one hand, who is mad for honor and will do anything for it and Falstaff on the other, who cares nothing for honor, in fact, doesn't even want to move toward getting it—it's far too dangerous to try to get things like that—Hal achieves the real thing. He pays the debt he never promised. He does defend his father, and he does defend the kingdom. It is the king's military duty to defend the realm.

Part II is set largely in a civil context. Hal is placed again within an opposing pair. Again, Falstaff is one side; the anarchic Falstaff, who robs, who abuses the draft, who doesn't pay his debts. On the other side is the highest legal figure in the land, the Lord Chief Justice, whose personal name is not given, merely his title, so he almost seems an allegorical character standing for justice. Falstaff believes that since Hal is his friend, once Hal becomes king, Falstaff will have all the laws of England at his commandment— "we can take any man's horses." In that context, Hal rejects Falstaff and adopts the Lord Chief Justice as his surrogate father. Hal reforms in Part II, rising to justice and good rule. He fulfills the royal duty of ordering the realm.

The Renaissance was much concerned with good government. They write many treatises on how to rule well. Nicolo Machiavelli wrote *The Prince*. Thomas Elliott wrote *The Governor*. Thomas More wrote *A Biography of Richard III*, which is actually a treatise on how to govern badly. It's meant as a negative example, not really an accurate biography of Richard. A number of poets contributed to a huge volume called *A Mirror for Magistrates*, which give the biography of a number of great people: kings, rulers, dukes, whatnot, and all magistrates are meant to look into that mirror and find good and bad examples. *Henry IV Parts 1 and 2* is Shakespeare's contribution to the literature of good government, to the modern problem of how we order a civil state, and it is a remarkably comprehensive contribution.

Henry IV—The Life of Falstaff
Lecture 16

[Falstaff] is not only one of the great creations in the drama of the English-speaking peoples; like Hamlet, he has taken on a life independent of the plays, become a figure in the mental world of English-speaking peoples. He's an intensely significant character.

Falstaff, the Shakespearean character most frequently mentioned in surviving comments on Shakespeare's plays from his own time, remains one of his two or three most enduring creations, a dominating figure in the mythology of English-speaking peoples. Like Hamlet, he has been interpreted and re-interpreted. To avoid excessively abstract intellectualization, it is wise to remember that on stage he is an imposing physical figure, a very fat man.

Although Falstaff appears in two history plays, he is not based on a historical person. Instead, he is an adaptation of various theatrical types. He derives from the Vice, the tempter figure, in medieval morality plays. Hal, however, is not deceived by him, as the protagonists of morality plays were by the Vice. He derives from the *miles gloriosus*, the braggart soldier of ancient Roman comedy. Unlike that prototype, however, he is not humorless. He derives from the parasite, the sponger of classical life and comedy and of early Elizabethan comedy. Unlike

James H. Hackett as Falstaff in *Henry IV.*

the parasite, however, he gives as well as takes. He derives from the medieval court jester who entertains the prince, but he is also an acute social critic.

His characteristic action is to turn things upside down, to invert the established order of things. Excusing highway robbery, he claims it as his vocation. Inventing a story to cover his cowardice in the Gadshill robbery, he accuses Hal and Poins of cowardice and tells a tale that is obviously unbelievable. He turns the serious concerns of the world into a game, a game that has no fixed rules but is pure improvisation. He inverts conventional morality by accusing Hal of corrupting him. Although he himself is old, he says that members of the staid elder generation "hate us youth." On the battlefield, he plays dead to stay alive. Hal observes that Falstaff is like quicksilver; he can change roles very rapidly.

Although Falstaff appears in two history plays, he is not based on a historical person.

As Hal comes to represent leadership, he embodies what we now call the Protestant Ethic: a form of this-worldly asceticism that stresses devotion to duty, sobriety, and working for the public welfare. Hal's version of the Protestant Ethic is unusual in that it is always present in him, even during his early experience as a wastrel, but it becomes apparent only over time. Falstaff comes to embody everything that is the opposite of this Protestant ethic; he represents the ethic of pleasure and self-fulfillment, and the rejection of the Establishment and its values and pretensions.

Hal's rejection of Falstaff at the end of Part 2 is a great, almost mythical moment in Western civilization, codifying a deep division in human nature as we have known it. It is one of the great marks of the abundance of Shakespeare that he creates and contains this moment, while he rejects neither Hal nor Falstaff. ∎

Essential Reading

Shakespeare, *Henry IV, Parts 1 and 2.*

See BBC-TV videotapes of *1 and 2 Henry IV*.

Hunter, "Shakespeare's Comic Sense as It Strikes Us Today: Falstaff and the Protestant Ethic."

Wilson, *The Fortunes of Falstaff*.

Questions to Consider

1. Would you allow your twenty-year-old son to spend time with a hard-drinking, fornicating, funny old thief with a claim to military distinction? (Note that Falstaff does have a knighthood; at some point someone in authority thought he had behaved meritoriously on a battlefield.)

2. What significant differences exist between Falstaff as he appears in Part 1 and Falstaff as he appears in Part 2? Consider not only his personal characteristics—his way of speaking, his treatment of other people, his health, for example—but the kinds of things Shakespeare gives him to do, the sorts of scenes he appears in. Note for example that in Part 2 he appears only twice with Prince Hal, in 2.4 (where Hal is disguised for most of the scene) and 5.5 (where Hal has just been crowned king).

Henry IV—The Life of Falstaff
Lecture 16—Transcript

I've devoted a lecture to *Henry IV, Parts I and II*, talking chiefly about the king, the prince and Hotspur. I barely mentioned Falstaff. He requires more space; he takes more space. Falstaff is probably Shakespeare's most enduringly popular creation. Certainly, he was mentioned more often in contemporary comment on Shakespeare's plays than any other character that Shakespeare created. Nowadays, he is argued over at least as often as Hamlet. He is not only one of the great creations in the drama of the English-speaking peoples; like Hamlet, he has taken on a life independent of the plays, become a figure in the mental world of English-speaking peoples. He's an intensely significant character.

In this lecture, I'm going to be interpreting a lot, probing the meaning of his actions and his words. But I do not want Falstaff himself to disappear amid a fine-spun web of abstract intellectualizing, a web of commentary. I don't want to get too far away, or let you forget, the physical presence of the man. Shakespeare never gets too far away from it. His words, what others say of him, and above all, the physical presence of the man, never let us escape from the central fact about Falstaff on the stage. The central fact is that he is fat; not plump, not chubby, nor portly, but corpulent, stout, rotund, obese, fat. To use Shakespeare's own words, he is a "bed-presser," a "huge hill of flesh," a "greasy tallow-catch." His belly is "as gross as a mountain, open, palpable;" "when has thou last seen thy knee?" In the center of this intensely political play, there is a "stuffed-cloak bag of guts," who eats, drinks, sleeps, and snores, and has no politics. At the center of the body politic, the state, the human organizations devised to fill our collective needs, is the human body itself.

This fat figure has various theatrical sources. Note theatrical, not historical. When I wrote a book about the real history behind Shakespeare's history plays, I barely mentioned Falstaff. Falstaff is largely an invented character coming out of theatrical traditions. It's useful, in understanding him, to understand what those traditions were, and how Shakespeare has adapted them. I'll mention four in particular. There is the "Vice," from the medieval morality plays. The morality plays were allegorical plays in which a representative figure, Youth or Mankind, was tempted by vices and encouraged by virtues. Often the vices were reduced to a single Vice with a capital V, whose job it was to ensnare Youth, to lead Youth on to idleness, gluttony, lechery and so forth, and to embody those sins himself. In fact, Hal calls Falstaff a "vice," a "reverend vice," a "gray iniquity," a "father ruffian," a "vanity in years." The terms are all paradoxical; vice, iniquity, ruffian, vanity, those are all terms for the Vice, but to have him reverend, gray, father or in years, old, that's unusual. The Vice is usually young.

Henry IV uses the pattern of the old morality plays, presenting a young man, in this case, Prince Hal, being tempted by an embodiment of the world, the flesh, and the devil. The pattern is used, but it is also modified. Hal, after all, is not deceived; it's he who calls Falstaff those names. In the normal morality play, Youth does think that the Vice is telling him something good to do: "Isn't it fun to be slothful, drunken, lecherous, and so forth?" Hal is perfectly well aware of what is going on. What is significant is the effect that Falstaff could have on Hal. Certainly this is the effect that the king thinks that Falstaff is having on Hal, but the relationship is not developed in the strict morality way.

The second source comes from ancient Roman comedy, the *miles gloriosus*, the boastful soldier: the soldier who comes into the city proclaiming how many countries he has conquered, how many provinces he has sacked, how many maidens he has raped, full of his own exploits. Usually he has actually done these things; sometimes he has not. Falstaff is this kind of braggart soldier who boasts about his military exploits. You must remember that he is a knight; he is Sir John Falstaff. At some point, someone in authority thought he had done something distinguished on a battlefield and had given him that knighthood. In the case of Falstaff the adaptation is that it is all lies, all exaggerations. A more important adaptation is that the ancient Roman *miles gloriosus* was a deadly serious figure; he expected to be taken at his own merit, at his own claim for military glory. Falstaff makes the claim, but it is never clear whether he really means people to believe it. In fact, some of the stories that he tells about his exploits are quite unbelievable, and he's far too smart to think that people would believe them.

Third source, also from classical comedy, and from classical life itself: the parasite or sycophant, the hanger-on who leeches onto other people and lives off them, a very common social phenomenon in a hierarchically-organized society where it's more difficult for people to go out and find jobs. They have to attach themselves as servants or functionaries to great people, who have much land and possessions, and hope they can make themselves useful and get paid for it. The parasite from classical comedy also turns up in Elizabethan comedy as a sponger, a trickster, a mocker, and these things Falstaff does. He never pays his own bills at the tavern; Hal pays them for him, or Mistress Quickly just hopelessly goes on adding to the tab, knowing that she'll never get paid. But again, there's a modification. Falstaff is not totally a taker; he also gives, he entertains. He's the sort of man whom you don't mind paying the bill in the tavern for, because he was such fun at the tavern. While you were drinking all that stuff that you are paying for, he was telling the funniest stories around.

The fourth, and last, source for the time being is the fool, the court jester. He is the prince's jester, and the jester exists to divert the lord, prince, king whom he serves with verbal wit, dexterity, verbal gains, comic inventions, pranks and so forth. In this case, however, it isn't nearly a fantasy that he's entertaining the prince with. For much that Falstaff says is quite true; much of it embodies a quite accurate criticism of the great people around, of kings and lords and princes in the commonwealth.

Falstaff is thus a paradoxical figure. Yes, you could say he is vicious, he is a vice, but he's also tonic. He is life-enhancing. Yes, he's parasitical, but he's generous. Yes, he tells lies, but he doesn't expect to be believed. Yes, he exploits his friends, but they still love him. Yes, he laments his age, his clumsiness and particularly his bulk, his fatness, and yet he is extraordinarily nimble and quick—nimble and quick mentally, light on his mental feet. He is a Lord of Misrule; he presides at the tavern, as surely as King Henry presides at the court at Westminster and Hotspur presides in the camp of the rebels out in the battlefield. In fact, he deliberately mocks that kind of sitting in state. There's a scene, the great tavern scene in *Henry IV, Part I*, the end of Act II, where he pretends to be the king momentarily, thrones himself in a wooden chair, and puts a cushion on his head to represent the king's crown. As Lord of Misrule, he advocates the good life; pleasure is more important than work, idleness is more fun than industry, enjoying oneself is more important than satisfying others or worrying about the future, or taking care for the welfare of the state, honor, and politics.

The chief means by which he does these things is to turn everything upside down, to invert the normal order of things. Let me take one example from the tavern scene I've already mentioned, at the end of Act II. This tavern scene follow upon a highway robbery that Hal, Falstaff, Poins, Bardolph, Nym and the rest of the crew have carried out on Gadshill, only it's been a highway robbery with a twist. Hal and Poins deliberately separated themselves from Falstaff and the others, let Falstaff and the others rob the merchants—who were going to Canterbury, or coming from Canterbury; I've forgotten which—of their money, and then, in disguise, set upon Falstaff and Bardolph and company, and robbed them.

Therefore, when Falstaff comes back to the tavern—supposedly having carried out this robbery, although having been deserted by Hal and Poins—he's got to account for the lack of money. Where's the dough? He has to say something, so he starts by picking on the faults of Hal and Poins: "You are cowards. What did you do? Why weren't you there to help us?" Then he expands the account of the robbery into a magnificent story, a story about how they did, indeed, carry out the robbery, but then they were set upon by others and robbed in turn. They were set upon by "two buckram men," and as he fought them, he took four of their points in his target. There are suddenly four buckram men, and they go on multiplying to seven buckram men, and eleven buckram men. Finally, he would have beaten even the eleven buckram men, had not "three misbegotten knaves in Kendal green" attacked him from behind.

He's doing several things here. He is escaping a tough situation, telling a wonderful and fantastic story. This is an essential part of the comedy of Falstaff. He's an escape artist. Our delight in him is in the ingenious methods of avoiding or extricating himself from an awkward spot. He was the one who ran away during the Gadshill robbery when Hal and Poins set on them disguised, but he reverses the cowardly accusation to attack them. He tells this story, which nobody is going to believe, and that itself attracts so much attention, is so amusing, that people can forget about the initial problem. He gets out of an awkward spot—not with the direct valor and quarrelsomeness of Hotspur, who of course would fight his way out with a sword; not with the anxious planning of King Henry, who has reckoned on all contingencies and arranged backup plans for any emergency; or with the long-range strategy of Prince Hal that I was talking about in the previous lecture. Instead, he gets out of awkward situations with spontaneous inventiveness, with improvisation. He is, to adapt a modern form, a stand-up comedian, who can talk his way out of any situation. By this means, by this improvisation, he creates holiday. He creates carnival. The world is a serious business, an anxious business where kings must meet rebellions, an insecure place. Falstaff considers the world to be a game, a revel.

Once they get through the buckram men section of this great tavern scene, in comes a messenger from the court, Sir John Bracy, to bring the news of the rebellion. The king wants the prince to turn up at court; the prince has got to help in meeting the rebellion, and obviously the king is going to rebuke the prince for his wastrel behavior. Falstaff takes that situation and turns it into another game. "Hal, you are going to be horribly rebuked tomorrow. What are you going to say to your father? Hey, let's practice it. Let's have a little tea group session in which I'll pretend to be the king and I'll rebuke you, and you answer for yourself." Then they switch roles; the prince takes the role of his father, and Hal answers for Falstaff. They turn it into a play of its own.

Falstaff is really a mythical figure, a god of physical pleasures, and a god of imaginative pleasures, a Saturnalian figure who presides over our merrymaking. We all feast at the Boar's-Head Tavern from time to time in our lives. We all pay homage to this particular kind of Bacchus god, and Falstaff embodies him enormously. He embodies him because he acts so well. This is all varieties of acting: the improvisation; the lies; the entertainment. He is supposedly leading Hal astray; he accuses Hal of leading *him* astray. At Gadshill, young men on a spree, oppressed by an older generation; he himself is old, but he says of the merchants, "They hate us youth." In the tavern, he is the courageous stalwart man vexed by the cowardice of his friends, who left him to fight alone against 11 buckram men. And on the battlefield, where things get really serious, finally, at the end of Part I, he turns out to have in his holster not a gun, but a bottle of sack. He plays dead in order to stay alive. Those soldiers running around there, the Earl of Douglas and Hotspur they're far too dangerous—and he just flops down and pretends to be a corpse in order to continue living. "This is the strangest fellow," says Hal to his brother, Prince John, at the end of the play. And he's strange, partly because he can act so well; he can shift roles so rapidly. He is quicksilver, which is all the more surprising in a fat man. He is never the same thing for more than a few minutes, always resourceful, always chameleonic, always shifting that huge hill of flesh into a new shape, and even remolding it into the ideal shape of himself.

When he is pleading to Hal not to be rejected in that game where Hal is playing the king and he is playing Hal, he talks about the virtues of this man Falstaff: Banish your other bad companions, by all means:

> Banish Peto, banish Bardolph, banish Poins; but for sweet Jack Falstaff, kind Jack Falstaff, true Jack Falstaff, valiant Jack Falstaff, and therefore the more valiant, being, as he is, old Jack Falstaff, banish not him thy Harry's company, banish not him thy Harry's company. Banish plump Jack, and banish all the world!

That's a wonderful metamorphosis, to take the fatness, the huge hill of flesh and make it sweet, true, and merely plump. You banish that, you banish all the world. Hal, of course, is willing to do it; his very quiet response to that speech is, "I do. I will," which brings us back to the confrontation between Hal and Falstaff, my ultimate goal in this lecture.

We can criticize Falstaff. We can criticize him for being detached from serious concerns. In essence, Falstaff is asking "What's so important about a well-run state? Why spend all this fuss and concern about who wears the crown? What does it matter, so long as we have food and drink? What does it matter if we get good soldiers?" He abuses the draft. There are several scenes in which he does it, one offstage in Part I, but one onstage in Part II, which is much more striking, where he allows all the hardy, strong men to buy their way out of the draft and takes, instead, the weak, the ragged, the sickly. But why not have the weak, the ragged and sickly? If the people going to the war are going to get killed, they'll fill a pit as well as others. Let the healthy ones survive. Why on earth do you worry so much about honor?

Falstaff is utterly without principle. You cannot really call him a liar, a coward, a thief, an abuser of the draft, a sponge on Mistress Quickly, as I have been saying he is, or make any of the moral objections that spring naturally to the moralists' lips. He doesn't share the principles that would validate such charges. He calls into question the very existence of principle itself. Eat, drink and be merry; act your way through. That is what Hal must object, and that is why there's a great confrontation between the two at the end of Part II of *Henry IV*.

Let me generalize here about what is going on. I said part of this would get quite intellectual. Hal is a leader, a prince who has designed a career that will lead him to the crown. What do we want in a leader? Justice, perhaps mercy; competence, efficiency, effectiveness; inspiration when necessary, the ability to inspire us to our best abilities; above all, I think, devotion to duty. We want him to be concerned with our protection, with our welfare, to be absorbed with that task, to take on the burden. It's a big burden. This is the play where the king has the most famous line Shakespeare wrote for any king—"uneasy lies the head that wears the crown." We want the king to be forethoughtful, industrious, resourceful, shrewd, and devoted to the job. Hal eventually proves to be so. As a Renaissance prince, he proves to be as devoted to his duty in the world, as devoted as any medieval man might be devoted to a religious vocation. I make that comparison because I am following the instruction of an old professor of mine, now retired— Robert Hunter, who would put the contrast between Hal and the prince in the context of the whole growth of the early modern world, the growth of Puritanism and the growth of capitalism. He urged me, when we first talked about Hal, Falstaff and the king, to read Max Weber, to read the book *The Protestant Ethic and the Spirit of Capitalism*, and think about the play in the terms provided by Weber.

Weber points out that the Protestant ethic is essentially a notion of worldly asceticism, labor in the worldly sphere, labor on a career in the world, be it business or government, with the intensity or devotion that the Middle Ages had brought to the religious life, to the monastic life. Weber saw the heart of the Protestant ethic in Luther's idea of "the calling." You may cease to be a monk, you may abolish the monasteries, but you do not abolish the worth of asceticism, of self-denial that lies within monasticism. Rather, he transferred that dedication from the monastery to the affairs of the world. Duty in worldly affairs is the highest form of moral activity that an individual could assume. You labor in your vocation, you are devoted to public welfare, you postpone personal gratifications, and you pay the debt you never promised, to use Prince Hal's phrase. In the four centuries since Puritanism stamped its distinctive mark on Western culture, particularly Anglo-Saxon culture, English-speaking culture, we have tried, many of us, to raise our children in this way. Hal's version of the Protestant ethic is unusual only in that he appears to be a wastrel at first; he really has this Protestant scheme of devotion to his job going all the time. When he becomes king, then it becomes apparent that he has been embodying dutiful devotion all the time.

In this context, Falstaff is everything that the Protestant ethic is not. He eats, drinks, and is merry. He makes no thought for the morrow. He mocks every serious value in the culture: honor, valor, truthfulness. He parodies the idea of a vocation. He says, quoting from Paul, "'Tis no sin for a man to labor in his vocation," and then adds, "My vocation is highway robbery." He arranges for constant Carnival, instead of Lent. He plays instead of working. Far from the new Protestant ethic, he's something close to the old romantic notion of "Merry England," Robin Hood and his Merry Men in Sherwood Forest, as opposed to the Sheriff of Nottingham and King John. He's something close to an ethic that has arisen in the late twentieth century—the counterculture that got going in the late 60s, that saw its values in personal warmth, in psychological fulfillment, not in asceticism or public duty, an ethic that is founded on a thorough skepticism about the establishment and what the establishment defines as public duty, often in its own self-serving interest. The final confrontation of the lean young prince at the end of Part 2, when he has just been crowned king, and the fat old knight, is the confrontation between the dedication to public life and the enrichment of private life.

Hal rejects Falstaff. That rejection has excited an enormous amount of argument among Shakespearean critics. Is he right to do so? Isn't it cruel that he does it? Moreover, the response to rejection has influenced response to the whole of the two plays: those who find Hal's rejection of Falstaff ("I know thee not, old man. Fall to thy prayers"), those who find that rejection a needlessly public and preachy putdown of Falstaff usually also find the whole Lancastrian tribe of kings to be a bunch of cold opportunists. Those who approve the rejection of Falstaff, those who say that Hal must put a stop to the pretension of this fat old rogue who thinks he has all the laws of England at his commandment, also usually approve of the Lancastrian kings, of their effort to preserve public order under difficult circumstances.

The argument over which side to take here, which side Shakespeare means us to take, has been going on since the beginning of the eighteenth century for three centuries. Any scene that so polarizes audiences for three centuries clearly evokes deep divisions in the human condition, at least the human condition as it existed in recent Western culture. If one of the functions of myth is to dramatize conflict that lie at the heart of our culture, then Shakespeare has created a most powerful myth here in this last confrontation between the young king and his old companion. The Protestant ethic, with its devotion to duty, hard work, sobriety and self-sacrifice, confronts warmth, loyalty, merriment, merrymaking and skepticism about the establishment.

This conflict, indeed, governs the two plays. The body politic is supported by all the fictions it generates of kingship, honor, and the common weal, yet Shakespeare ensures that we know they are fictions. The king himself was once a rebel, and honor is possessed by him that died o' Wednesday; what use is it to him? Many, in fact, don't do very well in the common weal. Balancing the body politic is the human body itself, best summed up in Falstaff—fat, disorderly; appetitive; shrewd; and rich in the fullness of living. Hal, as king of the body politic, must reject Falstaff, the body impolitic, but Shakespeare does not reject Falstaff, nor does he reject Hal for rejecting Falstaff.

Henry V—The Death of Falstaff
Lecture 17

> You must remember that in Shakespeare's day people believed in a literal Hell, that if one died unreconciled with God, one would suffer for all eternity.

This is a different kind of lecture from those I have been giving. Instead of talking about a big subject, a genre, a theme, a leading character, I want to do a close-up on detail. I want to show you the abundance of Shakespeare in a short passage. I will take about forty lines and show you the richness of their texture, share with you the ways in which Shakespeare can provoke in us—readers and playgoers—a multitude of emotional and intellectual responses. This will be what critics call a close reading. The passage is in *Henry V*, the first forty lines of Act 2 Scene 2, when the Hostess of the tavern describes to Pistol, Nym, Bardolph, and the Boy the death of Falstaff.

It is a simple passage. I have deliberately *not* chosen a stretch of high-flown verse rich in metaphor and mythological allusion. It is prose, they are down-to-earth characters grieving the death of a dear friend, not rising to royal eulogy but simply talking about what happened at the deathbed. A youngster could understand the basic sense without explanations. But it is remarkably rich in its effect upon an attentive audience.

The premise of the scene involves some emotional complication. These are comic characters, but at the moment they are sad. The audience will be sad too. The original audience in 1599 may have been not only sad but also surprised. They had been promised, in the epilogue to Shakespeare's previous history play, *Henry IV Part 2*, that the sequel, pursuing Prince Hal as king and his conquest of France, would also contain more adventures of Falstaff. The character has appeared in two or three plays already. He was a great public favorite. A serial character ought not to die. I am reminded of an old cartoon, of a boy sitting up in bed late at night, reading, with an expression of horror on his face. He's just reached the death of Sherlock Holmes. And of course, Conan Doyle wasn't allowed to get away with killing Holmes;

he had to go on, write more stories, invent some way of getting him out of that waterfall.

Why Shakespeare decided to kill Falstaff is a matter open to speculation; but *since* he decided to kill him, he had to give him an appropriate send-off. Consider who Falstaff was: an embodiment of tremendous vitality, a man who joked and drank and schemed and fornicated and saw through the public pretenses of kings and social order. A man witty in himself and the cause of wit in other men. The greatest drinking buddy, the greatest boon companion in English, or any other literature I know. To say that he is dead is almost to say that life itself is dead, or at least that all the *earthly* delight of life is dead. So there is great reason for sorrow. But the scene is not wholly sad.

Let's take it line by line. The characters come on as Pistol and the other men are departing King Henry's war in France. The Hostess, who has now married Pistol, begs to accompany them a short part of the way.

> **Hostess.** Prithee, honey-sweet husband, let me bring thee to Staines.
>
> **Pistol.** No, for my manly heart doth yearn.
>
> Bardolph, be blithe; Nym, rouse thy vaunting veins;
>
> Boy, bristle thy courage up; for Falstaff he is dead,
>
> And we must yearn therefore.

That's the only bit of verse in the scene, and it's verse because Pistol likes to talk in the manner of ranting old plays. He's another imitator of Marlowe's Tamburlaine, like the prince of Morocco in *The Merchant of Venice*, fond of big alliterative phrases like "vaunting veins." But the inflated rhetoric merely makes more abrupt what Pistol actually tells us, "Falstaff he is dead." The guy's gone; he's not going to appear in the play. True, we were told in an earlier scene that he was sick, but throughout the *Henry IV* plays, Falstaff had been moaning about his diseases and discomforts: they didn't stop him from joking and lying and fornicating, let alone living.

Bardolph responds with the direct simplicity of grief and loyalty:

> **Bardolf.** Would I were with him, wheresome'er he is, either in heaven or in hell.

But that raises a frightful possibility that the Hostess quickly rejects:

> **Hostess.** Nay, sure, he's not in hell; he's in Arthur's bosom, if ever man went to Arthur's bosom.

You must remember that in Shakespeare's day people believed in a literal Hell, that if one died unreconciled with God, one would suffer for all eternity. This is a prospect too horrible for the Hostess to contemplate about the fate of her dear friend. He must be in Heaven. But there's a funny little twist in the line. Her biblical reference is a little shaky. She's made a mistake about the parable of the rich man and Lazarus, from the Gospel of Luke:

> And there was a certain beggar named Lazarus, who was laid at the gate, full of sores, and desiring to be fed with the crumbs that fell from the rich man's table. Moreover the dogs came and licked his sores. And it came to pass that the beggar died, and was carried by the angels into Abraham's bosom. The rich man also died, and was buried; and in hell he lifted up his eyes, being in torments, and seeth Abraham afar off, and Lazarus in his bosom.

(Luke 16.20-23)

That parable is very well known, regularly read as a Gospel lesson in church, and Abraham's bosom has thereby become a familiar phrase for Heaven. We may laugh a little, that the hostess, while asserting herself so strongly, gets it wrong. Oh well, Abraham, Arthur, they both begin with A, what does it matter?

The Hostess goes on:

> **Hostess.** 'A made a finer end, and went away an it had been any chrissom child.

Now a "chrissom child" is a newly baptized infant. Cleansed by baptism of Original Sin, too young to commit any sins on its own, such a child, if it died, would go straight to Heaven. There is no doubt about salvation here. The Hostess goes on:

> **Hostess.** 'A parted even just between twelve and one, even at the turning of the tide.

We have here two familiar images for death, midnight and the ebb tide. Midnight and the ebb tide occur regularly, naturally. They are not things to be feared. Falstaff's death is made to seem easy and gentle physically as well as spiritually. We are consoled by such a description.

The hostess continues:

> **Hostess.** After I saw him fumble with the sheets, and play with flowers, and smile upon his fingers' end . . .

Falstaff was apparently delirious, hallucinating on his deathbed. The Elizabethans embroidered their sheets with colored thread. Evidently Falstaff was plucking at such colored sheet-borders, perhaps imagining he was in a garden, picking flowers, perhaps the first garden he had played in as a child. Maybe his death wasn't only easy, it was happy. That at least was my thought about that line, until two years ago, when I delivered a public lecture on the subject. The next day I got a message from my doctor, who'd heard the lecture. He told me that plucking at the sheets, or at imaginary things in the air, is a symptom of patients in the later stages of alcoholic liver disease, hepatic encephalopathy.

Shakespeare is clearly drawing on some experience of watching an alcoholic die. And since Falstaff was indeed a heavy drinker, I'm afraid my doctor's tough interpretation of the lines is far more convincing than my earlier sentimental one. Even the Hostess knows that these gestures are a sign of the coming end. Let me give you her full sentence:

> **Hostess.** After I saw him fumble with the sheets, and play with flowers, and smile upon his fingers' end, I knew there

was but one way; for his nose was as sharp as a pen,
and 'a babbled of green fields.

She knew that there was but one way, and the sharp nose is another clear medical sign. Early in the history of medicine, Hippocrates and Galen recorded the apparent sharpening of the nose as a sign of approaching death. The face seems to lose flesh so that the bone structure stands out, an effect also noticeable in cancer patients, and particularly clear when the person has been fat, as Falstaff was. As for the green fields, well, we already know the shakiness of the Hostess's hold on famous Biblical texts, but she really ought to have recognized what Falstaff was saying when he babbled of green fields:

The Lord is my shepherd; I shall not want.

He maketh me to lie down in green pastures:

He leadeth me beside the still waters.

He restoreth my soul:

He leadeth me in the paths of righteousness for His name's sake.

Yea, though I walk through the valley of the shadow of death,

I will fear no evil: for thou art with me;

Thy rod and thy staff they comfort me.

(Psalm 23)

He was trying to pray, to utter the 23rd Psalm, the great psalm of trust and faith in the Lord even at the point of death.

The Hostess continues:

Hostess.	"How now, Sir John," quoth I, "what, man? be o' good cheer." So 'a cried out, "God! God! God!" three or four times.

Now that to me is the most mysterious line in the Hostess' narrative. *How* did Falstaff cry out "God! God! God!"? Was he still humbly praying? Was it a cry of greeting—did he imagine he saw God welcoming him into heaven? Was it a cry of terror, as he saw an angry God, like the Christ of Michelangelo's *Last Judgment*, hurling the sinners down to hell? Any of those three is possible, and we just don't know, since we are getting this account second-hand. Maybe the hostess knew, and her tone of voice in reporting his cry can be relied on, but we know that she's better at facts than at their implications. Indeed, the next thing the Hostess says is really ghastly. In response to Falstaff's cry to God, she says she replied:

Hostess.	Now I, to comfort him, bid him a' should not think of God. I hoped there was no need to trouble himself with any such thoughts yet.

What terrible advice to give a dying man! (She "knew there was but one way.") And Elizabethans would recognize it as especially terrible advice. They were experts on deathbeds. Slight digression here. You can tell much from an age by its favorite self-help books—what topics do people try to master in their lives? The Victorians were concerned with class. Having made their money in industrial fortunes, they wanted to behave as if they were born to it. So their most popular self-help books were books of etiquette: how to behave as if you were born noble, how to give dinner parties and write letters. My generation grew up in the sixties, we were preoccupied with sex. So we made bestsellers of books on the art of intercourse, *The Joy of Sex*, how to achieve the "big 'O.'" Nowadays it's money. In my local bookstore, I see books on investing, how to navigate the shoals of the economy, *Five Ways to Get Rich*.

Well, for Shakespeare's England, it was death. The most important moment of life was the moment of dying, because all eternity depended on it. Dying was a public act, not conducted behind screens in a hospital, but in the family bed, with the family, the friends, and the neighbors gathered round. And there was plenty of printed advice available on how to prepare, how to repent, how to pray, what final temptations to ward off. There was a medieval treatise, the *Ars Moriendi,* that got into print as soon as Gutenberg invented the press and spread all over Europe in vernacular translations. There is the medieval play *Everyman.* Erasmus wrote *A Comfortable Exhortation against the Chances of Death.* Thomas More wrote a dialogue with an almost identical title. Francis Bacon wrote an essay, "On Death." A man named Lupset wrote *A Compendious and Very Fruitful Treatise Teaching the Way of Dying Well.*

The most interesting case is a book known at the time as "Parsons on resolution." The actual title is *A booke of Christian exercise appertaining to resolution, that is, shewing how that we should resolve our selves to become Christians indeed, to live and die well.* It was published in 1582, when Shakespeare was eighteen years old. The author, Robert Parsons, was a Jesuit priest, and naturally the advice contains some matters, such as prayer to saints and instruction on purgatory, things that Catholics accepted but Protestants rejected. But Protestants thought that it was a good book, too. So an Anglican clergyman named Edmund Bunny went over it, cut out the papist parts and put Protestant stuff in those places, and republished it three years later. And over the next twenty years or so, which were the years of Shakespeare's writing career, some fifteen new editions were published, either the Parsons Catholic version or the Bunny Protestant one. People must have been buying this book, or the printers wouldn't have churned out so many editions. And of course, contrary to what the Hostess says to Falstaff, what all these books say is that the dying person should be thinking of God, intently, continuously. When she tells Falstaff not to trouble himself with God, most Elizabethans would be as horrified as we would be if we heard some one advising children to accept rides from strange men. And yet, and yet, we know what the Hostess is doing. She's a kindly woman, and she wants people to be comfortable and happy, so why trouble yourself with ugly thoughts like divine judgment?

There's one more bit of her narrative.

> **Hostess.** 'A bade me lay more clothes on his feet. I put my hand into the bed and felt them, and they were cold as

any stone. Then I felt to his knees, and so upward and
upward, and all was cold as any stone.

Now when I first read this play in college, I had three responses to those
words. The first was a pure gut response. I found it spooky. The idea that the
feet can be so cold, that they are dead, while the mind is still working, and
the mouth can speak—the idea that death creeps so slowly up the body, plain
frightens me.

The second was to think, I've heard something like that before. And indeed I
had. What I had heard, or rather read, was this:

The man who gave him the hemlock now and then looked at his
feet and legs. After a while he pressed his foot hard, and asked if
he could feel. He said, "No." And then his legs, and so upward and
upward, and showed us that he was cold and stiff.

That is Plato, in *The Phaedo*, describing the death of Socrates. And I'm really
not sure what to say about that coincidence. Is it merely a coincidence? Or
did Shakespeare, as he invented the death of Falstaff, happen to think of
Plato's description, remember how effective it is, and just lift it? Or does he
mean something by it? Is there some analogy between the wise old Greek,
whose wisdom so outraged his own city that they killed him, and Falstaff the
jester who could see through the pretenses of the great men of his own time.
I'm afraid I must leave you to ponder on that.

I had a third response. I'm afraid I sniggered. I thought of the Hostess
putting her hand on the flesh of Falstaff's feet, and then upward and upward,
and I giggled. And then I said to myself, come on, Peter, stop being such an
adolescent. This is supposed to be one of the great passages in Shakespeare
and all you can think of is the Hostess's hand on Falstaff's private parts. Grow
up, guy. So I grew up, and I became a Shakespeare scholar, and eventually I
found out that I had been right to snigger. "Cold as any stone"? I found out
that in Elizabethan English, the word "stone" can mean "testicle." It is their
ordinary word for that organ of the body. Holinshed reports that at the battle
of Shrewsbury the earl of Douglas was wounded "in the stones." Of course
it also means "a rock." The Hostess isn't being intentionally obscene, and

the men she's talking to don't respond that way. But most members of the audience would have noticed the accidental obscenity. This moving passage about a beloved character's death ends with a bawdy joke.

The scene continues in dialogue (professor's commentary is in brackets).

Nym.   They say he cried out of sack.

[The dying Falstaff wanted one more mug of the strong wine he was fond of.]

Hostess.   A, that a' did.

Bardolph.   And of women.

Hostess.   Nay, that 'a did not.

[She's upset at that idea, that Falstaff could be asking for more sex while he was dying.]

Boy.   Yes, that 'a did, and said they were devils incarnate.

[Oh, that's okay then, if he was crying out not *for* a woman but *against* women, who had led him into sin... But the Hostess doesn't understand fancy words like "incarnate."]

Hostess.   'A never could abide carnation, 'twas a color he never liked.

Boy.   'A said once the devil would have him about women.

[That is, he would be damned because of his loose sex life. And the Hostess admits:]

Hostess.   'A did in some sort, indeed, handle women, but then he was rheumatic, and talked of the whore of Babylon.

Another unconscious pun from the Hostess, he did *handle* women—Falstaff certainly did, but she means *handle* in the sense of talk about, discuss. At one moment on the deathbed he mentioned the whore of Babylon. Why on earth would he talk about her? Well, it's one more Biblical reference that the Hostess doesn't seem to recognize:

> [And the angel said] unto me,
>
> I will show unto thee the judgment of the great whore that sitteth upon many waters;
>
> With whom the kings of the earth have committed fornication,
>
> And the inhabitants of the earth have been made drunk with the wine of her fornication.
>
> So he carried me away in the spirit into the wilderness:
>
> And I saw a woman sit upon a scarlet-colored beast, full of the names of blasphemy, having seven heads and ten horns
>
> And the woman was arrayed in purple and scarlet color, and
>
> Decked with gold and precious stones and pearls,
>
> Having a golden cup in her hand full of abominations and filthiness of her fornication;
>
> And upon her forehead was a name written, MYSTERY, BABYLON THE GREAT, THE MOTHER OF HARLOTS AND ABOMINATIONS OF THE EARTH.
>
> (Revelation 17.1-5)

That terrifying passage has been used as a text for many sermons, hellfire and damnation sermons, sermons threatening sinners. Falstaff was clearly thinking of his sins, fearing damnation for his drunkenness and fornication.

The Boy has one more line:

Boy.   Do you not remember, he saw a flea stick upon
                  Bardolph's nose, and said it was a black soul burning
                  in hell?

The joke about Bardolph's nose, repeated many times through the Henry plays, is that he too is a heavy drinker, and his nose has turned red with the alcohol. And I love the "Do you not remember...?" It marks a change in tone, a modulation from direct grief into reminiscence. These people have something wonderful to talk about. They can sit around of an evening, chatting like this, saying "Do you remember when he said this?" "Do you remember when he did that? How funny that was! How lucky we were to know such a remarkable man!" A new feeling comes into the scene. They are no longer mourning, but in a mood both happy and sad, a mood we call bittersweet. But even that is emotionally complicated, because the particular joke the Boy recalls is not a purely merry one, it's a joke about damnation. They don't want to think about Falstaff going to Hell, but the possibility does recur.

Let me generalize about all this. What I've been doing here is entering into Shakespeare's imagination. He imagined fully the death of Falstaff. He imagined Falstaff in easy moments of illness, sleeping like "a chrissom child." He imagined Falstaff in hope and prayer, plucking at the sheets ends, hallucinating. He imagined Falstaff feeling his feet go cold. He imagined the Hostess fondling Falstaff's balls. He imagined Falstaff crying out for sack (fortified wine, his favorite drink), crying out for women (or against women—it's hard to be sure). He imagined Falstaff ranting out of the book of Revelation, seeing his fornications embodied in the wine of the scarlet woman.

He imagined a scene that was peaceful, hopeful, bawdy, silly, childish, drunken, lecherous, and terrifying, terrifying both physically and spiritually. All at once, in only forty lines. No single performance can highlight everything, but it is all there. I haven't made any of this up: I've been pointing out where it all lies in Shakespeare's words. Different performances will bring out different aspects of the abundance. And the more we ourselves know the more we can be alert to the abundance as we read him.

This is the point in the course when I lay my cards face up on the table: this man is a genius. He can write anything he wants, on a complex multifaceted scale. He's a genius on the order of Michelangelo, the Michelangelo of the Sistine Chapel ceiling.

What's on the ceiling of the Sistine Chapel? Well, there are three major elements to that vast composition. Going down the center of the vault are nine narrative scenes from Genesis, from God creating light, through Adam and Eve onto Noah and the Flood. On the curve of the vault are twelve large figures, Hebrew prophets and their female classical equivalent, the Sibyls of ancient Rome. And the third principal element is twenty male figures, young nude atlantes, supporting on their shoulders the narrative scenes out of Genesis, turned and twisted in nearly every possible human posture. And what is it all about? Art historians have discussed that at length; I'm asking as an ordinary educated person who has been there, who has asked what does the whole of this amount to? I lay down on the floor of the Chapel and tried to take the whole thing in, tried to find the sense, the emphasis, the organization. And I discovered something very curious. You can read it in at least three ways, and it makes sense in each way.

My first instinct was to go for the narrative. The scenes from Genesis are central. This is a historical epic, it's about an action, God's creation of the world and his first interactions with mankind. In that context, the prophets and sibyls fit in, they *see* these events and convey them to ordinary mortals, and the events are of course physically supported by the male nudes. But, if you shift your focus a little, the prophets and sibyls gain greater prominence. They are in fact larger than the Genesis figures, and closer to us since they are on the curve of the vault. Then the ceiling becomes a composition concerning vision, inspired vision, artistic vision, the sort of ability possessed by mystics and artists to see deeply into the truth and to record what they see.

> **Different performances will bring out different aspects of the abundance.**

The Genesis paintings become part of their context, *what* sages and sibyls and artists can see that they convey to ordinary mortals. And you can shift once again, and focus on the male nudes. They are not larger, but there are so many of them, their powerful arms and backs and legs are at work throughout the whole composition. It becomes a painting about human energy, muscular strength, the windswept exertions of the human race that are the basis for all action and vision in the earthly world. At which point I find it impossible not to think about the sheer physical labor that Michelangelo himself exerted to paint all that, lying on a scaffold. Each reading of the whole composition makes sense, each takes in a major thing that is really there and makes coherent sense with the others.

Shakespeare is like that in his abundance and the complexity of his composition. That is why there can be so many interpretations of his plays. So many good interpretations—I don't mean the crackpot ones where people merely insert their own obsessions. I mean interpretations that stress things genuinely there, because there is so much there, artfully inter-coordinated. What speaks to you at one particular reading, what one actor or director finds, is a genuine resonance with things pouring forth from a spacious plenty. ■

Essential Reading

Shakespeare, *Henry V*.

Supplementary Reading

Film by Kenneth Branagh. Judi Dench is excellent in this scene.

Footnotes on *Henry V*, 2.3, from Gurr (New Cambridge edition) or Taylor (Oxford edition).

Questions to Consider

1. What do you think might have happened, in the audience and to the play, if Shakespeare had decided to put the death of Falstaff on stage instead of having it described at second hand by the Hostess and her friends?

2. Why might Shakespeare have allowed Falstaff to die "with his boots on," as it were, instead of in battle serving his prince or in some other more dramatic or heroic manner?

Henry V—The Death of Falstaff
Lecture 17—Transcript

This is a different sort of lecture from the kind I have been giving. Instead of talking about a big subject, a major character, a theme, a genre, I want to do a close-up on detail. I want to show you the abundance of Shakespeare in a short passage. I will take about 40 lines and show you the richness of their texture, share with you the ways in which Shakespeare can provoke in us, readers and playgoers, a multitude of emotional and intellectual responses. This is what critics call a "close reading." For you to follow it best, it's good to have the passage in front of you. It's printed in your booklet, so you may get it out when you are watching this on video or hearing it on audio (please not if you are at the wheel of a car) and follow along phrase by phrase. Or you can get out an edition of Shakespeare; the passage is in the play *Henry V*, Act II, Scene III, the first 40 lines, when the hostess of the tavern describes to Pistol, Nym, Bardolph and the boy how Falstaff died.

It's a simple passage; I have deliberately *not* chosen a stretch of high-flown verse rich in metaphor and mythological illusion. It is prose; they are down-to-earth characters grieving the death of a dear friend, not rising to royal eulogy, but simply talking about what happened at the deathbed. A youngster could understand the basic sense of these words without explanations, but it is remarkably rich in its effect on an attentive audience.

The premise of the scene does involve some emotional complications. These are comic characters, but at the moment they are sad. The audience will be sad too; particularly, the audience in 1599 that first saw *Henry V*, will be sad and perhaps even surprised. Falstaff has appeared in several plays already. At the Epilogue at the end of *Henry IV Part 1*[sic Part 2], Shakespeare promised that he would come back in the sequel, *Henry V*. Now, he is welching on that promise; he's killing him off instead. Serial characters ought not to die. I'm reminded of an old cartoon of a boy sitting up late at night, reading in bed with an expression of horror on his face; he's just arrived at the death of Sherlock Holmes. Of course, Conan Doyle wasn't allowed to get away with killing Sherlock Holmes; his audience made him go on, write more stories, invent some way to get Holmes out of that waterfall. Why Shakespeare decided to kill Falstaff is a matter open to speculation, but since he did decide to kill him, he had to give him an appropriate send-off. Consider who Falstaff was: an embodiment of tremendous vitality; a man who joked, drank, schemed, fornicated, and saw through the public pretenses of kings and social order; a man witty in himself, and the cause of wit in other men; the greatest drinking buddy in literature that I know. There is great reason to be sad. But the scene is not, in fact wholly sad.

It begins fairy abruptly. Pistol announces, by line 4, "Falstaff, he is dead," and Bardolph responds with the direct simplicity of grief and loyalty, "Would I were with him, wheresome'er he is, either in heaven or in hell!" A moving statement of friendship. But that raises a frightful possibility in the mind of the Hostess. "Nay, sure, he's not in hell: he's in Arthur's bosom, if ever man went to Arthur's bosom." You must remember that in Shakespeare's day, people believed in a literal Hell. If one died unreconciled with God, one would suffer for all eternity, a prospect too horrible for the Hostess to contemplate about the fate of her dear friend; he must be in heaven. But there's a funny twist in her line. Her Biblical reference is wrong; she's made a mistake about the parable of the rich man and Lazarus from the Gospel of Luke. The original text goes like this:

> There was a certain beggar named Lazarus, who was laid at the gate, full of sores, and desiring to be fed with the crumbs that fell from the rich man's table. Moreover the dogs came and licked his sores. And it came to pass that the beggar died, and was carried by the angels into Abraham's bosom. The rich man also died, and was buried; and in Hell he lifted up his eyes, being in torments, and seeth Abraham afar off, and Lazarus in his bosom.

The parable is very well known; it's regularly read as part of church lessons "Abraham's bosom" has become a familiar expression, a synonym for Heaven in the Western culture as a result of that passage. We, therefore, may chuckle a little at the Hostess for getting it wrong, while asserting herself so strongly. Oh well, Abraham, Arthur, they both begin with A, what does it matter?

The Hostess goes on: "'A made a finer end, and went away an it had been any chrissom child." A "chrissom child" is a newly baptized infant. It ha been cleansed by baptism of original sin, but since it is still an infant, it's far too young to have committed any sins of its own. Such a child, if it died, would go straight to Heaven. There is no doubt about salvation here. The Hostess is quite sure of it.

She goes on: "'A parted even just between twelve and one, even at the turning o' th' tide." That's quite lovely; two familiar images for death, midnight and the ebb tide. Midnight and the ebb tide occur regularly, naturally. They're not things to be feared. Falstaff's death is made to seem easy and gentle physically, as well as spiritually, the chrissom child. We are consoled by such a description.

The Hostess goes on: "After I saw him fumble with the sheets, and play with flowers, and smile upon his fingers' end..." Falstaff was apparently delirious on his deathbed, hallucinating. The Elizabethans often decorated their sheets with colored thread, embroidered them, and evidently Falstaff was plucking at that colored embroidery, perhaps imagining he was in a garden. I get that idea because he was playing with flowers. Perhaps in his last moments he'd gone back to his childhood and was remembering the first garden he ever played in as a child. Maybe the death wasn't only easy, it was happy. At least, that was my thought about that line until two years ago. I delivered a public lecture on the death of Falstaff. The next day, I got an e-mail from my doctor, who'd been present at the lecture. He told me that plucking at the sheets, or plucking imaginary things out of the air, is a symptom of patients in the later stages of alcoholic liver disease. It's called hepatic encephalopathy. Shakespeare is clearly drawing on some experience he had had of watching an alcoholic die, and since Falstaff was indeed a heavy drinker, I'm afraid my doctor's tough interpretation of the line is far more convincing than my earlier sentimental one is. Even the Hostess knows that these gestures are a sign of the coming end. Let me give you her full sentence:

> After I saw him fumble with the sheets, and play with flowers, and smile upon his fingers' end, I knew there was but one way; for his nose was as sharp as a pen, and 'a babbl'd of green fields.

She knew there was but one way; he was dying, and the sharp nose is another clear medical sign. Quite early in the history of medicine, Hippocrates and

Galen noticed it, recorded the apparent sharpening of the nose as a sign of approaching death. The face seems to lose flesh so that the bone structure stands out. It's an effect particularly noticeable in cancer patients, and it's particularly clear when the patient has been fat, as Falstaff was. Suddenly the bone's sticking out. As for the green fields—he babbled of green fields— we already know the shakiness of the Hostess' grasp of the Bible, but she really ought to have recognized what Falstaff was saying when he babbled of green fields.

> The Lord is my shepherd; I shall not want.
> He maketh me to lie down in green pastures:
> He leadeth me beside the still waters.
> He restoreth my soul: ...
> Yea, though I walk through the valley of the shadow of death,
> I shall fear no evil, for Thou art with me,
> Thy rod and thy staff, they comfort me.

He was trying to pray, trying to recite the 23rd Psalm, the great Psalm of hope and trust in the Lord, even at the point of death.

The Hostess continues:

> 'How now, Sir John!' quoth I 'What, man, be o' good cheer.' So 'a cried out 'God, God, God!' three or four times.

That I find to be the most mysterious line in the Hostess's account. How did Falstaff cry out "God, God, God"? Was this prayer, continuing the 23rd Psalm, or was it a cry of greeting? Did he imagine he saw God welcoming him into heaven? Or was it a cry of terror? Did he see an angry God, like the Christ in Michelangelo's *Last Judgment*, flinging the sinners down to hell? Any of those three is possible, and we just don't know, since we're getting this story secondhand. Maybe the Hostess knew at the time, and he tone of voice in reproducing Falstaff perhaps can be relied upon. But we know she's better at getting facts than getting implications. Indeed, the next thing the Hostess says is really ghastly. In response to Falstaff's cry to God, she says she replied,

Now I, to comfort him, bid him 'a should not think of God; I hop'd
there was no need to trouble himself with any such thoughts yet.

What terrible advice to give a dying man. She knew he was dying; she knew
there was but one way. The Elizabethans would've recognized it as especially
terrible advice. They were experts on death. A slight digression here: you can
tell a lot about a period, a generation, from the self-help books that they like.
The Victorians were obsessed with class. Having made all that money in
the industrial revolution, they wanted to behave as if they had been born to
it. Their favorite self-help books were the books of etiquette that told them
how to write letters, how to dress properly, how to entertain properly, how
to behave as if they were upper class. My generation came to age in the 60s;
we were obsessed by sex, so we made bestsellers out of all those books on
the art of intercourse, *The Joy of Sex*, how to achieve the big O. Nowadays,
I think it's money. In my local bookstore, I see books on investing: *How To
Manage The Shoals Of The Economy, Five Ways To Get Rich*.

For Shakespeare's England, the favorite subject that people would buy a
book to help them out with was death. The most important moment of life
was the moment of dying, because all eternity depended upon it. Dying was
a public act, not conducted behind screen in hospitals, but in the family bed,
with the family, friends and neighbors assembled to witness it. There was
plenty of printed advice available on how to prepare: how to repent; how to
pray, what final temptations to ward off. There was a medieval treatise called
the *Ars Moriendi*, which got into print as soon as Gutenberg invented the
press and spread all over Europe in the various European languages. There
is the medieval play, *Everyman*. Erasmus wrote *A Comfortable Exhortation
against the Chances of Death*. Thomas More wrote a dialogue with almost
exactly the same title. Francis Bacon wrote an essay on death.

The most interesting case, because it's exactly Shakespeare's time, I
discovered recently. There is a book known as "Parsons On Resolution," at
least that's the way the Elizabethans referred to it. The actual title is *A Book
of Christian Exercise Appertaining to Resolution, thatis, Showing How We
Should Resolve Ourselves to Become Christians Indeed, to Live and Die
Well*, which doesn't strike us as a title that would exactly sell itself off the
rack right away, but this did. It was published first in 1582, when Shakespeare

was 18 years old. The author, Robert Parsons, was a Jesuit priest, and therefore naturally the advice contained some Catholic material, prayers to saints, talk about purgatory, things that Catholics accepted, but Protestants did not. But the Protestants thought it was a good book too. An Anglican clergyman named Edmund Bunny went over it, cut out the Catholic parts, put Protestant stuff in those places and republished it three years later. There was no copyright law to prevent him from doing this. Over the next 20 years or so, which are the years of Shakespeare's active playwriting career, some 15 new editions were published. I went through them in the British Library last summer, either the Parsons Catholic version or the Bunny Protestant version. People must have been buying this book. Publishers don't keep grinding it out that way unless they've got the sales.

Of course, contrary to what the Hostess says to Falstaff, what all these books say is that the dying person should be thinking of God continuously. When she tells Falstaff not to trouble himself with any such thought, most Elizabethans would be horrified, as horrified as you would be if you heard me telling a child, "Accept rides from strange men." Yet we know what the Hostess is doing. She's a nice, kindly woman; she wants people to be happy and comfortable. She doesn't want them to have any disconcerting thoughts about death. Why worry yourself with something ugly like divine judgment? We feel perfectly warm toward her, even when we're horrified by her.

There's one more bit of her narrative: "'A bade me lay more clothes on his feet;"—more bedclothes—"I put my hand into the bed and felt them, and they were cold as any stone; then I felt to his knees, and so upward and upward, and all was cold as any stone."

When I first read this play in college, I had three responses to those words. One was a pure gut response – I found it spooky. The idea that the feet can be cold, can be dead, while the mind is still alive, while the mouth is still speaking, struck me as genuinely scary. The idea that death can creep up the body so slowly just plain frightens me, still does. Another was to think, I've heard something like that before, and indeed I had. What I heard, or rather read, was this:

The man who gave him the hemlock now and then looked at his feet and legs, and after a while he pressed his foot hard and asked if he could feel. He said no, and then his legs, and so upward and upward, and showed us he was cold and stiff.

That is Plato in the dialogue known as the *Phaedo*, describing the death of Socrates, and I'd read it the previous year in a philosophy class. I'm really not sure what to say about that coincidence. Is it merely a coincidence, or did Shakespeare, as he invented the death of Falstaff, happen to think of Plato's description, remember how effective it is, and then just steal it? Or does he mean something by that theft? Is there some analogy between the wise old Greek, whose wisdom so outraged his own city that they killed him, and Falstaff the jester, who could see through the pretensions of the great men of his time? I'm afraid I must leave you to ponder on that.

I had a third response, and actually, chronologically, it was my first response, to the line about the Hostess feeling up from the feet. I'm afraid that I sniggered. I thought of the Hostess putting her hand on the flesh of Falstaff's feet and moving upward and upward and I giggled. Then I said to myself, "Come on, Peter, stop being such an adolescent. This is supposed to be one of the great passages in Shakespeare, and all you can think of is the Hostess's hand going up on to Falstaff's private parts. Grow up." So, I grew up, or tried to, and I became a Shakespeare scholar, and I found out that I had been right to snigger. "Cold as any stone"—I found out that in Elizabethan English, the word "stone" could mean "testicle." It is the ordinary word for that organ of the body. Holinshed, the historian, reports that at the Battle of Shrewsbury, the Earl of Douglas was wounded "in the stones." Of course, it also meant "rock." The Hostess isn't intentionally being obscene, and the men she's talking to do not respond in that way. But most members of audience will have noticed the accidental obscenity. This moving passage about a beloved character's death ends with a bawdy joke.

The scene then continues in dialogue. Nym says, "They say he cried out of sack." That is, the dying Falstaff asked for more liquor on his deathbed, his favorite strong wine. The Hostess agrees, "Ay, that 'a did." Bardolph says, "And of women." But the Hostess is shocked. "Nay, that 'a did not;" upset by the idea that Falstaff could be crying out for more sex on his deathbed, But the boy intervenes. "Yes, that 'a did, and said they were devils incarnate." That's okay then; he was crying out against women, not for women, against women for having led him into temptation.

But the Hostess doesn't understand fancy words like "incarnate": "'A could never abide carnation; 'twas a colour he never liked." And the boy goes on, "'A said once the devil would have him about women." That is he'd go to hell because of his fornications. The Hostess admits, "'A did in some sort ... handle women; but then he was rheumatic, and talk'd of the whore of Babylon." Again, we have a pun from the Hostess, an unconscious one. Falstaff did, indeed, handle women, quite physically, quite frequently. But she means handle in the sense of discuss, talk about, and he talked about women on his deathbed. At one moment, he mentioned the whore of Babylon. Why on earth would he talk about her? It's one more Biblical reference that the Hostess doesn't seem to recognize. I quote from the Book of Revelation:

> [And the angel said] unto me, ...
> I will show unto thee the judgment of the great whore that sitteth upon many waters:
> With whom the kings of the earth have committed fornication, and the inhabitants of the earth have been made drunk with the wine of her fornication.
> So he carried me away in the spirit into the wilderness: and I saw a woman sit upon a scarlet coloured beast, full of names of blasphemy, having seven heads and ten horns.
>
> And the woman was arrayed in purple and scarlet colour, and decked with gold and precious stones and pearls, having a golden cup in her hand full of abominations and filthiness of her fornication:
>
> And upon her forehead was a name written, MYSTERY, BABYLON THE GREAT, THE MOTHER OF HARLOTS AND ABOMINATIONS OF THE EARTH.

That terrifying passage has been used as a text for many sermons, hellfire and damnation sermons. Falstaff was clearly thinking of his sins, fearing damnation for his drunkenness and his fornication.

The boy has one more line, "Do you not remember 'a saw a flea stick upon Bardolph's nose, and 'a said it was a black soul burning in Hell?" I love that "do you not remember." Do you not remember? It's a modulation in tone. We've moved from direct grief for the loss of Falstaff, to a memory of Flastaff. These characters will do this many times, sitting around the fireplace of an evening, saying "Do you remember the time he said this?" Do you remember the time he did that? Weren't we lucky to know such a wonderful person?" It is no longer straight mourning; it is the mood we call bittersweet, where there is grief, but there is also pleasure. He will provide them with other merry evenings just in the remembering of his life. A new feeling comes into the scene, but even that is a complicated feeling, because the particular joke that the boy recalls is not a purely merry one. He saw a black flea on Bardolph's nose, which is bright red, because Bardolph drinks a lot too, and it reminds him of a black soul burning in Hell. They don't want to think about Falstaff going to Hell, but the idea somehow keeps coming back.

Let me generalize about all this. What I've been doing is entering into Shakespeare's imagination. He imagined fully the death of Falstaff. He imagined Falstaff in easy moments of illness, sleeping like a "chrissom child." He imagined Falstaff in hope and in prayer, plucking at the sheet's end, hallucinating. He imagined Falstaff feeling his feet go cold. He imagined the Hostess fondling Falstaff's private parts. He imagined Falstaff crying out for sack, crying out against women. He imagined Falstaff ranting out of the Book of Revelations. He imagined a scene that was peaceful, hopeful, bawdy, silly, childish, drunken, lecherous and terrifying, terrifying both physically and spiritually, and all in less than 40 lines. No single performance could highlight all of that, but it's all there. I haven't made any of this up; I've been pointing out where it is in the words. Different performances will bring out different aspects of this abundance, and the more we ourselves know, the more we can be alert to the abundance as we read the passage.

This is the point where I lay my cards on the table and say this writer is a genius. He can write anything he wants, on a complex, multifaceted scale. He's a genius on the order of Michelangelo, the Michelangelo of the Sistine Chapel ceiling. What's on the ceiling of the Sistine Chapel? There are three major elements to that vast composition. Going down the center of the arc is a series of nine narrative scenes from the Book of Genesis: God creating light, God creating the world, Adam and Eve, the Fall, all the way to Noah's flood. On the curve of the vault on either side are twelve large figures, the ancient Hebrew prophets and their classical equivalents, the Roman Sibyls, female prophets. The third principal element in that ceiling composition is 20 nude young men, and they are supporting the central narrative scenes, the male body twisted at every possible angle. Michelangelo's showing off, saying "I can paint the body this angle, that angle, this perspective, whatever, any way I want." What is all that complication about? I'm not asking as an art historian who has devoted volumes to this subject; I'm asking as an ordinary educated person who has been there, seen it, lay down on the floor and tried to say, "What is this about? What am I supposed to look at? Where's the emphasis?"

I discovered something very curious. You can read that ceiling in at least three ways, and it makes sense each way. My first instinct, of course, was to go for the narrative; the scenes from Genesis are central. This is an historical epic. It's about an action, God's creation of the world, His dealings with mankind. In that context, the prophets and the Sibyls fit in, they see these events and record them, convey them to ordinary people. The events, of course, are physically supported by the male nudes. But if you shift your focus a little, the prophets and the Sibyls gain central prominence. They are, in fact, physically bigger than the figures from Genesis, and they're a little closer to us because they're on the curve of the vault. Then the ceiling becomes a composition concerning vision, artistic vision, spiritual vision, the sort of ability possessed by mystics, saints, and artists, to see deeply into the truth and then embody it in a form that can reach less gifted people. The Genesis paintings become part of their context; they become what is seen by a prophet or a Sibyl. You can shift once again and focus on the male nudes. They're not larger, but there are so many of them that their powerful arms, backs and legs are at work through the whole composition. It becomes a painting about human strength: muscular energy, the windswept exertions of the human race that are the basis for all action and vision in the world.

Shakespeare is like this in his abundance and the complexity of his composition. This is why there can be so many interpretations of his plays. I don't mean the crackpot ones where people put in their own obsessions. I mean interpretations that stress things genuinely there, artfully inter-coordinated, what speaks to you at one particular reading, what one actor or director finds is a genuine resonance with some of the things pouring forth from a spacious plenty.

Henry V—The King Victorious
Lecture 18

> Since 1920 ... both directors in the theater and scholars in the academy have had deep misgivings about this play. They have regularly seen it, as it were, with bifocals. Long range, it is a play celebrating a heroic king who inspires his country to an outstanding victory. Close up, it is not celebratory, but satiric; it exposes the brutality of war and the connivance of politicians who resort to war to achieve their own self-serving purposes.

Twentieth-century response to *Henry V* has been double-sided. It can be seen as celebratory and patriotic. It can also be seen as critical and satiric exposure. This doubleness has been clear in times of public debate over particular wars. Vietnam influenced Michael Kahn's direction of a savage presentation of *Henry V* at Stratford, Connecticut, in 1969. The Falklands war and conflict in northern Ireland influenced Kenneth Branagh's film version in 1989, which vividly illustrated the human costs of war.

The play supports both readings. The vigorous Choruses that open each act celebrate the king and his enterprise, and the Agincourt victory is highlighted as an epic achievement. On the other hand, the play highlights the ugly and costly side of war. Henry is urged by self-interested churchmen to wage war on France. While in northern France, Henry consents to the execution of his old tavern crony, Bardolph. During the battle, he ruthlessly orders the slaughter of French prisoners who have surrendered. A common soldier offers a very inglorious and unchivalric account of death in battle.

Dualism neglects the variety of experience in the play. There are many different kinds of soldiers in the play:

- Henry speaks of a rampaging slaughterer and rapist.

- Henry evokes the heroism of ancestral warriors.

- Soldiers are knights bound in brotherhood.

- A soldier may be a pedant.

- A soldier may be afraid.

- A soldier may be eager for battle.

- A soldier may be an athlete.

- A soldier may be a beast.

- A soldier may be a fake.

Henry himself plays many roles. He is an able politician and diplomat, as shown in his message to the French ambassadors in response to the Dauphin's insult. He dispenses justice (as shown in his consent to the execution of Bardolph) and mercy (as shown in his pardon of a man who has slandered him). He is a warrior and leader of men. He is a lover. While wooing the French princess, he graciously pretends to be a rube in order to put her at ease.

Henry both sees that kingship is a fiction and uses it well.

Henry both sees that kingship is a fiction and uses it well. He deconstructs kingship into a set of stage props, as illustrated in his soliloquy on Ceremony the night before the battle of Agincourt. He realizes that kingship is a fiction, with nothing real about it except the responsibility. He reconstructs kingship by asserting his mastery of the props. ■

Essential Reading

Saccio, *Shakespeare's English Kings,* chapter 4.

Shakespeare, *Henry V.*

Film of *Henry V* by Kenneth Branagh or by Laurence Olivier.

Introduction to *Henry V*, Gurr (New Cambridge edition) or Taylor (Oxford edition).

Loehlin, *Henry V: Shakespeare in Performance.*

Rabkin, "Rabbits, Ducks, and *Henry V*."

Questions to Consider

1. Consider each of Henry's major public speeches. What role is he playing in each one? By what means? For what audience? To what end?

2. Compare Henry to any modern political leader you know well. Compare the Olivier film with the Branagh film: cuts, decisions on how to play particular scenes, use of comedy, lighting, means of filming the battle, placement of climax, etc.

Henry V—The King Victorious
Lecture 18—Transcript

Henry V is a play with an elementary structure. King Henry declares war upon the French in Act I; he wins it at the Battle of Agincourt in Act IV. He reaps the fruits of victory in Act V, a treaty with the French that makes him heir to the French crown and gives him the hand of the French princess in marriage. The victory at Agincourt, against extraordinary odds and with very few casualties on Henry's own side, made him England's great hero king of the later Middle Ages, remembered as such in Shakespeare's time and to the present. His triumph is the object at which the whole tetraology of Lancastrian history plays aim. Richard II had been a legitimate king, but incompetent. Henry IV had been highly competent, but a usurper, and therefore always vulnerable. Henry V is legitimate, at least to the extent of having inherited the crown from his father, and he's very able indeed.

Since 1920, however, both directors in the theater and scholars in the academy have had deep misgivings about this play. They have regularly seen it, as it were, with bifocals. Long range, it is a play celebrating a heroic king who inspires his country to an outstanding victory. Close up, it is not celebratory, but satiric; it exposes the brutality of war and the connivance of politicians who resort to war to achieve their own self-serving purposes. This doubleness of the play is now the orthodox opinion. In 1972, a scholarly review of a production at Stratford laid it down as an axiom. That there have always been two sides to *Henry V* is surely obvious, for in it, the pro-war and anti-war feeling are both perfectly explicit. In 1997, a Dartmouth colleague of mine, James Loehlin, published an excellent stage history of the play in the twentieth century. He structured his discussion around the two poles that he called the official play, which is patriotic, heroic, and celebratory—the secret play, which is critical and subversive. Possibly those most influential academic essay on the play, the one most frequently reprinted, most influential on college teaching, is by Norman Rabkin. It's called *Rabbits, Ducks, and Henry V*. Rabkin compared the play to a well-known optical illusion, a cartoon which can be perceived either as a rabbit or as a duck, depending on how you focus on it. You just can't see both simultaneously.

Actually, it has not always been obvious that the play has two sides. Before the twentieth century, the play was regularly performed as a straightforward patriotic celebration. It was produced with great lavishness on occasions of national rejoicing in England. A few people disliked it, most notably at the beginning of the nineteenth century, the Romantic critic William Hazlitt, and at the end of the nineteenth century, the Irish playwright George Bernard Shaw. But they did not reinterpret Shakespeare's text; they just condemned Shakespeare for having written a jingoistic piece celebrating an empty headed warmonger.

The effort to reinterpret the text, to claim that it is secretly satiric, came significantly in 1919, immediately after World War I, when an Englishman who had, in fact, fought in that war, published an essay claiming Shakespeare had written an ironic exposure of the brutalities of war; and once this view was born, it did not long remain a secret. During and after controversial wars in our century, this take on the play has been expressed with particular fervor. In 1969, in America, as the protests against American involvement in Vietnam boiled through our politics, Michael Kahn directed a savage presentation of the play at Stratford, Connecticut. In 1989, influenced by Britain's engagement in the Falklands, and by his own childhood in Northern Ireland, Kenneth Branagh created a film version of *Henry V* that quite vividly exposes the costs of war.

Sometimes this interpretation is tinged with class prejudice. People speak of the play as if Shakespeare wrote the patriotism for the commoners; the more sophisticated, upper-class people would see the satire. The play does offer a good deal that will support this kind of bipolar or binary interpretation. On the one hand, there are vigorous choruses opening each act, celebrating the king and his enterprise. There is a clear climactic structure that I've already mentioned, focusing on victory at Agincourt, an epic achievement. When two noblemen die in battle, they are given a glowing epitaph: "In this glorious and well-foughten land / We kept together of our chivalry." On the other hand, Henry is urged into war by bishops whose chief aim is to protect ecclesiastical endowments. There's an odd lurch between the opening chorus and the first scene that follows. The opening chorus gets the audience all excited with talk of war between "two mighty monarchies [with] high upreared and abutting fronts." The next thing that happens is, we see not two mighty monarchies, but those two bishops, and they talk, not of saving souls, but saving money. As his army crosses northern France, Henry consents to the execution of one of his old tavern cronies, Bardolph, without acknowledging that he ever knew the man. If earls and dukes fall gloriously on a field well foughten in chivalry, a common soldier gives us an account in battle that is most inglorious and unchivalric:

> All those legs and arms and heads, chopp'd off in a battle, shall join together at the latter day and cry all 'We died at such a place;'some swearing, some crying for a surgeon, some upon their wives left poor behind them, some upon the debts they owe, some upon their children rawly left. I am afeard there are few die well that die in a battle.

All these things are there. One is repeatedly invited into heroic patriotism and then disturbed by the realities of warfare. To see the play as a kind of rabbit/duck, to argue that it is fundamentally binary in its effect, is by no means a stupid idea.

There are problems, however, with this dualistic interpretation. It is not as if the Shakespeare I know offers us the simplicities of political rhetoric, to say that there are only two sides here, black and white, pro-war and anti-war. Outside the moralism of agitprop theater, dualism is rarely appropriate to stage experience. A rabbit/duck is an intellectual puzzle, a static construction. There are no rabbit/ducks in theatrical prop rooms. When we watch a play, moreover, we're not building a case for or against a character or an event. We hear and see many words, many tones, and many actions. If there are poles, they're not isolated; they are connected by a dense web of abundant possibilities.

In the play of *Henry V*, soldiery provides one such spectrum of human possibility. Soldiers come in all shapes and sizes. When King Henry wishes to frighten the governor of Harleur into surrender, he describes "the flesh'd soldier, rough and hard of heart, / With conscience wide as hell, mowing like grass / Your fresh fair virgins and your flow'ring infants." This blind and bloody sadist will rape maidens, impale children, and smash the white heads of old men against walls. Such a soldier does not actually appear onstage in the play, but Henry, at that moment, is pretending to be such a soldier, and is therefore creating the image of such a soldier in the mind of the governor in order to get him to submit. Henry also evokes soldiers whose energy derives from a valiant and tireless past: "You noblest English, / Whose blood is fet from fathers of war-proof! /Fathers that, like so many Alexanders, / Have in these parts from morn till even fought." Have in these parts from morn till even fought—that last phrase, oddly, makes mortal combat sound like a rather pleasant way to spend a summer afternoon, if you're so inclined.

Soldiers are also knights. The distinguishing characteristic of knights are two: they desire honor, and they maintain a brotherhood that recognizes and confers honor.

> But if it be a sin to covet honour,
> I am the most offending soul alive.
> No, faith, my coz, wish not a man from England. ...
> We would not die in that man's company
> That fears his fellowship to die with us. ...
> We few, we happy few, we band of brothers;
> For he to-day that sheds his blood with me
> Shall be my brother. ...

This sort of soldier comes in a group, a roundtable, an Order of the Garter, but a soldier can also be a peasant. The Welsh captain Fluellen is one such; he's read all the ancient and modern accounts of warfare and insists on the precise way of doing things: "Look you, the mines is not according to the disciplines of the war; the concavities is not sufficient." A soldier may fear the approaching combat: "We see yonder the beginning of the day, but I think we shall never see the end." Or, he may be eager for it: "The Dauphin longs for morning." He longs to eat the English. A charismatic king may describe the soldiers as trim, eager athletes: "I see you stand like greyhounds in the slips, / Straining upon the start." But a captain in the trenches may revise that image in grittier words: "Up to the breach, you dogs!" A soldier may also be a boastful coward: "For Pistol, he hath a killing tongue and a quiet sword; by means whereof 'a breaks words and keeps whole weapons."

In the previous lecture, I talked about the variety of emotions evoked by the death of Falstaff. Such a range of possibilities is not unique to that one scene of the play. It pervades *Henry V*. All sorts and conditions of men become soldiers, so we have all sorts and conditions of soldiers. The variety is most manifest in the king himself. He is a hero and a conniving politician, and he is a lot of things in between. Most of all, Henry V, the grown Prince Hal, is a role player. He knows there's really no such thing as a king, only a man doing a king's job, playing the roles required of a king. So, he is a politician, particularly when dealing with other people who have their own axes to grind, like the bishops.

He is also a diplomat; he is very polite to the French ambassadors in the first act, and when they insult him with the tennis balls, he tells them exactly where they get off. The tennis balls are meant to suggest that Henry is merely a young playboy; that's the Dauphin's intention in sending them. A young playboy, not a king at all. Henry seizes them as an opportunity to assert his own vigor, strength and control of his affairs.

> We are glad the Dauphin is so pleasant with us;
> His present and your pains we thank you for.
> When we have match'd our rackets to these balls,
> We will in France, by God's grace, play a set
> Shall strike his father's crown into the hazard.
> Tell him he hath made a match with such a wrangler
> That all the courts of France will be disturb'd
> With chaces.

Rackets and balls are literal here, but he continues the tennis language. He will play a set, he hath made a match, the courts of France are both tennis courts and royal courts, and a chace is not only the pursuit of a fleeing enemy, it is also a double bounce in a tennis game, by which you lose the point. Henry has, in effect, seized the Dauphin's serve and smashed it right back at him. Henry continues:

> Tell the Dauphin I will keep my state,
> Be like a king, and show my sail of greatness,
> When I do rouse me in my throne of France; ...

> I will rise there with so full a glory
> That I will dazzle all the eyes of France,
> Yea, strike the Dauphin blind to look on us.

Note that he switched there from "I" to the royal plural "us":

> And tell the pleasant Prince this mock of his
> Hath turn'd his balls to gun-stones, and his soul
> Shall stand sore charged for the wasteful vengeance
> That shall fly with them; for many a thousand widows
> Shall this his mock mock out of their dear husbands;
> Mock mothers from their sons, mock castles down;
> And some are yet ungotten and unborn
> That shall have cause to mock the Dauphin's scorn.

This is in part a propaganda stunt, the Shakespearean equivalent of a good sound-bite, a quick answer. The English have already decided, for their own reasons, to invade France before the Dauphin's tennis balls even arrive at the English court, but the tennis balls give Henry an opportunity to place the principal blames for the war on the Dauphin. Henry is also converting his old playboy image into something truly threatening; a sportsman of real skill and determination, who can seize the enemy's weapon and use it against him. "If you think I'm a player, Dauphin, at least I'm a player-king." He does do with remarkable resourcefulness, sticking throughout to the language the Dauphin had meant as an insult, the tennis language. Mock, mock, mock, mock... that's the sound of a tennis game as the ball goes back and forth across the court. It's the sound of a tennis game, but it has turned deadly.

The king is also a dispenser of justice, executing the traitors who had plotted against him, and agreeing to the execution of Bardolph. It really is unpleasant to hang an old friend, to be sure. Bardolph has pillaged a French church. Henry has explicitly forbidden despoiling the French; he wants to rule the French peacefully; he claims France as his own. He doesn't want a population seething in resentment, Therefore, he uses Bardolph's theft as a way of making his point to the rest of the soldiers. It's very hardheaded, but it's not purposeless. Henry can also dispense mercy. He pardons a man who had slandered him, saying merely that the wretch must have been drunk.

Henry is, of course, a warrior, above all, a leader of men, and an oratorical wizard who can call forth the best from his army. He can project an imaginative vision of a band of brothers, a vision that can stir the soul, a vision that can ennoble our relations with one another and lift ordinary people to extraordinary effort when the need is upon them. He is also a lover, and he woos the princess at the end of the play. There I find him truly gracious. He pretends to be a country rube, who lacks the rhetoric of courtship; "you'd think I was such a plain king, I'd sold my farm to buy my crown." It's a very pleasant little scene; we enjoy it enormously. It is only when we come to think about it afterwards, we realize this is absurd. Henry has demonstrated one kind of eloquence after another through four and one half acts. Surely, he ought to be able to speak to a woman too. But his role-playing here is a deliberate attempt to make Katharine more comfortable, and to make himself more comfortable in a tight situation. This is a diplomatic marriage; there's no personal choice involved. For political reasons, the king of England must marry the Princess of France, whether the two care about each other or not. This is the seal on the victory, and they both know it; that's why she's been learning English. Henry's little act of behaving like a bumpkin creates a friendly atmosphere; the country rube he plays is extremely likable. He's so charming, they can get along easily with each other. It creates a relaxed atmosphere for them as people, within the framework of political necessity.

All these are roles that Henry plays. As the death of Falstaff provokes a prism of emotional possibilities, Henry is a multifaceted prism of kingship, the facets being displayed, discarded and recombined across the many scenes of the play. The final and most important point I must make about Henry's roles is that he knows they are roles. We see him confront that, confront the necessities that his position inflicts upon him in his one soliloquy. This is the speech on ceremony, the night before the Battle of Agincourt:

> What infinite heart's-ease
> Must kings neglect, that private men enjoy!
> And what have kings that privates have not too,
> Save ceremony, save general ceremony?
> And what art thou, thou idle ceremony?
> What kind of god art thou, that suffer'st more
> Of mortal griefs than do thy worshippers?

What are thy rents? What are thy comings in?
O ceremony, show me but thy worth!
What is thy soul of admiration?
Art thou aught else but place, degree, and form,
Creating awe and fear in other men?
Wherein thou art less happy being fear'd
Than they in fearing.
What drink'st thou oft, instead of homage sweet,
But poison'd flattery? O, be sick, great greatness,
And bid thy ceremony give thee cure!
Think'st thou the fiery fever will go out
With titles blown from adulation?
Will it give place to flexure and low bending?
Canst thou, when thou command'st the beggar's knee,
Command the health of it? No, thou proud dream,
That play'st so subtly with a king's repose.
I am a king that find thee; and I know
'Tis not the balm, the sceptre, and the ball,
The sword, the mace, the crown imperial,
The intertissued robe of gold and pearl,
The farced title running 'fore the king,
The throne he sits on, nor the tide of pomp
That beats upon the high shore of the world,
No, not all these, thrice-gorgeous ceremony,
Not all these, laid in bed majestical,
Can sleep so soundly as the wretched slave,
Who, with a body cramm'd and vacant mind,
Gets him to rest, fill'd with distressful bread…"

That speech deconstructs kingship. The only thing that differentiates kings from other people is the ceremony surrounding them. But the word "ceremony" is repeated in the speech with increasing irony, until it becomes meaningless. Titles and homage may cause awe and fear in other men, but they do not bring happiness or heart's ease to the king. Ceremony cannot cure sickness, in the king or in the subject. In fact, ceremony is simply a set of theatrical props: the scepter; the sword; the robe. Somebody pulls them out of a trunk back there and puts them on the king the day they march him into

Westminster Abbey, then they pack all those pretty little things away, and they tell the man to stand nightwatch alone, while everyone else is asleep. Kingship is a fiction, with nothing real about it except the responsibility. That's real; the king will get the blame when something major goes wrong.

Buried in the middle of that demolition, however, there is something else—a statement of identity: "I am a king that find thee; and I know." When you read Shakespeare, stay alert for simple sentences that being with the phrase "I am," particularly when they're uttered by the protagonist of the play. They are crucial, the moment of recognition, the moment of self-awareness, sometimes called by Aristotle's term *anagnorisis*, the moment when the major character makes a statement about what he or she is. I will come back to this kind of thing later in the course, when I handle the tragedies, using examples like King Lear late in his play, saying to his beloved Cordelia, "I am a very foolish, fond old man." That is, I am just an aged human being— no more insistence on rank, royalty, or even the authority of a father.

Henry V has that sort of self-recognition here. "I am a king that find thee, and I know." Despite the emptiness of ceremony, despite the fact that there really is no such thing as a king, only a man doing a king's job, bearing the king's responsibility, "I am a king." I am a king because I know. I am a king because I know how false it all is. I know that being king is a fiction, and I know how to make the fiction work. I know how to make the fiction do the work it must do in the world. That's what kingship really is, that knowledge.

There is one more thing I must point out about this speech. There is not only the deconstruction of kingship and ceremony, and the statement of personal identity. There is also the third step. There is a reassertion. Most deconstructionists merely clear the ground; Henry, and William Shakespeare, not only clear the ground, but they build on the vacant space. Listen once again to a chunk of this ceremony soliloquy. Hear the rhythm of the lines when Henry starts listing the accoutrements of the king:

> 'Tis not the balm, the sceptre, and the ball,
> The sword, the mace, the crown imperial,
> The intertissued robe of gold and pearl,
> The farced title running 'fore the king,

> The throne he sits on, nor the tide of pomp
> That beats upon the high shore of the world."

That's rather wonderful, especially that last dozen words, "the tide of pomp / That beats upon the high shore of the world." That is a striking image of majesty and power. In the process of deconstructing kingship, Henry reconstructs it in the crescendo of those lines. I can't ask for anything more majestic, anything more charismatic than that. There is no such thing as a king. "I am a king that find thee, and I know." Most of Shakespeare's kings are weak, like Richard II, or they're wicked, like Richard III, or they hang on by the skin of their crafty teeth, like Henry IV. Of all Shakespeare's kings, Henry V can most falsely and most truly say, "I am a king."

Chart of Shakespeare's Plays

This chart suggests the general course of Shakespeare's career as a playwright by listing all his plays vertically according to genre and horizontally according to date of probable first performance. In many cases the dates given arise from limited evidence that scholars interpret in different ways.

Date	Comedies	Histories	Tragedies	Romances
1589–1593	The Two Gentlemen of Verona The Comedy of Errors The Taming of the Shrew	Henry VI Part 1 Henry VI Part 2 Henry VI Part 3 Richard III	Titus Andronicus	
1594–1596	Love's Labor's Lost A Midsummer Night's Dream	King John Richard II	Romeo and Juliet	
1596–1598	The Merchant of Venice The Merry Wives of Windsor Much Ado about Nothing	Henry IV Part 1 Henry IV Part 2		
1599	As You Like It	Henry V	Julius Caesar	
1600			Hamlet	
1601	Twelfth Night			
1602			Troilus and Cressida	
1603	All's Well That Ends Well			
1604	Measure for Measure		Othello	
1606			Macbeth	

Date	Comedies	Histories	Tragedies	Romances
1607			Antony and Cleopatra	Pericles
1608			Coriolanus	
1609			Timon of Athens	Cymbeline
1610				The Winter's Tale
1611–1613		Henry VIII		The Tempest
				The Two Noble Kinsmen

Other plays in which Shakespeare appears to have had a hand include:

- *Edward III*, a history performed before 1595 and printed in 1596 some scenes probably by Shakespeare.

- *Love's Labor's Won*, a comedy by Shakespeare with this title is mentioned in a book published in 1598 and printed before 1603. No copy is now known. Possibly it is one of the comedies listed above with an alternative title.

- *Sir Thomas More*, a history surviving in manuscript, to which Shakespeare contributed some scenes, perhaps around 1604.

- *Cardenio*, apparently a collaboration with Fletcher based on Cervantes, performed around 1613, never printed, now lost.

Timeline

Major Events in Politics, the Theater, and Shakespeare's Life

(See the Chart of Shakespeare's Plays for probable dates of individual plays.)

1509–1547......................................Reign of Henry VIII. He presides over the English Reformation, severing England from the Church of Rome. He begets three children who survive him, one each by the first three of his six wives. Small troupes of players tour the country.

1547–1553......................................Reign of Henry's son Edward VI. *The Book of Common Prayer* establishes an English liturgy for the Church of England.

1553–1558......................................Reign of Henry's elder daughter, Mary I (Bloody Mary). A Catholic, she restores England to Roman obedience. She marries Philip of Spain but dies childless.

1558...Accession of Henry's younger daughter, Elizabeth I. In the first years of her reign, the Protestant (Anglican) church is re-established by the Act of Supremacy (Elizabeth declared to be "Supreme Governor of the Church in England") and the Act of Uniformity (church attendance required upon pain of fines). *The Book of Common Prayer* is revised and republished. English translations of the Bible become standard: the Bishop's Bible for church use and the Geneva Bible for private reading. William Cecil (later Lord Burghley) serves as Elizabeth's chief secretary.

1560s .... Theatrical companies named after their patron lords begin regularly playing at nonce sites in London, as well as touring the country and playing at Court when asked. A purpose-built theater called the Red Lion is built in the London suburb of Stepney (it appears not to have lasted long).

1564 .... William Shakespeare born in the market town of Stratford-upon-Avon, Warwickshire, son to glover John Shakespeare and his wife, Mary Arden Shakespeare.

1568 .... Elizabeth's cousin, Mary Queen of Scots, having misruled Scotland since 1561 and having been forced to abdicate in favor of her infant son James VI, flees to England. She is kept confined in various castles, but by letter repeatedly conspires with various English and continental Catholics to take Elizabeth's crown.

1569–1570 .... Elizabeth puts down northern rebellion in favor of Mary Queen of Scots. Pope Pius V proclaims Elizabeth excommunicated and deposed.

1570s	Two outdoor amphitheaters are built for playing in the northern outskirts of London, The Theatre and The Curtain. Over the next four decades some seven other large theaters are built in the northern outskirts and on the south bank of the Thames River, but usually only two or three are in operation at any given time. Two small indoor theaters within London are used by companies consisting of choirboys.
1577	Francis Drake sets sail around the world (returns and is knighted in 1580). Raphael Holinshed publishes the first edition of *Chronicles of England, Scotland, and Ireland.*
1579	Thomas North publishes his English version of Plutarch's *Lives,* the major source for Shakespeare's plays on Roman subjects.
1582	Shakespeare (aged eighteen) marries Anne Hathaway (aged twenty-six).
1583	Susanna, Shakespeare's elder daughter, born. The Queen's Men are established with the celebrated comic actor Richard Tarlton. They become the leading company in London and on tour for the decade.
1585	Hamnet and Judith, Shakespeare's twin son and daughter, born. Failed attempt to establish an English colony at Roanoke.

Later 1580s.................................... The Elizabethan drama becomes
a significant literary as well as
commercial activity with the plays
of Christopher Marlowe, John Lyly,
Thomas Kyd, and Robert Greene.
Sometime at the end of this decade,
Shakespeare starts acting and writing.

1587... Mary Queen of Scots beheaded for
complicity in plots against Elizabeth.
Second edition of Holinshed's
Chronicles, a major source for
Shakespeare's plays on English history
and for *King Lear, Macbeth,*
and *Cymbeline.*

1588... With the backing of Pope Sixtus V,
Philip II of Spain sends the Spanish
Armada against England. It is defeated
and dispersed by English ships and
English weather.

1590... Edmund Spenser published the first
three books of *The Faerie Queene,* the
great Elizabethan epic poem (remainder
published in 1596).

1592... Earliest surviving reference to
Shakespeare as an actor and playwright
(a sneering allusion by Robert Greene,
including a line parodied from *3 Henry
VI*) and the earliest surviving account
of a performance of a Shakespeare play
(an enthusiastic description by Thomas
Nashe of the audience's emotional
response to *1 Henry VI*).

1593–1594....................................Marlowe killed in a tavern brawl.
A severe outbreak of plague keeps
the London theaters closed for some
eighteen months. Theater companies
are disrupted. Shakespeare turns to
writing narrative poetry, publishing
Venus and Adonis and *The Rape of
Lucrece.* When the playhouses reopen,
all playing in London is in the hands of
two newly consolidated companies: the
Lord Admiral's Men at the Rose, with
Edward Alleyn as their leading actor
and Marlowe's plays in their repertoire,
and the Lord Chamberlain's Men at
the Theatre, with Richard Burbage as
leading actor, Will Kemp as leading
comic, and Shakespeare as
chief playwright.

1596...Shakespeare secures the grant of a
coat of arms for his father, giving the
family the right to describe themselves
as gentlemen, members of the gentry
class. Shakespeare's son Hamnet dies
at age eleven. Ben Jonson's career
as a playwright begins. Robert Cecil
becomes Secretary of State as his father,
Burghley, moves toward retirement.

1597...Shakespeare buys New Place, a large
house in Stratford. The owner of
the Shoreditch land upon which the
Theatre stands refuses to renew the
lease and attempts to take over the
building, which is owned by Richard
Burbage and his brother. The Lord
Chamberlain's Men play at the Curtain.

1599... The Lord Chamberlain's Men tear down
the Theatre and use its timbers to build
the Globe Theater on the south bank of
the Thames. They play there until 1642.

1601... The earl of Essex, Elizabeth's last
favorite, rebels against her and is
executed. Shakespeare's father dies.

1603... Death of Elizabeth I, accession of
James I (James VI of Scotland). In
the subsequent reshuffling of Court
patronage, the Lord Chamberlain's Men
become the King's Men, by which name
they are known for the rest of
their career.

1604... James I concludes peace with Spain
(England has been technically and
often actually at war with Spain since
the Armada). At the Hampton Court
Conference, James commands a new
English translation of the Bible.

1605... Francis Bacon publishes *The
Advancement of Learning.* Gunpowder
Plot to blow up the royal family, and
parliament (Guy Fawkes being one of
the conspirators) is discovered.

1606... Francis Beaumont and John Fletcher
begin their career as playwrights.

1607... Captain John Smith settles Jamestown.
Shakespeare's daughter Susanna marries
John Hall, physician of Stratford.

1608 .... Shakespeare's mother dies.
Shakespeare's granddaughter, Elizabeth
Hall, born (dies 1670, his last
surviving descendant).

1609 .... The King's Men, having taken over the
indoor theater in the Blackfriars district
formerly used by boy companies, use
it for their winter performances, while
continuing at the Globe in the summers.
Several other small roofed theaters
within London come into regular use
in the following decades, eventually
becoming more important than the
large amphitheaters in the suburbs.
Shakespeare's *Sonnets* published,
apparently without his cooperation.

1611 .... The King James Version of the Bible is
published, and gradually becomes the
standard English translation.

1612 .... About this time Shakespeare retires to
Stratford. He appears to have written
several of his last plays in collaboration
with Fletcher, who then takes over as
principal playwright for the King's Men.

1613 .... The Globe theater burns down during
a performance of Shakespeare's and
Fletcher's *Henry VIII*. It is rebuilt and
reopens the next year.

1616 .... Shakespeare's daughter Judith marries
Thomas Quiney, a Stratford vintner.
Shakespeare dies at Stratford. Ben
Jonson publishes his poems and plays in

folio format under the title of *Works,* the first time such lavish publication had been given to contemporary stage-plays in England.

1618 .... Thirty Years War starts in Europe.

1620 .... English Pilgrims settle on the coast of Massachusetts.

1623 .... Death of Anne Hathaway Shakespeare. Two of Shakespeare's fellow actors, John Hemings and Henry Condell, publish in folio format *Mr. William Shakespeare's Comedies, Histories, and Tragedies* (now called by scholars the First Folio). The volume contains thirty-six plays, of which eighteen had previously been available in cheap quarto format, and eighteen had been unpublished. Not included are some plays now thought to have been at least partly written by Shakespeare.

1625 .... Death of James I, accession of his son Charles I.

1642 .... Parliament passes an act forbidding all playacting in England and closing the theaters. The theater companies dissolve.

1649 .... Charles I is executed after losing a civil war to parliamentary forces led by the Puritan Oliver Cromwell and being tried for treason against his own people. The monarchy is abolished and England declared a Commonwealth.

1660... Within two years of Cromwell's death, the monarchy is restored in the person of Charles I's son, Charles II. Theater is once again allowed in England. By this time, all the playhouses established in the 1560–1642 period have been demolished or adapted to other purposes. Some of the plays of Shakespeare, Jonson, and Beaumont and Fletcher are revived in new theaters.

1700–1800...................................... Shakespeare's plays continue in production, often in adapted versions suited to the changing tastes of the times. He comes to be regarded as the greatest of English playwrights; actors become famous for their performances in his major roles. The plays begin to receive scholarly editions and commentary.

Glossary

action: used in these lectures in three related but differing senses. (1) Any physical movement on stage: entrances, duels, kissing, falling to the ground, crossing the stage. (2) The collective ongoing movement of the play, including not only physical movement but also dialogue, display of emotion, etc.; the movement of the story as a whole. (3) What a play is "about," usually put in a summary phrase; the action of *Richard II* is the fall of a king, the action of *The Taming of the Shrew* is named in its title, the action of *King Lear* might be described as Lear's self-discovery.

amphitheatres: also called "public theaters," large polygonal buildings in the suburbs of London, the playing-spaces of theater companies starting in the 1560s (see **hall theatres**). The audience stood in an unroofed yard around a large stage projecting from one wall, or sat in three stories of galleries surrounding the yard. Performances took place in the afternoon by natural light. Elizabethan accounts refer to their capacity as 2,000 or 3,000 people. The foundations of two, the Rose and the Globe, have been recently discovered. A full-size replica of the Globe has been built near its original site on the south bank of the Thames and now produces Shakespeare and other Elizabethan playwrights from May to September.

anagnorisis: (Gk: "disclosure," "recognition") the sudden revelation of important information, such as the real identity of a disguised character. In discussion of tragedy, it has come to be used especially for the protagonist's recognition of his faults, or of his real nature and position.

anti-Stratfordian: a person who believes that the plays performed and printed as William Shakespeare's were written by someone else and passed off under Shakespeare's name in a conspiracy to protect the identity of the real author. Anti-Stratfordians have proposed many different candidates for the authorship, most frequently Francis Bacon, Christopher Marlowe, and the earl of Oxford.

catharsis: the purgation of emotions. Aristotle considered the aim of tragedy to be the purgation of the emotions of pity and fear. The precise meaning of his brief statement has been disputed.

chorus: in Greek drama, twelve or fifteen characters stood aside (largely) from the action and commented on it in choral lyrics to which they danced. In Elizabethan drama, a chorus is one person, speaking as representative of the acting company, usually presenting a prologue, epilogue, and other extra-dramatic speeches to frame the action.

climax: a moment in a play or a scene in which emotional tension or interest is at its highest, usually marking a turn in events.

company: a group of actors working together to put on plays. The Lord Chamberlain's Men were a legally chartered company consisting of six or eight sharers (the senior members who put up the money, organized the productions, paid playwrights and others for their work, played the leading roles, and took whatever profits there were), hired men (who for wages played minor parts and worked as theater functionaries), and several boys (apprenticed to senior members, playing the roles of women and children). There were also Elizabethan companies consisting entirely of boys, managed by a schoolmaster, choirmaster, or other adult.

conflict: the struggle(s) with which a play is concerned, between the protagonist and forces opposing him. Opposition may be provided by another character (the antagonist), by the protagonist's own conflicting desires, or by outside forces such as society, fate, the gods.

convention: the tacit agreement between actors and audience that certain stage actions correspond to certain experiences that might be difficult to reproduce realistically. In the Elizabethan theater, entrance with a torch signified that the scene was taking place at night. The term can be extended to practices of play-writing, such as the "aside" that can be heard by the audience but not by other characters on stage, or ending the play with an epilogue that directly addresses the audience requesting their applause, or the pretense that disguise makes a person utterly unrecognizable.

denouement: the resolution of the plot, in which the complications are unraveled and solved. Given the many plot lines of most Elizabethan plays, the denouement can be quite an elaborate scene.

dramatic irony: the term "irony" refers in general to a phrase or situation in which there are two levels of experience that contrast with each other. A dramatic irony occurs when the audience knows more than the characters do about the identity, the intentions, or the situation of a character.

dramaturgy: the art of writing plays.

Elizabethan: the adjective describing any person or thing dating from the reign of Elizabeth I (1588–1603). The equivalent adjective for the reign of James I (1603–1625) is Jacobean, of Charles I (1625–1649), Caroline. Many scholars use "Elizabethan" as an omnibus term to cover things (especially the plays) of all three reigns.

flaw: a fault or failing in a character, usually having consequences in the plot. Some critics hold that a flaw in the protagonist (what Aristotle called "*harmartia*") is crucial to the structure of a tragedy; others find the theory less useful.

exposition: information about events happening offstage or prior to the action of the play.

foil: a character used to provide contrast that will set off the qualities of another character. Shakespeare frequently uses dissimilar characters put in similar situations as foils to each other. Prince Hal uses the metaphor of foil (a metal used as background setting for a jewel) when outlining his plan to let his past behavior highlight his future reformation (*1 Henry IV*, 1.2).

folio: a book format: a single sheet of printing paper is printed on each side with two blocks of type and then folded once, creating two double-sided leaves, four pages. A book composed of such folded sheets was a large and lavish form of publication, used chiefly for history, theology, and other prestigious matter. Ben Jonson's printing of his play in folio was considered unusual and hubristic, but it set an example followed by Hemings and Condell for their collected edition of Shakespeare's plays.

hall theaters: often called "private theaters," these were smaller, roofed-over performance spaces, illuminated by candles, with the whole audience seated, charging higher prices than the amphitheaters. Used by companies consisting wholly of boys until about 1609, when the King's Men began the custom of using hall theaters for winter performances. Other adult companies followed suit.

hamartia: Aristotle's term for "failure" or "error" applied to the protagonist of a tragedy. Sometimes erroneously termed "tragic flaw," this term really applies more to what the character does than to any inherent flaw. Acting out of overweening pride (i.e., out of hubris) is often an example of *hamartia*.

pace: the speed at which a scene is acted, sometimes deducible from the way it is written.

peripety: a sudden reversal of fortune.

property (prop): an object used in the action of a play; e.g., a sword, a crown.

protagonist: in Greek drama, the "first actor"; i.e., the actor who played the largest role. By extension, the term means the central character in any play. In this sense, the word is more useful than "hero," since it may without awkwardness refer to a woman (Rosalind is the protagonist of *As You Like It*) and it avoids the favorable moral connotations of "hero": many plays have villains, such as Richard III and Macbeth, as protagonists. Strictly speaking, there can be only one protagonist in a play, but usage varies on this.

Puritans: Radical Protestants, those who wished to carry the reformation of the Church of England further, purifying doctrine, ritual and church government of elements still left from Roman Catholicism.

quarto: a book format: a single sheet of printing paper is printed on each side with four blocks of type and then folded twice, creating four double-sided leaves, eight pages. Single plays were usually published in this inexpensive format and sold unbound, with the folded pages merely stitched or tacked together.

soliloquy: a speech spoken by an actor alone on the stage.

speech prefix: in a written playtext, the name appearing before a speech indicating who is to speak the words.

stage direction: in a written playtext, a statement indicating an actor's movements: e.g., "Enter Lear," "Exit Queen," "he dies." Elizabethan plays are usually sparse in stage directions compared to the lengthy descriptions given by Shaw and O'Neill, but often the reader may notice implicit stage directions in the spoken lines. When Cordelia says to Lear, "No, sir, you must not kneel," clearly Lear has at least begun to kneel down.

suburb: as now, a town or settlement immediately outside a city, in Shakespeare's case, London. The associations of the term are quite different from those of today: they could be regarded as places of vice. Since London itself was ruled fairly strictly by the Lord Mayor and Aldermen, the owners of taverns, brothels, and theaters found it convenient to locate their establishments in suburbs.

Biography of William Shakespeare

Biographical information about William Shakespeare is sketchy: we know that he was born in Stratford-upon-Avon in England and was baptized on April 26, 1564. Although we celebrate April 23 as his birthday, the exact date is not known. His parents, John and Mary Arden Shakespeare, were solid citizens of Stratford, his father a tanner and glover and a dealer in farm produce, as well as a holder of various local offices. Nicholas Rowe, in his 1709 biography of Shakespeare, reported that William attended a grammar school, the King's New School at Stratford-upon-Avon, where Latin works would have formed the basis of the curriculum. In November 1852, at age eighteen, Shakespeare married Anne Hathaway, who was eight years older than he was. Their first child, Susanna, was born in May of the following year, and three years later the couple had twins, Hamnet and Judith, in February 1585.

The first reference to Shakespeare as an actor and dramatist in London came in 1592, in a critical mention in a work by another playwright, Robert Greene, who called Shakespeare "an upstart crow." Between 1592 and 1594, plague forced theatres to suspend performances. By late 1594, when Shakespeare was listed as a member of Lord Chamberlain's company, there were several plays to his credit (see timeline). From 1594 to 1601, Shakespeare was successful as a dramatist and actor in Lord's Chamberlain's Men, and, in 1599, his family was granted rank as gentlemen and was granted its own heraldic coat of arms. William Shakespeare was a part-owner of the best-known Elizabethan theatre, the Globe, which was built in 1599. After Elizabeth I died and King James I ascended the throne in 1603, Shakespeare's company became the King's Men and enjoyed the king's patronage. In 1608, Shakespeare and his company signed a twenty-one-year lease for the Blackfriars Theatre.

Surviving records attest to Shakespeare as a substantial property owner in Stratford and in London. He suffered the deaths of his son Hamnet in 1596, his father in 1601, his brother Edmund in 1607, and his mother in 1608. He returned to Stratford to live in 1611 or 1612 and died there on April 23, 1616. The largest share of his estate went to his married daughter Susanna, and a dowry went to his recently wed daughter Judith; by law, a third of the estate went to his wife Anne, although there was little mention of her in his will.

During Shakespeare's lifetime, some of his plays and poems were published without his permission. The sonnets were published in 1609, apparently without Shakespeare's involvement. The first complete edition of the plays, the First Folio of 1623, was based on manuscript copies and on prompt-books used by actors in the plays, materials that were collected by Shakespeare's fellow actors John Heminges and Henry Condell. There are no known surviving manuscript copies of any Shakespearean plays.

Bibliography

Primary Texts

Primary reading on Shakespeare consists of the plays themselves, which are available in many modern editions. Since Shakespeare wrote 400 years ago, the present lecturer recommends a text with good explanatory footnotes. Paperback series such as Signet, Bantam, and New Penguin offer a single play per volume with footnotes and introductions. Some also offer an account of Shakespeare's life, an account of stage history, and lists of supplementary reading. They are easily portable, and one need buy only the plays one wants.

One-volume complete works of Shakespeare offer the similar footnotes and introductions for all the plays, plus substantial prefatory material on Shakespeare and his times, documentary material, and fuller bibliographies. Although such a large book is cumbersome, the lecturer recommends any of the following:

The Complete Works of Shakespeare, ed. David Bevington, 4th edition updated, Addison Wesley Longman, 1997. (Used by the lecturer)

The Riverside Shakespeare, ed. G. Blakemore Evans, Houghton Mifflin, second edition, 1997.

The Norton Shakespeare, based on the Oxford Edition, ed. Stephen Greenblatt, W. W. Norton & Co., 1997. (The most comfortable of the three to carry and read. Some of its textual innovations have been disputed. The general introduction is good; some of the introductions to individual plays are tendentiously political).

Serious study of an individual play benefits from the more substantial multi-volume complete works of Shakespeare, of which there are three outstanding series:

The oldest is the *New Arden Shakespeare*, published by Methuen from 1952 to 1982. These volumes are gradually being replaced with a re-editing known as "Arden 3," published by Thomas Nelson and Sons.

Two newer series are the *Oxford Shakespeare* and the *New Cambridge Shakespeare*, which started appearing in the 1980s from the University Presses of Oxford and Cambridge, respectively, and are not yet complete. These three series, publishing one play per volume in both hardback and paper cover, offer comprehensive introductions and detailed notes referring to the most recent scholarship and interpretation. Below are listed the plays in this course, with the names of the Arden, Oxford, and Cambridge editors. When no editor is listed, that particular play has not yet been published in that series:

Hamlet—Jenkins (Arden, 1982). Hibbard (Oxford, 1987). Edwards (Cambridge,1985).

Henry IV Part 1—Humphreys (Arden, 1960). Bevington (Oxford, 1987). Weil (Cambridge, 1997).

Henry IV Part 2—Humphreys (Arden, 1966). Weis (Oxford, 1998). Melchiori, (Cambridge, 1989).

Henry V—Craik(Arden,1995).Taylor(Oxford,1984).Gurr(Cambridge,1992).

Julius Caesar—Daniell (Arden, 1998). Humphreys (Oxford, 1984). Spevack (Cambridge, 1988).

King Lear—Foakes (Arden, 1997). Halio (Cambridge, 1992).

Macbeth—Muir (Arden, 1951). Brooke (Oxford, 1990). Braunmiller (Cambridge, 1997).

Measure for Measure—Lever (Arden, 1965). Bawcutt (Oxford, 1991). Gibbons (Cambridge , 1991).

The Merchant of Venice—Brown (Arden, 1955). Halio (Oxford, 1993). Mahood (Cambridge, 1987).

Othello—Honigmann (Arden, 1997). Sanders (Cambridge, 1984).

Richard II—Ure (Arden, 1956). Gurr (Cambridge, 1984).

Richard III—Hammond (Arden, 1981).

Romeo and Juliet—Gibbons (Arden, 1980). Evans (Cambridge, 1984).

The Taming of the Shrew—Morris (Arden, 1981). Oliver (Oxford, 1982). Thompson (Cambridge, 1984).

Troilus and Cressida —Bevington (Arden, 1998). Muir (Oxford (1982).

Twelfth Night—Lothian & Craik (Arden, 1975). Warren & Wells (Oxford, 1994). Donno (Cambridge, 1985).

The New Arden Shakespeare is also available as a one-volume complete Shakespeare without notes or introductions, for those who want a "clean" text, uncluttered by scholars.

Secondary Material

Adelman, "'This Is and Is Not Cressid': The Characterization of Cressida." *The (M)other Tongue: Essays in Feminist Psychoanalytic Interpretation*, ed. Shirley Nelson Garner et al. Ithaca: Cornell University Press, 1985.

Altick, Richard D. "Symphonic Imagery in Richard II." Publications of the Modern Language Association, 62 (1947), 339–365.

Andrews, John F., ed. *William Shakespeare: His World, His Work, His Influence*. New York: Scribner, 1985. Essays by sixty modern scholars summarizing available knowledge of the Elizabethan world (volume I), Shakespeare's works (volume II), and the subsequent history of interpretation, production, and adaptation of those works (volume III).

Barber, C.L. *Shakespeare's Festive Comedy*. Princeton: Princeton University Press, 1959. A major book on the form and significance of the comedies.

Barkan, Leonard. "The Theatrical Consistency of Richard II ." *Shakespeare Quarterly*, 29 (1978), 5–19. Characteristic texture and effects of the play.

Bate, Jonathan. *The Genius of Shakespeare*. New York: Oxford University Press, 1998. The best recent general book on Shakespeare (much better than Harold Bloom's over-promoted volume or the biography by Park Honan) dealing with the life, the career, and the nature of his genius.

Beckerman, Bernard. *Shakespeare at the Globe*. New York: Macmillan 1962. The structural patterns and theatrical effects of plays in Shakespeare's time.

Booth, Stephen. *King Lear, Macbeth, Indefinition and Tragedy*. New Haven Yale University Press, 1983. Rich and supple readings of the plays, starting from the expectations we bring to tragedy.

———. "On the Value of Hamlet." In Kastan's collection of Hamlet essays listed below. This distinguished essay deals with the apparent incoherences and changes of focus in the play.

Bradley, A.C. *Shakespearean Tragedy: Lectures on Hamlet, Othello, King Lear, Macbeth*. London: Macmillan, 1904. A classic book on these four plays. The culmination of nineteenth-century criticism, this book was more influential than any other in determining notions of Shakespearean tragedy for the first half of the twentieth century.

Briggs, Julia. *This Stage-Play World: English Literature and its Background 1580-1625*. New York: Oxford University Press, 1983. A useful, brief account of the intellectual and social backgrounds of Shakespeare's age.

Bullough, Geoffrey. *Narrative and Dramatic Sources of Shakespeare*. 8v London: Routledge & Kegan Paul and New York: Columbia University Press, 1957–1975. A magnificent resource reprinting all of the sources of Shakespeare's plays with discussion of the ways in which he used them.

Cavell, Stanley. *Disowning Knowledge in Six Plays of Shakespeare.* Cambridge: Cambridge University Press, 1987. Essays on *Othello* and *Hamlet*, and an especially detailed and sensitive analysis of *King Lear* by a philosopher who has specialized in problems of aesthetics and value.

Coghill, Nevill. "The Basis of Shakespearean Comedy." *Essays and Studies*, n.s. 3 (1950), 1–28. Reprinted in Anne Ridler, ed., *Shakespeare Criticism*, 1935–1960. London: Oxford University Press, 1963. Comic theory, with a detailed reading of *The Merchant of Venice.*

———. *Shakespeare's Professional Skills.* Cambridge: Cambridge University Press, 1964. Contains an excellent essay on *Troilus and Cressida.*

Cook, Ann Jennalie. *Making a Match: Courtship in Shakespeare and His Society.* Princeton, 1991. Authoritative handling of marriage laws and customs in Shakespeare's time, and how Shakespeare uses them.

Danby, John F. *Shakespeare's Doctrine of Nature: A Study of "King Lear."* London: Faber, 1948.

Danson, Lawrence. *The Harmonies of The Merchant of Venice.* New Haven: Yale University Press, 1978. Book-length discussion of the play.

Dollimore, Jonathan & Alan Sinfield, eds. *Political Shakespeare: New Essays in Cultural Materialism.* Ithaca: Cornell University Press, 1985. Essays by "new historicists" and "cultural materialists" who concentrate on the ways in which literary texts participate in the social and political struggles of the era in which they were produced and in the eras in which they have been consumed.

———. *Radical Tragedy.* Chicago: University of Chicago Press, 1984. This feisty social and political reinterpretation of Renaissance tragedy includes a striking essay on *King Lear.*

Drakakis, John, ed. *Alternative Shakespeares.* London: Methuen, 1985. Essays by British feminists, Marxists, deconstructionists and other post-structuralist critics contesting the traditional liberal-humanist Shakespeare.

Goldman, Michael. *Shakespeare and the Energies of Drama*. Princeton 1972. Focuses on stage dynamics and audience responses. Very perceptive on *Hamlet, Henry V*, and *King Lear*.

Greenblatt, Stephen Jay. *Shakespearean Negotiations: The Circulation of Social Energy in Renaissance England*. Berkeley: University of California Press, 1988. Includes "Invisible Bullets," a famous recent essay reinterpreting the history plays in terms of contemporaneous issues of class and culture.

Gross, John. *Shylock: Four Hundred Years in the Life of a Legend*. London Chatto & Windus, 1992.

Gurr, Andrew. *The Shakespearean Stage, 1574-1642*. Cambridge University Press, 3rd. ed., 1992. A compendium of scholarly information concerning the playhouses, and performance circumstances of Shakespeare's time.

Hawkins, Sherman. "The Two Worlds of Shakespearean Comedy." *Shakespeare Studies, 3* (1968), 62–80. Characteristic structural patterns and their significance.

Heilman, Robert B. "The Taming Untamed, or, The Return of the Shrew." *Modern Language Quarterly, 27* (1966), 147–61. An effort to restore the farcical nature of the play.

Howard, Jean E. *Shakespeare's Art of Orchestration: Stage Technique and Audience Response*. Urbana: University of Illinois Press, 1984. An illuminating account of Shakespeare's dramatic techniques.

Hunter, Robert G. *Shakespeare and the Comedy of Forgiveness*. New York: Columbia University Press, 1965. Essays on the comedies that deal with sin and repentance.

———. *Shakespeare and the Mystery of God's Judgments*. Athens: University of Georgia Press, 1976. Issues of free will and damnation in *Richard III, Hamlet, Othello,* and *Macbeth*.

Bibliography

————. "Shakespeare's Comic Sense as it Strikes us Today: Falstaff and the Protestant Ethic," in David Bevington and Jay L. Halio, eds., *Shakespeare: Pattern of Excelling Nature*, Newark: University of Delaware Press, 1978.

Kahn, Coppelia. *Man's Estate: Masculine Identity in Shakespeare.* Berkeley: University of California Press, 1981. A psychological study of male self-definition in the plays.

————. "*The Taming of the Shrew*: Shakespeare's Mirror of Marriage." *Modern Language Studies, 5* (1975), 88–102. Deplores the farcical treatment of women.

Kastan, David Scott, ed. *Critical Essays on Shakespeare's Hamlet.* New York: G. K. Hall, 1995. Outstanding essays on Hamlet written since 1965.

————. "Proud Majesty Made a Subject: Shakespeare and the Spectacle of Rule." *Shakespeare Quarterly*, 37 (1986), 459–75. A major article on the stage deposition of kings, especially Richard II.

Kernan, Alvin B. "The Henriad: Shakespeare's Major History Plays." In Kernan, ed., *Modern Shakespearean Criticism*, New York: Harcourt, Brace, and World, 1970. Classic statement of the ruling themes of the Lancastrian tetralogy of history plays.

————. "The Plays and the Playwrights," in *The Revels History of Drama in English*, ed. Clifford Leech & T.W. Craik. Volume III. London: Methuen, 1975.

Kirsch, Arthur. *The Passions of Shakespeare's Tragic Heroes.* Charlottesville: University Press of Virginia, 1990.

Kitto, H.D.F. *Form and Meaning in Drama.* London: Methuen, 1956. This book on Greek tragedy has a fine chapter on *Hamlet*.

Knight, G. Wilson. *The Wheel of Fire.* Oxford: Oxford University Press, 1930. Includes a famous essay on the "Othello music."

Leech, Clifford. *Tragedy.* London: Methuen, 1969. A useful brief account c efforts to define tragedy.

Leggatt, Alexander. *Shakespeare's Comedy of Love.* London: Methuen, 1974 A perceptive book on love and social behavior in Shakespeare.

Lewis, C.S. "Hamlet: The Prince or the Poem." This classic essay is reprintec among other places, in the Kernan collection listed above.

Lindenberger, Herbert. *Historical Drama.* Chicago: University of Chicag Press, 1975.

Loehlin, James. *Henry V: Shakespeare in Performance.* New York: S Martin's Press, 1996.

Mack, Maynard. *Everybody's Shakespeare.* Lincoln: University of Nebrask Press, 1993. A great scholar-teacher's essays on the tragedies, including a excerpt from his book *King Lear in Our Time* and his classic piece originall published as "The World of Hamlet."

McElroy, Bernard. *Shakespeare's Mature Tragedies.* Princeton: Princeto University Press, 1973.

Miola, Robert S. *Shakespeare's Rome.* Cambridge: Cambridge Universit Press, 1983.

Neely, Carol Thomas, "Women and Men in Othello*." The Woman's Par Feminist Criticism of Shakespeare*, ed. Carolyn R. S. Lenz et al, Urbana University of Illinois Press, 1980. Summary of major criticism on the play leading to a helpful feminist reinterpretation.

Neill, Michael. *Issues of Death: Mortality and Identity in Englis Renaissance Tragedy.* Oxford: The Clarendon Press, 1997. A recent book o the big issues of tragedy, with fine sections on *Hamlet* and *Othello.*

Ornstein, Robert. *A Kingdom for a Stage: The Achievement of Shakespeare History Plays.* Cambridge, Mass: Harvard University Press, 1972. A subt and sensitive response to Shakespeare's history plays, with an eye on the serious ethical issues they raise.

Rabkin, Norman. *Shakespeare and the Problem of Meaning.* Chicago: University of Chicago Press, 1981. Includes sensitive accounts of the multiple meanings of *The Merchant of Venice* and *Henry V.*

————. "Troilus and Cressida: The Uses of the Double Plot." *Shakespeare Studies*, 1 (1965), 99–136.

Rose, Jacqueline. "Hamlet—the 'Mona Lisa' of Literature." In the Kastan collection listed above. A recent meditation on readings of the play.

Saccio, Peter. *Shakespeare's English Kings.* New York: Oxford University Press, 2nd ed., 2000. An account of the medieval history that Shakespeare modified in writing his history plays.

————. "Shrewd and Kindly Farce." *Shakespeare Survey, 37* (1984), 33–40. A fuller statement of the argument in Lecture 6.

Schoenbaum, Samuel. *William Shakespeare: A Compact Documentary Life.* New York: Oxford University Press, rev. ed., 1987. The most reliable and sensible of the many available biographies of Shakespeare.

Shapiro James. *Shakespeare and the Jews.* New York: Columbia University Press, 1996. The fullest account of this difficult subject.

Sher, Antony. *The Year of the King.* New York: Limelight Editions, 1987. A distinguished actor's account of preparing and playing the role of *Richard III.*

Sterling, Brents. "'Or Else This Were a Savage Spectacle.'" *Shakespeare: Modern Essays in Criticism*, ed. Leonard Dean. New York: Oxford University Press, 1961. The use of ceremony in Julius Caesar.

Stevenson, David L. *The Achievement of Shakespeare's "Measure for Measure."* Ithaca: Cornell University Press, 1966.

Taylor, Gary. *Reinventing Shakespeare*. New York: Oxford University Press, 1989. A witty account of the ways in which Shakespeare was been reinterpreted by succeeding generations.

Tillyard, E. M. W. *The Elizabethan World Picture*. London: Chatto & Windus. 1943. How some people of the 16th century imagined their world to be organized.

————. *Shakespeare's History Plays*. London: Chatto & Windus, 1944. A classic study of the history plays, now widely disagreed with.

Williams, Penry. *The Later Tudors: England, 1547-1603*. Oxford: Oxford University Press, 1995. Currently the most useful introduction to the history of the period. Chapters 10–13, on the social order, religion, and family structure, are very relevant to readers of Shakespeare.

Wilson, J. Dover. *The Fortunes of Falstaff*. Cambridge: Cambridge University Press, 1964.

————. *What Happens in Hamlet*. Cambridge: Cambridge University Press. 1935. An old study, still valuable for understanding the ghost.

Films and Videos

If you want to see Shakespeare and do not live or travel near on of the Shakespeare theatre companies, there are many films and videos, some fairly faithful to Shakespeare's scripts, some heavily adapted (in English and other languages). A complete listing up to 1989 is available in Kenneth S. Rothwell and Annabelle Henkin Melzer, *Shakespeare on Screen* (New York and London: Neal-Schuman, 1990). Leading English-language versions are:

The Complete Plays done by BBC and Time-Life. All the plays, some good, some not so good, videotaped in the late 1970s and early 1980s. Not commonly available at local video rentals, but can be secured from Insight Media (1-800-233-9910) or Ambrose Video Publishing (1-800-526-4663). May be available at good public or university libraries.

Individual plays often available by catalog sales or at video rental stores:

1. Three directed by and starring Laurence Olivier:

Henry V (1944)

Hamlet (1948)

Richard III (1955)

Olivier also plays the title role in the 1965 filmed version of a National Theatre Production of *Othello*, directed by Stuart Burge, and Shylock in a 1974 TV video on Jonathan Miller's National Theatre Production of *The Merchant of Venice*.

2. Three directed by and starring Orson Welles:

Macbeth (1948)

Othello (1952)

Chimes at Midnight (1966), also called *Falstaff*; script put together from parts of *1 Henry IV, 2 Henry IV* and *Henry V.*

3. Three plays directed by and starring Kenneth Branagh:

Henry V (1989)

Much Ado About Nothing (1993)

Hamlet (1996: the complete text, four hours long)

4. Three plays directed by Francisco Zeffirelli:

The Taming of the Shrew (1966, starring Richard Burton and Elizabeth Taylor)

Romeo and Juliet (1968, starring Olivia Hussey and Leonard Whiting)

Hamlet (1990, starring Mel Gibson, Glenn Close, and Alan Bates)

5. Various directors:

A Midsummer Night's Dream (1935, a Hollywood black-and-white spectacular directed by Max Reinhart, with the young Mickey Rooney, James Cagney, Olivia de Havilland, and others, with Mendelsohn pouring from the sound track; great fun)

Julius Caesar (1953, directed by Joseph Mankiewicz, with James Mason, John Gielgud, Marlon Brando)

Macbeth (1971, directed by Roman Polanski; remarkably bloody)

Macbeth (1979, Ian McClellan and Judi Dench, based on Trevor Nunn's 1976 RSC production; very good acting, but hard to find)

Richard III (1995, starring Ian McClellan, set in a Fascist Britain of the 1930s)

Othello (1995, Lawrence Fishburne, Kenneth Branagh)

Twelfth Night (1996, directed by Trevor Nunn, starring Imogen Stubbs, Nigel Hawthorne, Helena Bonham Carter, Ben Kingsley)

King Lear (1983, directed by Michael Elliott, starring Laurence Olivier, for Granada TV, 1983)

Romeo and Juliet (1996, directed by Baz Luhrmann, set in Verona Beach, Florida, and shot in MTV style, with Leonardo DiCaprio, Claire Danes)

Al Pacino's *Looking for Richard* (1996) is about the problems of producing *Richard III* for a modern audience. It contains scenes from Shakespeare's play.

Midsummer Night's Dream (1999; directed by Michael Hoffman, Italy/UK, set in late Victorian Italy (the lovers ride bicycles), with suitable operatic music; a fairy world of special effects supervised by the lush figures of

Michelle Pfeiffer and Rupert Everett and the charmingly bewildered Bottom of Kevin Kline.

Shakespeare in Love (1998, directed by John Madden, screenplay by Tom Stoppard, US/UK); multiple Oscar®-winning film; Tom Stoppard's dialogue is replete with outrageous anachronisms; the story is charming and the jokes are sly; the theatres, streets, and costumes are authentic; and the acting, especially that of Gwyneth Paltrow and Judi Dench, glows.

Notes

Notes

Notes

Notes

Notes

Notes

Notes